£5
HRB

SOCIETY AND THE LYRIC
a study of the Song Culture
of eighteenth-century Scotland

SOCIETY
AND THE LYRIC

a study of the Song Culture
of eighteenth-century Scotland

THOMAS CRAWFORD

1979

SCOTTISH ACADEMIC PRESS
EDINBURGH

Published by
Scottish Academic Press Ltd
33 Montgomery Street, Edinburgh EH7 5JX

First published 1979
SBN 7073 0227 7

Printed in Great Britain by
R. & R. Clark Ltd, Edinburgh

CONTENTS

PREFACE

This work is meant as a contribution both to Burns Studies and to the definition of Scottish culture in the eighteenth century.

It is complementary to a number of books and articles which have appeared during the past fifteen years. First, there was James Kinsley's 'The Music of the Heart' in *Renaissance and Modern Studies*, VIII (1964), 5-52, which saw Burns's songs as the triumphant realisation in practice of a dominant tendency in mid-eighteenth-century critical theory, exemplified for example in Beattie when he said that music 'never appears to the best advantage but with poetry for its interpreter'. Then followed David Daiches, *The Paradox of Scottish Culture* (London, 1964), a succinct analysis of the whole civilisation of which the lyric culture forms a part. The musical background and its organisation were treated in David Johnson's *Music and Society in Lowland Scotland in the eighteenth century* (London, 1972), while Burns's songs as unities of tune and verse – an aspect totally excluded from the present volume – were examined by Cedric Thorpe Davie in 'Robert Burns: Writer of Songs' in *Critical Essays on Robert Burns*, ed. D. A. Low (London, 1975) and above all by Catarina Ericson-Roos, *The Songs of Robert Burns: a study of the unity of Poetry and Music* (Studia Anglistica Upsaliensis, Uppsala, 1977). Mary Ellen B. Lewis, in contrast, has concentrated on the songs Burns did *not* write, where his activity was that of a collector – sometimes an incompetent one by modern standards, who could not resist altering what he found. Her article, ' "The joy of my heart": Robert Burns as Folklorist' in *Scottish Studies*, XX (1976), 45-67, is a contribution to yet another area barely touched upon in the pages which follow.

There is, however, one volume which the present book is specifically designed to complement – my own anthology *Love, Labour and Liberty*, published by the Carcanet Press (Manchester, 1976). *Society and the Lyric* is, amongst other things, a commentary on the lyrics in that collection and many pieces which are merely quoted here are there printed in full. The anthology makes plain the connection between Burns and the earlier lyric tradition in a much more direct manner than the present study does. It is divided into twenty-six brief sections according to content, each of them ending with pieces by Burns which demonstrate conclusively that

Burns was the apogee of the whole lyric tradition. The two books, then, support each other, and should if possible be used together.

Society and the Lyric developed out of an inquiry into the verbal sources of Burns's songs. I had not been long at the project before I came to see that their sources were not words on the page or even tunes on the lips, but song-types, many traceable to the sixteenth century and even earlier. Like all artistic forms, these types are congealed content — 'social experience solidified'[1] — just as, on other levels, individual words and inherited melodies are social experience solidified. The song-types are not dead and passive, however, but serve as tools to be used and foci for emotional control: they are a means of giving shape and meaning to the experience of ordinary men and women both in performance and composition. And they have the same function both for the anonymous composers of 'oral' folk-song and the later writers of the literate phase.

The song-types are the organising principles of a medium (almost in the sense in which language itself is a medium of communication); the products of that medium are the artifacts of a 'song culture'. Investigation soon showed that it is merely a matter of the angle of vision whether one considers the song culture as a single unity or as a bundle of disparate strands. It seemed more useful to concentrate on the whole rather than the parts, to stress the interrelation of opposites rather than their mutual exclusion. The medium was used not just by Burns's 'compeers, the common people', but by the *whole* people — lairds and merchants as well as farmers and artisans, lawyers' wives as well as beggars' doxies, as an indispensable part of their daily living. Just as it is misleading to see in Burns the victim of a paralysing linguistic dichotomy ('good' Scots for ever at war with 'effete', unnatural English),[2] so it is wrong to think of the lowland Scottish song-culture of the eighteenth century as split down the middle into 'good' folk-song and 'bad' tea-table or art song.

Indeed, conditions were in some ways similar to those prevailing in both Scotland and England two hundred years before. Writing of the early Tudor period, John Stevens found that at that time there existed not only folk-songs 'made by the people', but also, and alongside of these, other popular songs which he defines as 'composed or adapted to meet the people's taste, and current amongst them. "People" in the present context means "the nation at large." . . .'[3] In *Society and the Lyric*, 'people' means 'the lowland Scottish people at large, of all classes'. Tea-table songs were the popular songs of the upper and middle classes, and if they were any good at all they gradually became known among the whole people. Everybody, high and low, was aware of folk and stall (i.e. broadside or chap-book) songs.

Throughout the book I emphasise that the lyric strand in eighteenth-century Scottish culture was not narrowly or parochially Scottish, but a part of a general, all-British lyric culture. And I stress again and again the medium was there to be *used*, by all sorts of persons for all sorts of purposes. Eighteenth-century Scotland produced two major works 'of a certain length' in which popular sung lyrics formed part of a larger dramatic whole – the 1729 text of Allan Ramsay's *The Gentle Shepherd* and Burns's *Love and Liberty* (*The Jolly Beggars*), written in 1785. The book is in a sense structured around these two works. Ramsay's pastoral drama is examined at length in chapter V, while the final chapter, chapter X, ends with a treatment of Burns's cantata.

Acknowledgements are due to the E. A. Hornel Trust for permission to reproduce songs from the St. Clair (Mansfield) Manuscript, to the British Library Board and the Trustees of the National Library of Scotland for materials in broadsides held by the British Museum and the National Library of Scotland respectively; to Harvard College Library for verses in Peter Buchan's manuscript *Secret Songs of Silence*; to the Nottingham Reference Library and Edinburgh and Glasgow University Libraries for material in their possession; and to the Yale Editions of the Private Papers of James Boswell and the McGraw-Hill Book Company for 'Cut him down Susie' and 'Gif ye a dainty mailing want', as well as for passages quoted from the Boswell Journals. Similar acknowledgements are due to the Regents Press of Kansas for an excerpt from James Thomson, *Letters and Documents*, ed. A. D. McKillop; to the Oxford University Press for texts from the *Letters* of David Hume, F. A. Pottle's *The Literary Career of James Boswell*, and the Oxford Standard Authors' *Burns*; and to the Scottish Text Society for quotations from their editions of Ramsay and Fergusson.

I must also thank the Carnegie Trust for the Universities of Scotland and the Canadian Universities Foundation for fellowships which furthered my researches into Scottish lyrics and songs, and McMaster University, Hamilton, Ontario for hospitality and support. Of the many individuals who have helped me with information or in discussion, three merit my especial gratitude – Dr Emily Lyle, Mr Hamish Henderson, and Dr MacDonald Emslie, all of Edinburgh.

Aberdeen   December, 1978

REFERENCES

1. Ernst Fischer, *The Necessity of Art* (Harmonsdworth, 1963), p.152.
2. See my *Burns: a study of the Poems and Songs* (Edinburgh and Stanford, 1960), henceforth cited as *Burns, passim* and, more recently, James Kinsley, 'Burns and the Peasantry 1785' in *Proceedings of the British Academy*, LX (1974), 1-21.
3. J. Stevens, *Music and Poetry in the Early Tudor Court* (London, 1961), p. 41.

Chapter I

INTRODUCTORY

In countries with a strong tradition of puritanism there has always been a tendency to look down on sung lyrics because they do not take up much room on the page and their idea-content is often slight. It is hardly surprising, then, that critics — especially in Scotland — have disagreed violently about the place of Burns's songs in the whole course of his poetic development. Two main views have been put forward in the hundred and eighty years since the poet's death.

The first holds that Burns's increasing preoccupation with fitting words to tunes after 1787 was a kind of treason to poetry, which ought always to prefer larger and more complex forms. Thus although Sir Walter Scott liked many of the songs, and although he was careful to say, 'Let no one suppose that we undervalue (them)', it is clear that in practice he *did* undervalue them:

> . . . we cannot but deeply regret that so much of his time and talents should have been frittered away in compiling and composing for musical collections. . . . But the writing of a series of songs for large musical collections, degenerated into a slavish labour which no talents could support, led to negligence, and above all, diverted the poet from his grand plan of dramatic composition.[1]

R. L. Stevenson was of the opinion that after 1787 Burns 'rarely found courage for any more sustained effort than a song' and that 'it is not the less typical of his loss of moral courage that he should have given up all larger ventures, nor the less melancholy that a man who first attacked literature with a hand that seemed capable of moving mountains, should have spent his later years in whittling cherry-stones';[2] and a similar austerity seems to be implied in the value judgements of David Craig in his *Scottish Literature and the Scottish People 1680–1830* (1961), where he spends by far the greater time on the satires and other poems in the vernacular.[3]

The second assessment of the place of the songs in Burns's literary career was put forward in the very same year as Scott's review by

Francis Jeffrey, when he prophesied that they would 'transmit the name of Burns to all future generations'.[4] Echoed and developed by Hazlitt, Carlyle, Tennyson, W. E. Henley, J. C. Dick, David Daiches, James Kinsley and many lesser commentators, this judgment has almost completely ousted the conception of Scott and Stevenson, and it is certainly the view of ordinary Burnsians and folk-singers who include Burns songs in their repertoire. J. de Lancey Ferguson,[5] perhaps the best of all American writers on Burns, argued with great eloquence and conviction that the true bent of Burns's genius was towards the lyric, and that even the great satirical and comic poems of the Kilmarnock period were deviations from his true mission in life. I myself believe that Burns never surpassed his best lyrics, and that even yet no one has explored all their ramifications.

The implications of this view are two-fold, applying (i) to the criticism of the songs as individual works of art and (ii) to the songs in relation to their sources. At the level of words without music, a Chinese specialist in English literature, Dr Wen-Yuan-Ning, has emphasised that rather different criteria are required from the 'complexity' and 'subtlety' which are so often held to be the supreme values in literary art. Broadcasting on 25th January 1944 he said that Burns's treatment of common incidents and feelings reminded him very much of the poetry of his own country, 'where the maximum effect of vastness and grandeur is conveyed through simple and common incidents; the shadow cast by bamboos on the wall, the flight of wild geese in autumn, or the sound of temple bells in the evening'.[6] Such effects have indeed a subtlety of their own, requiring different techniques of attention from those commonly applied to the lyrics of Donne or a poem like Coleridge's 'Ancient Mariner'.[7]

For a total criticism of Burns's songs, verbal analysis is not enough, and another dimension—the musical—must be added. Burns's favourite method of composition is well known. In almost every case he took a traditional melody and then fitted words to it. Here is the famous account of how he intended to find verses for the tune, *Laddie, lie near me*:

> Laddie, lie near me—must *lie by me*, for some time.—I do not know the air; & untill I am compleat master of a tune, in my own singing, (such as it is) I never can compose for it.—My way is: I consider the poetic Sentiment, correspondent to my idea of the musical expression; then chuse my theme; begin one Stanza; when that is composed,

which is generally the most difficult part of the business, I walk out, sit down now & then, look out for objects in Nature around me that are in unison or harmony with the cogitations of my fancy & workings of my bosom; humming every now & then the air with the verses I have framed: when I feel my Muse beginning to jade, I retire to the solitary fireside of my study, & there commit my effusions to paper; swinging, at intervals, on the hind-legs of my elbow-chair, by way of calling forth my own critical strictures, as my pen goes on.[8]

Burns is probably exaggerating: the rhythms of riding and walking and the influence of the fields, streams and bushes of the lowland countryside, did not go into the making of all his songs, and his self-conscious picturing of himself as a refined Man of Feeling obscures the amount of traditional material which he uses: phrases, individual lines, perhaps a chorus or a germinal stanza as well as the tune. When at last the definitive work on Burns's songs is written, verbal and musical analysis will go together, song by song and stanza by stanza. James Kinsley has shown how this can be done in a pioneering analysis of 'John Anderson my jo, John', 'Mary Morison' and 'Willie brew'd a peck o' Maut',[9] and the method has been used on a fairly large number of songs by Catarina Ericson-Roos, though much still needs to be done.[10]

It is, however, with another aspect of Burns's primacy in song — his relation to his verbal sources — that the present study is concerned. From the early nineteenth century on, editors and critics have indulged in the sort of source-hunting which traces individual lines and verses to previous songs and poems, and the poet has been shown to have borrowed from here, there and everywhere.[11] And now that the results of all these minute inquiries have been sifted, digested and summed up in the notes to the individual songs in Professor Kinsley's monumental edition,[12] it would seem that little fresh information of this kind can be expected: future inquiries will be content to dot the i's and cross the t's, that is all. In the end sources are social, and to study them is to study society. The words on the page of any literary work are of value because they are the utterance of a man speaking to men. These words, and such larger units as scenes and chapters, are arranged in formally beautiful patterns which it is the business of aesthetic criticism to evaluate. Outside the purely literary structure and texture as experienced by a reader are five relationships, each contradictory and each sustained by its own tensions — (i) that between the poem and its author; (ii) that between the author and his society; (iii) that between social classes, local regions and other groups and sub-cultures within his society; (iv) that between his society and other societies; and (v) that between his society and its past. It is in these five relationships that the 'reality prior to the poem' (or play, or novel) largely consists: and the systematic study of literature embraces *both* the formal qualities within the work (the poet's utterance temporarily considered as a thing-in-itself rather than as a term in a relationship) and the establishment of connections between that work, that *utterance*, and the 'reality prior to the poem'. The present volume has in mind the last four of these relationships — in particular, those between the various classes in eighteenth-century Scotland and between the popular cultures of Scotland and England; its aim is to help the reader to see how Burns's songs are linked to the ways of life of his century.

And it draws heavily on three types of material produced mainly but not exclusively in Scotland: (a) manuscripts; (b) printed broadsides, chapbooks and slips; (c) printed song-books, with or without music. The most important of the existing manu-scripts compiled before 1825 are:

(1) Elizabeth Cochrane's Song Book (*c.* 1730). Harvard College Library, MS. Eng. 512.

(2) Agnes Thorburn Creighton: A Collection of Old Songs (1818) Ewart Public Library, Dumfries.

(3) David Herd's MSS. (*c.* 1766). British Museum, Add. MSS. 22311-2. One folio of these MSS. is in the Edinburgh University Library, La. II, 358.2.

(4) Robert Jamieson's Brown MS. (1783). Edinburgh University Library, La. XIII. 473.

(5) William Motherwell's MSS. (*c.* 1825). *Ballad Book* in Glasgow University Library MS. Murray 501, also MSS. Robertson 6, 12 and 15, and a notebook in Pollok House, Glasgow.

(6) A Miscellaneous Collection of MSS. in the National Library of Scotland, MS. 893, bound in one volume.

(7) The Miscellanies of Sir Walter Scott in the National Library of Scotland, and other MSS. of Scott in the N.L.S. and at Abbotsford.

(8) 'The Collection of an old lady's complete set of ballads' (Sir Walter Scott's title, 1805–7 and 1818): at present in Broughton House, Kirkcudbright.

(9) Elizabeth St. Clair's Manuscript (1770–80): at present in

Broughton House, Kirkcudbright, and previously known as the Thomas Mansfield Manuscript.

(10) Thomas Percy's Papers (MSS. sent from Scotland to Bishop Percy after 1765). Harvard College Library.

(11) Thomas Wilkie's MS. Notebooks (1813–15). National Library of Scotland, MSS. 121-3; 877.

(12) William Tytler's Brown MS. (1783). Old Clune House, Aldourie.[13]

Nos. 4 and 12, the Jamieson Brown MS. and the Tytler Brown MS., record part of the repertoire of a particular singer, Mrs Brown of Falkland, and are extensively treated by David Buchan in *The Ballad and the Folk* (London, 1972). Five of these manuscripts date from the early nineteenth century,[14] and are less important than the others, since they mix nineteenth with eighteenth-century material. The most crucial from the point of view of lyrical song before Burns, are David Herd's MSS. (which Burns may well have seen), only seven of whose 370 items remain unprinted either by Herd himself, by Child in his standard collection of Popular Ballads, or by Hans Hecht in his *Songs from David Herd's MSS.* (Edinburgh, 1904);[15] and the St. Clair Manuscript, which was lost for much of this century until rediscovered by William Montgomerie. Its compiler, Elizabeth St. Clair, was born *c.* 1738, the daughter of an Edinburgh advocate, and died in 1811; in 1773 she married Lieut.-Col. James Dalrymple, third son of Sir James Dalrymple of Hailes, and for most of her life she was a friend of Alison Cockburn, author of one of the two main sets of 'The Flowers of the Forest' ('I have seen the smiling/Of Fortune beguiling'). She also knew Hume's friend Sir Gilbert Elliot and his sister Jean, who wrote the other main text of 'The Flowers of the Forest' ('I have heard a lilting/At our ewes' milking'). Her MS. includes twenty traditional ballad texts and many orally transmitted folk-songs and fragments (some overlapping with texts in the Herd MSS.), as well as songs copied from print and songs composed by Mrs Cockburn and other members of the Dalrymple-Elliot-Cockburn circle.[16]

But most of my evidence comes from printed sources. Of these the most interesting, and the most difficult to cover with any approach to completeness, are the white-letter broadsides, chapbooks containing ballads and songs, and the song sheets, the latter being sometimes 'slips' or galley 'pulls' containing one or more songs. It seems evident that broadsides and chapbooks printed by the popular printers of Aldermary Churchyard, London, and such northern English centres as Newcastle-upon-Tyne and York, were widely circulated by itinerant pedlars and ballad-singers. It is often impossible to state when or where a broadside or chapbook was printed because of the lack of a date or printer's name, and the inclusion of specifically Scottish songs is by no means an infallible guide, as these were often printed in London chapbooks or sheets, presumably for sale in both Scotland and England. Furthermore, since Scottish popular printers included a fair proportion of English songs in their productions, and since Irish collections printed both Scots and English songs, one is led to conclude that the song market was at this time an all-British one.

As the eighteenth century advanced, broadsides and chapbooks printed in Scotland itself became increasingly common. Many song chapbooks were issued by the printers J. & M. Robertson of Glasgow between 1780 and 1810, and other printers in Paisley, Falkirk, Stirling, Dumfries, Edinburgh and elsewhere exploited the popular market about the same time. Material originating in English black-letter broadsides of the seventeenth century was reprinted in Scottish chapbooks of the early nineteenth century, such as those printed by T. Johnston of Falkirk and M. Randall of Stirling (c. 1815). For example, one Randall chap includes *The Maid's Complaint for Jockey* (l.1. 'Love did first my thoughts employ'), a pseudo-Scots song of the type published in London by Thomas Durfey in the late seventeenth century; in another, *The Frigate Well-Mann'd* (l.1. 'In blows a fresh and pleasant gale'), a woman is compared to a frigate in a way that was standard in Durfey's time. These correspondences could be multiplied, and they help to document the close connection between Scottish song and the English broadside tradition.

Most literary historians recognise a specific 'broadside' or 'stall' type of song; but its existence does not preclude the appearance of other kinds of song in the printed material sold at stalls and carried into the countryside by travelling packmen. This is well-illustrated by a collection of 42 white-letter broadsheets in the British Museum,[17] apparently printed at Aberdeen in 1775 or 1776. They contain a fairly high proportion of comic songs, including some of the 'Merry Muses' type; many Scottish songs, some of which have a specific Aberdeen reference, and quite a large number of English ones. One broadsheet prints the English *Blind Beggar's Daughter of Bethnal Green* (l.1. 'It was a blind beggar had long lost his sight'), together with the Scottish *Bonny Highland Lad* (l.1. 'Down by yon shady grove'). Two more of these Aberdeen broadsides were reprints of well-known English productions, *The Berkshire Lady's Garland: Or Bachelors of Ev'ry Station* and *The Bristol Garland: Or The Merchant's*

Daughter of Bristol. Of the few Child Ballads in this Aberdeen series, one is *Barbara Allen*, widely distributed throughout the British Isles and America; another is the English *Chevy Chase*. Finally, and even more typically, *The Roving Maids of Aberdeen's Garland*, dated 30th January 1776, contains as its third song the English *Golden Glove* (l.1. 'A wealthy young squire of Tamworth we hear').

Now Aberdeenshire has for centuries been one of the main centres of balladry and popular song in the British Isles. A surprisingly large number of Child's A texts (his main or favoured texts) turn out to be Aberdeenshire ones, and at the present day the North-East is richer than any other part of Scotland in the remains of the old popular song. Of some 10,000 variants of Lowland Scottish songs recorded by the School of Scottish Studies since 1945, several thousand are from the Aberdeen area alone. Many songs in the repertoire of present-day Aberdeen folk-singers are of English or Irish origin, and there seems to be a fairly common impression that such borrowing took place mainly during the nineteenth century. The existence of these late-eighteenth-century broadsides, however, documents the popularity of English material in this area as early as 1775, and one may well suspect that songs and ballads from the English broadsides entered oral tradition in Aberdeenshire at least a hundred years before this. It is perhaps significant that the first song-book ever printed in Scotland, Forbes' *Cantus* of 1662, was an Aberdeen production. It is a learned, not a popular song-book, representing the taste of an earlier generation, and with perhaps one or two exceptions, most of its songs, including those written by Scots, are in what looks like English on the printed page. Thus, in all probability, the song culture of Aberdeenshire was not simply all-Scottish, but all-British, at quite an early date.

Broadsides and chapbooks, then, are sometimes the closest we can get to popular tradition, and may have at least as much authority as manuscripts. They often contained songs which their printers acquired from oral tradition; while, conversely, townsfolk and country people might learn songs from printed copies, only to transmit them to others by oral communication, thus initiating the 'folk process' in the course of which some stanzas would disappear, and others perhaps be modified beyond all recognition.

The last primary sources to be considered are the printed song-books. Collections of words without music far outnumber those which print the music and most of the former are 12mo, 16mo, or 18mo volumes ranging from about 100 pages to 400 pages in length, with an elaborate title-page (often engraved) and an index of first lines. Even when known, authors' names are often suppressed;

where possible, the titles of well-known tunes to which the songs can be sung are mentioned; and sometimes the song-books will give the name of a well-known professional singer into whose repertoire the song has passed, such as Mrs Catley or Signor Tenducci. Song-books with music were often of folio or quarto size, and finely engraved. The *Perth Musical Miscellany* of 1786, 12mo, 347 pages, was the first pocket-book with music to be printed in Scotland, so far as I am aware. The best bibliography of Scottish song-books is that in J. C. Dick, *The Songs of Robert Burns: now first printed with the melodies for which they were written*, London, 1901, but it is far from complete. Some seventy-four song-books, with or without music, are known to have been published in Scotland before 1786. They contain between them approximately 3000 separate songs, and detailed examination shows that songs written by Englishmen appear to outnumber those of Scottish origin; that a large number of songs composed in Scotland are linguistically indistinguishable from English songs on the printed page; and that the pieces in the song-books are broadly speaking the same *sort* of songs as those in the chapbooks, slips, broadsides or manuscript collections. The song-books appear to print a larger number of art-songs than do other source-groups.

As will become clear, much Scottish art-song was in a folk or even a broadside tradition, and the fashion of writing new words, Scots or English, to old tunes — a *genre* sometimes called 'national song'[18] — inevitably blurred these differences. The distinction that is of the greatest value in the study of Scottish song literature before and immediately after Burns's time is the distinction between popular and artificial. By artificial song I mean a particularly insipid variety, often sung by professional singers at the public gardens of Ranelagh and Vauxhall, and at their northern counterparts in Edinburgh and Aberdeen. Such *artificial* songs were a peculiar sub-class of art-song, by no means identical with the whole of art-song; they were associated with a particular social group, the 'polite', and above all with the women of that group; and their idea-content was often that of the mid-eighteenth-century cult of sentiment. One Scotswoman who enjoyed and herself wrote this kind of artificial song was Burns's 'Clarinda' — Mrs Agnes McLehose: her relations with Burns were nothing other than an attempt to *live* according to the cult of sentiment.

All the other songs in the song-books may be subsumed under the single category of 'popular song'. By 'popular song' I mean a generic term which will cover (1) composed songs by popular writers of certain conventional types, sung to Scots or popular

English tunes; (2) slip or chapbook songs, generally shorter than broadside ballads and often printed under such titles as *Three Excellent New Songs, Seven Excellent New Songs*, etc.; (3) 'broadside' or 'stall' ballads — i.e. songs with a considerable narrative content, generally fairly long, and often showing signs of sheer padding; (4) folk-songs, subject to the laws that govern oral transmission, namely the co-existence for long periods of a fixed norm alongside of spontaneously occurring variations.

These five types of song did not appeal to five separate publics or even to two — the 'masses' and the 'educated'; they appealed in varying degrees to all of lowland Scotland. In 1786, the year when the Kilmarnock edition of Burns's poems made him famous overnight, at a moment of poise after he had written *The Jolly Beggars* but before he had begun to transmit songs to Johnson's *Museum* and Thomson's *Select Collection of Original Scotish Airs*, there existed in Scotland an extraordinary rich song culture, in which Scottish, English and Irish strands were intertwined into a whole that seems in retrospect to be more than the sum of its parts.

For far too long it has been customary to look only at the parts, to see them as in irreconcilable opposition to each other, as yet another illustration of a historical Myth — that the Scottish consciousness was disastrously split by the Union with England. A profound disharmony between reason and emotion, so the theory goes, was irrevocably linked to the linguistic split between the Scots and English tongues which had been developing since the Union of the Crowns in 1603: henceforth the rule was — feel in Scots, think in English, and never the twain shall meet — until, perhaps, the 'Scottish Renaissance' of Hugh MacDiarmid and his followers from the nineteen-twenties onwards. The theory is persuasively put forward in Edwin Muir's *Scott and Scotland* (London, 1936) and it underlies Lewis Grassic Gibbon's account of Chris Guthrie's education in *Sunset Song*, where his heroine is more than just a realistic character, but is also intended to be allegorical and to stand for Scotland:

> . . . two Chrisses there were that fought for her heart and tormented her. You hated the land and the coarse speak of the folk and learning was brave and fine one day and the next you'd waken with the peewits crying across the hills, deep and deep, crying in the heart of you and the smell of the earth in your face, almost you'd cry for that, the beauty of it and the sweetness of the Scottish land and skies. You saw their faces in firelight, father's and mother's and the

neighbours', before the lamps lit up, tired and kind, faces
dear and close to you, you wanted the words they'd known
and used, forgotten in the far-off youngness of their lives,
Scots words to tell to your heart, how they wrung it and
held it, the toil of their days and unendingly their fight.
And the next minute that passed from you, you were
English, back to the English words so sharp and clean and
true for a while, for a while, till they slid so smooth from
your throat that you knew they could never say anything
that was worth the saying at all.[19]

Some of the sharpest, cleanest and truest English words of the
whole eighteenth century were written by the Scottish historians,
philosophers and economists of the Enlightenment: and what they
said, it can hardly be denied, was supremely worth saying. But that
fact does not of itself dispose of the dissociation theory, though
modern revaluations of the poems and novels of the Anglo-Scots
Thomson and Smollett should perhaps give us pause. In his pene-
trating study of ballad structure and a ballad community, *The
Ballad and the Folk* (London, 1972), David Buchan adapts the theory
to explain why the educated Mrs Brown of Falkland, the greatest
transmitter of eighteenth-century ballad texts, was able to compose
letters in English by one method (ordinary writing) and ballads by
another (re-creation in performance). 'She composed ballads in
Scots because Scots was for her the language of *real* speech and *real*
feeling, and the total process of oral composition in Scots is simply
an extension of the basic dichotomy.'[20] The basic dichotomy was
even diagnosed by David Daiches as 'national schizophrenia',[21] and
he has applied the notion wholesale to all the songs of Burns's
century, erecting a clear and absolute division between the two main
classes of lyric — art (English) and folk (vernacular). To ram his
point home, he takes a little-known song from *The Charmer* (1765),
first published in Scotland in Volume II of *The Tea-Table Miscellany*
(1725):

> Now all thy virgin-sweets are mine,
>   And all the shining charms that grace thee;
> My fair Melinda, come recline
>   Upon my breast, while I embrace thee,
> And tell, without dissembling art,
>   My happy raptures on thy bosom:
> Thus will I plant within my breast
>   A love that shall forever blossom.

'How salutary', says Daiches, 'how very salutary after this to turn
to Burns on the same theme.' And he quotes 'The Rigs of Barley':

> I hae been blythe wi' Comrades dear;
>   I hae been merry drinking;
> I hae been joyfu' gathrin' gear;
>   I have been happy thinking;
> But a' the pleasures e'er I saw,
>   Tho' three times doubl'd fairly,
> That happy night was worth them a',
>   Amang the rigs o' barley.[22]

I am by no means certain that the two songs *are* on the same theme.
Burns's is on physical love and the exchange of hearts, not necessarily followed by marriage, whereas the *Charmer* song is a kind of
epithalamium, bearing the title 'On the marriage of the R.H.
Lord G———————— and Lady K———— C——————'.
Another point: when we ignore orthography, the difference between
the *Charmer* extract and the Burns lines is more the difference
between a high style and a colloquial style than between standard
English and a regional dialect, for Burns does not employ a single
word that would (given the accepted Southern pronunciation) have
been unknown in England. It is not a matter of two poets employing
different languages, but rather different registers or levels of usage
within the same language. Let me now quote from a less colloquial
register — from the well-known ballad 'William and Margaret' by
David Mallet, published in Edinburgh as an anonymous broadside
in 1723 *before* he left for London in August of that year and before
any English broadside or song-book version of the ballad had been
printed:

> When all was wrapt in dark Mid-Night,
>   And all were fast asleep,
> In glided Marg'ret's grimly Ghost
>   And stood at William's feet.
>
> Her Face was like the April-Morn,
>   Clad in a Wintry Cloud,
> And Clay-cold was her Lilly Hand,
>   That held her Sable Shroud.
>
> So shall the fairest Face appear
>   When Youth and Years are flown;
> Such is the Robe that Kings must wear,
>   When Death has riff'd their crown.[23]

This ballad imitation is moderately successful writing in English by a Scot in Scotland at the beginning of the century. For an additional piece of evidence from a Collection of Broadside Ballads in the National Library of Scotland, let us take these intensely political verses to the tune of 'Old Lang Syne'. They go back to the period immediately after the Union of 1707:

> O Caledon! O Caledon!
> How wretched is thy Fate.

Stanza V, which is fairly typical, runs:

> But oh! Alas, the Case is chang'd
> You'r wretched and forlorn,
> The hardships now impos'd on you
> By slaves are only born:
> Your antient Rights, which you so long
> Did with your Blood maintain,
> Are meanly sold and given up,
> And you dare scarce complain.[24]

As a third example I have chosen two stanzas from another broadside of the same period, concerning 'A bonny Lad of High Renown/ Who Liv'd in Aberdeen's fair town':

> My Love and I's like a Mine of Gold,
> planted in an island in the Sea,
> Where Boats and Barks and Men make bold
> in that curious island for to see.
> My Love and I's like a Mine of Gold,
> all cloathed o're on every side,
> Where Boats and Barks and Men make bold
> By that overflowing of the Tyde.[25]

And finally, a prose letter by James Thomson, author of *The Seasons*, written, as Mallet's ballad was, before he left his native country for England, and dated Edinburgh, 11th December 1724:

> You write to me that Misjohn and his Quadruped are
> making a large excentricall orbitt together with 2, or 3
> walletfulls of books which I suppose will be multiply'd into
> several more of papers befor they return. belike they have
> taken a trip into china, and then we shall have his travels.
> ther is one thing I hear storied (God forbid it be true) that
> his horse is metamorphosing into an ass. And by the last
> accounts I had of it, its lugs are shott up into a strange
> length and the cross was just begining to dawn upon its

shoulders and besides as it one day was saluting a cap-full of
oats (wonderfull to tell!) it fell a braying. I wish Nanny
Noble were so comfortably settl'd as you hint. tell Misjohn
when you see him that I have a bundle of worthies for him
if once I had receiv'd his packet. . . .[26]

The Thomson letter, owing a little to reminiscences of Don
Quixote and to the Augustan 'familiar style', is in the modified
standard language of a clergyman's son writing sixty years before
Burns. Any linguistic split, any basic inability to write easily in
English, should be evident here. But there is no such inability: there
is nothing but an ordinary letter, colloquial rather than dialectal,
but with some dialectal features. Thomson in his early letters
occasionally employs Scots morphology and syntax, as in the
paragraph following the one just quoted, where he has a weak
preterite inflexion 'com'd' instead of standard 'came': but in this
paragraph, as generally, the sentence patterns are those of everyday English and the only differences are in vocabulary — *Misjohn*
(Burns would have written 'Mess John'), the popular term for a
clergyman; *to story*, as a verb for 'to relate', and *lugs* for 'ears'. Such
a letter is every bit as Scottish in its own way as the stanza from
Burns's 'It was upon a Lammas night' which Daiches counterposed
to the *Charmer* song 'Now all thy virgin-sweets are mine': or, equally,
just as English.
    To return to lyric poetry: the situation was not in principle
different from that prevailing in the sixteenth century, when a
large number of English tunes and lyrics, 'popular' as well as 'art',
were known and sung in Scotland. But it did differ in the sheer
number of lyrics available, as well as in the currency of certain
types of popular and artificial songs which had arisen in the interval.
Reminiscing about his early reading Burns mentions that one of
the volumes which entranced him was a 'select Collection of English
songs' (note the significance of that word 'English'!). 'The Collection
of Songs was my vade mecum', he wrote. 'I pored over them,
driving my cart, or walking to labor, song by song, verse by verse;
carefully noting the true tender or sublime from affectation and
fustian. — I am convinced I owe much to this for my critic craft,
such as it is'.[27] Although it is still not absolutely certain which
miscellany Burns was referring to, the consensus of opinion is that
it was *The Lark*, printed for W. Gordon in the Parliament Close of
Edinburgh in 1765, and subtitled 'A Select Collection of the most
celebrated and newest songs, Scots and English'.[28] *The Lark* is an
excellent specimen of its kind. Its 324 pages print 321 songs that

enable us to sample the broadside, pastoral and artificial songs that were featured in the 'Tea-Table' division of popular lyrical taste, and it is significant that it also printed a few songs of the folk type. The bulk of its texts are taken over bodily from that best-seller among eighteenth-century miscellanies, Ramsay's *Tea-Table Miscellany*, or from Yair's *Charmer*. *The Lark* had no 'folk' texts that were not printed earlier by Ramsay or Yair.

The Lark, then, represented all sides of eighteenth-century Scottish song known to Burns, though in a rather distorted fashion: those which were not featured so strongly Burns supplemented from 'the compositions & Fragments which are daily sung' to Scots melodies by 'my compeers, the common people'.[29] To get some idea of these, one has to go to surviving manuscripts like the Herd MSS. and the St. Clair MS., to stall and slip songs, and to broadsides. Together, the song-books and the other classes of material preserve the popular lyric culture of the eighteenth century. In the following pages I attempt to analyse in some detail all the products of this culture apart from the folk ballads, and to indicate in my final chapter how they were summed up and transcended by Robert Burns.

REFERENCES

1.   [Scott], review of Cromek's *Reliques of Robert Burns*, in *Quarterly Review*, I (1809), 30-2.
2.   R. L. Stevenson, 'Some Aspects of Robert Burns', in *Familiar Studies of Men and Books* (London, 1923), p. 46.
3.   Pp. 72-135.
4.   [Jeffrey], review of Cromek's *Reliques*, in *Edinburgh Review*, XIII (1809), 263.
5.   In *Pride and Passion* (New York, 1939), pp. 247-8.
6.   B.B.C. Home Service, 25th January 1944: *Burns Chronicle* (1945), pp. 6-7.
7.   See, for example, Winifred Nowottny's analysis of the following two lines of 'O, open the door': 'The wan moon is setting ayont the white wave,/And time is setting with me, oh' (*The Language Poets Use*, London, 1965, pp. 140-1). And see also my *Burns*, pp. 257-67, on which I have drawn heavily in these first two pages.
8.   To Thomson (Sept. 1793), in *Letters of Robert Burns*, ed. J. de Lancey Ferguson, 2 vols. (Oxford, 1931), II, 200-1.
9.   'The Music of the Heart', *Renaissance and Modern Studies*, VIII (1964), 44-50.
10.   *The Songs of Robert Burns: a study of the Unity of Poetry and Music*, Studia Anglistica Upsaliensis (Uppsala, 1977).
11.   See *The Poetry of Robert Burns*, ed. W. E. Henley and T. F. Henderson (The Centenary Edition), 4 vols. (Edinburgh and London, 1896-7), henceforth cited as H. & H.: notes to Vol. III; *The Songs of Robert Burns*, ed. J. C. Dick (London, 1903); O. Ritter, *Quellenstudien zu Robert Burns 1773-1791* (Berlin, 1901) and *Neue Quellenfunde zu Robert Burns* (Halle, 1903).

12. *The Poems and Songs of Robert Burns*, ed. James Kinsley (The Oxford English
     Texts Edition), 3 vols. (Oxford, 1968), henceforth cited as Kinsley: notes
     in Vol. III cited as *P. & S.*

13. These are listed by William Montgomerie, *Bibliography of the Scottish Ballad
     Manuscripts 1730–1825*, Ph.D. thesis (Edinburgh, 1954) and in *Studies in
     Scottish Literature*, Vol. IV, No. 1 (July, 1966), 3-7. See also E. B. Lyle,
     'Child's Scottish Harvest', *Harvard Library Bulletin* XXV (1977), 125-54.

14. A sixth, not on this list, and dating principally from 1826–8, the Crawfurd
     MS. (Paisley Central Library, PC 1453-5) is of great importance for the
     previous century and therefore for Burns. See *Andrew Crawfurd's Collection
     of Ballads and Songs*, Vol. I, ed. E. B. Lyle, S.T.S. 4th Ser., 9 (Edinburgh,
     1976) and my review in *Scottish Literary Journal*, Supplement 5, Winter 1977,
     pp. 47-50.

15. W. Montgomerie, 'Some Notes on the Herd Manuscripts', *Edinburgh
     Bibliographical Society Transactions* (1948–55), III (1957), 291-8.

16. Much use of this MS. is made below, in Chapter 9.

17. B.M. 1346 m. 7. *Ballads*. See Chapter 8 below, where many of these are
     examined.

18. E.g. by Francis Collinson, *The Traditional and National Music of Scotland*
     (London, 1966) and David Johnson, *Music and Society in Lowland Scotland
     in the Eighteenth Century* (London, 1972). The term goes back further, *via*
     J. S. Blackie, *Scottish Song* (Edinburgh, 1889), to nineteenth-century
     German usage.

19. *Sunset Song* (1932): quotation from *A Scots Quair* (London, 1946), p. 28.

20. P. 69.

21. *Robert Burns* (New York, 1951), p. 1.

22. D. Daiches, *The Paradox of Scottish Culture* (Oxford, 1964), pp. 85-6;
     Kinsley, 8.

23. '*Margaret* and *William*, a Ballad. To the Tune of fair *ROSAMOND*',
     BM, 839.m. 23 (115).

24. *Old Scotch Ballads, Broadsides etc. 1679–1730*, NLS, Ry III.a 10 (71).

25. *Ibid.*, Ry III.a 10 (69).

26. *James Thomson (1700–1748) Letters and Documents*, ed. A. D. McKillop
     (Laurence, Kansas, 1958), pp. 1-2.

27. To John Moore (Mauchline, 2nd Aug. 1787) in *Letters*, I, 111-13.

28. H. Hecht, 'Burns lyrisches vade mecum: The Lark 1765', in *Archiv für das
     Studium der neueren Sprachen und Literaturen*, CXLIV (1922), 176-83.

29. *Robert Burns's Commonplace Book, 1783–1785*, ed. J. C. Ewing and D. Cook
     (Glasgow, 1938), pp. 37-8.

Chapter II

LOVE AND MARRIAGE

Every sub-group of the culture produced more songs on love than on any other subject, some of them purely conventional stereotypes, others showing real insight into the love and family life of eighteenth-century Scotland. To labour the obvious, Scotland, just like most other societies in Western Europe, was a money economy where the male sex dominated, and where both upper and middle classes increased in refinement as the century advanced.[1] A male-dominated family structure had been inherited from the medieval past, even although there is some speculation that in pre-Norman times Pictish society may have been matriarchal, with quite other sexual mores;[2] this structure applied to labourers, farmers and craftsmen as well as to those in a more comfortable station; and it was even enshrined in folk belief. Thus superstition had it that a girl who went before a boy to the baptismal font would pay dearly for her mistake. In the words of the minister of S. Ronaldsay at the end of the century:

> Within these last seven years the minister has been twice
> interrupted in administering baptism to a female child
> before the male child. When the service was over, he was
> gravely told that he had done very wrong, for, as the female
> child was first baptised, she would on her coming to years
> of discretion, most certainly have a strong beard, and the
> boy would have none.[3]

At the other end of the social scale, the same unquestioned notion of man's place is to be found in the words which William Creech, bookseller and publisher of Robert Burns, puts into the mind of an imaginary Louisa as she writes about her daughter:

> . . . in my life I never told her that beauty had, or ought to
> have, one single grain of merit essential to her well-being:
> On the contrary that there is no other way to make herself
> happy, but by endeavouring to cultivate those lasting
> accomplishments of which men never tire – A well-taught
> honest mind. . . .

I have an utter abhorrence for wit at any rate, unless it is
in a sensible good-natured man's keeping; but in a wife, it is
productive of many ills . . . I do insist upon it, the only
(light) woman ever can shine in is that which borrows its
lustre from their husbands.[4]

There were two tensions which influenced the love-behaviour of
every class — first, that between instinct and intellect, and that
between love and money or property. For the first contradiction an
important document is *Of Venery, Or of the Commerce of the Two Sexes*[5]
by the Rev. Robert Wallace (1697–1771), Moderator of the General
Assembly in 1743, Dean of the Chapel Royal and Chaplain in
Ordinary to George II in 1744. In spite of his cloth, Wallace
examines sexual behaviour in an utterly dispassionate and enlightened way. He finds that, in both sexes, its sole basis is lust. Yet
the official view is that for a woman 'no lust intermixes' even when
she appears sexually excited: the man 'must always provoke her and
lead the way'. Experience, says Wallace, teaches differently. He
rejects Platonic Love as impossible, and from his observation of
contemporary Scotsmen and Scotswomen he concludes:

Seldom I believe can a man admire the good qualities of a
fine woman's mind and conduct without a secret wish to be
familiar with her person. Virtue, honour, prudence may
restrain him from any indecency, but his regard is allways
mixed with something sensuall. If his health & the
temperament of his body be vigorous he would gladly rush
into her embraces: What women feel I know not but
perhaps the most bashfull virgin or chastest matron may not
be without the same sort of passionate Desires.

Scottish writers and English travellers often postulate a golden age
of sexual purity in eighteenth-century Scotland, especially before
1750 or 1760.[6] Yet Wallace, writing privately, and with the experience of the first half of the century in mind, appears to suggest
otherwise:

I think fornication should be Disscouraged, but be only
gently punished. It ought to be accounted a very great blot
even upon a woman's character. . . .[7] Those who profess to
make love an art, those who study it, often prefer a married
woman even during her marriage, to their own wives or to
virgins. The world have certainly gone into foolish
whimsicall, unnaturall, absurd, ill founded conceits on this

head. It would be much better if fornication gave less
scandall & there was less jealousy of wives and misstresses.

The reverend Moderator concedes that promiscuity 'is bad & must
be prevented. But a woman's being enjoyed by a Dozen in proper
circumstances can never render her less fit or less agreeable to a
thirteenth, if proper care is taken of all necessary decencies'. The
'necessary decencies' he envisages are, in fact, the details of a
utopian pattern of frequent and freely dissolvable marriages. 'I
would have no venereal commerce to take place between the two
sexes but in consequence of a contract entered into publickly before
witnesses & with certain ceremonies. I would give parents, relations,
and friends an opportunity to advise, but no negative on the
parties.' Wallace's ideal scheme has its parallels, perhaps even its
roots, in the customs and marital habits of the lower classes; and
his extreme emphasis on freedom of contract, as we shall see, is
merely a further development of the Calvinist ethic of the Kirk of
which he was so heterodox a member.

For a lower-class parallel, let us take a case which came before
the Presbytery of Irvine in 1762:

> A man 'acknowledged that marriage lines had passed betwixt
> him and a certain woman – that he had consented to the
> said marriage lines – that they both swore to be true to one
> another for two years, and, in case they did not like one
> another to be parted then' – and he added that, 'if the
> Moderator would free him, he would acknowledge marriage
> with her for two years'.[8]

As a general rule the peasantry have led freer and less inhibited
sex-lives than the middle classes. The Irvine case would seem to
substantiate this.[9]

Freedom of contract, the belief that marriage should be based
on the couple's own unimpeded choice, apart altogether from the
interests of relatives and, presumably, from monetary considera-
tions, had always been supported by the Kirk. Indeed, it is part of
the general Protestant ethic. In his *Table Talk* Luther says: 'The
substance of matrimony is the consent of bride and bridegroom;
and I advise that ministers interfere not in matrimonial questions,
but leave them to lawyers and magistrates'.[10] Milton's conception
that true marriage is a fusion of mind and spirit as well as body
would, by implication, preclude any sort of marriage for material
gain ('we know it is not the joining of another body will remove
loneliness, but the uniting of another compliable mind').[11] And

Samuel Rutherford told the Westminster Assembly of Calvinist Divines in 1644: 'Marriage is only the consent of parties; a vow is annexed unto it'. The English Brownists and Cromwellian Independents regarded marriage as a civil contract; all that was necessary was for the couple to declare themselves married in the presence of witnesses, quite irrespective of any solemnisation, whether in church or before a minister,[12] while the Westminster Directory (for Presbyterians) stated categorically that 'parents ought not to force their children to marry without their free consent, nor deny their own consent without just cause'. Nevertheless, so great was the pressure of material interests that the Church is sometimes on record as acting directly against its own precepts. In 1704 the Kilmarnock kirk session 'ordered Archibald Fulton, and Margaret Wilson's proclamation to be stopped, in regard his parents were against it'. And in 1712 the minister of Galston refused to order proclamation of banns for his own session-clerk and a rich widow, at the behest of the lady's relations.[13] By and large, however, in the conflict between love and money, the Kirk was on the side of love — provided love issued in marriage, and the marriage was regular.

Two of the greatest blemishes on regular marriage were premarital intercourse and 'Penny Weddings' — that is, in the words of the minister of Drainie at the time of the old Statistical Account, 'when the expense of the marriage entertainment is not defrayed by the young couple or their relations, but by a club amongst the guests. Two hundred people of both sexes will sometimes be convened on an occasion of this kind.'[14] The merrymaking lasted for two or three days and scenes were sometimes positively orgiastic. It was in its opposition to pre-marital sex, and to the revelry and merriment of Penny Weddings that the Kirk showed itself most inimical to the instinctive life of the body: for example, in 1723 Mr Wyllie of Clackmannan is reputed to have said:

> There is a young generation got up worse than their fathers, they have dancing at their *contracts*. They'll provoke God to blast their marriage and lessen their affection for one another. Some idle vagabonds came to the town with fiddles. Put them out of the town and break their fiddles, and I'll pay them.[15]

Folk attitudes to sex tend towards a frank acceptance of the physical, and to be expressed in the memory of such institutions as handfasting, which the minister of Eskdalemuir describes as having existed in that parish in former times. An annual fair was held at the meeting of the Black and White Esks:

> At that fair it was the custom for the unmarried persons of
> both sexes to choose a companion according to their liking,
> with whom they were to live till that time next year. This
> was called *handfasting*, or hand in fist. If they were pleased
> with each other at that time, then they continued together
> for life; if not, they separated, and were free to make
> another choice. The fruit of their connexion . . . was always
> attached to the disaffected person.[16]

The spirit if not the documentary actuality of Penny Weddings
is rendered not so much in songs composed during the eighteenth
century itself as in poems of the former century which came down
through *Watson's Collection* or the *Tea-Table Miscellany*, to be
reprinted continually in the years that followed. The original
Scotch wooing appears to be 'Robeyn's Jok come to wow our
Jynny'[17] in the Bannatyne MS., dating from the sixteenth century,
but the text printed by Allan Ramsay and substantially reprinted
by Herd (1769) adapts the situation (and the objects and utensils
mentioned in the poem) to the eighteenth century. Jenny has
'burnist baith breast and brou' for the occasion, but when the
mother brags of her dowry, Jenny interrupts, giglot-like:

> Te hee quo' Jenny, Kick, Kick I see you,
>   Minny, yon makes but a mock
>   Deil hae the liers — fu lies me o' you.

The refrain line which follows serves to emphasise the young man's
oafish single-mindedness: 'I came to woo your Jenny, quo' Jock'.
The mother enumerates the tocher's items — goose, gryce, cock and
hen, sown acre, graip, flail, rusty whittle, and all the rest of them —
a list of homely artefacts, each with its sometimes slightly archaic
dialect term. The couple marry by declaration without benefit of
clergy, after which Jock sets down *his* property in a parallel in-
ventory. The most important objects listed from the woman's
point of view were, perhaps 'Twa lusty lips to lick a laiddle', and
the most stimulating

> Five hundred flaes, a fendy flock,
>   And are not thae a wakrife menzie,
> To gae to bed with Jenny and Jock?[18]

The song ends with a final comic insult:

> The rost was teuch as raploch hodin,
> With which they feasted Jenny and Jock.

In this song, whether in its eighteenth- or sixteenth-century version, the comedy concerns material goods and the social accoutrements of marriage as a community event, and there is no churching. 'Muirland Willie', however, also from *The Tea-Table Miscellany* and also, in all probability, based on a much earlier original, gives the couple the Kirk's blessing:

> This winsome couple straked hands,
> Mess John ty'd up the marriage bands.

In 'Muirland Willie' an orgiastic celebration follows, of the sort that won the Kirk's disapproval. The bridesmaids and 'our lads' dance to a wild reel when it is all over:

> Sic hirdum, dirdum, and sic din,
> Wi he o'er her, and she o'er him;
> The minstrels they did never blin,
>   Wi' meikle mirth and glee.
> And ay they bobit, and ay they beckt,
> And ay their lips together met,[19]
>   With a fal, dal, &c.

For the really orgiastic aspect of Penny Weddings, one has to go to 'The Kirriemuir Wedding', which probably dates from the late eighteenth century, though preserved only in a chapbook of the early nineteenth century. From the rhythm it seems almost certain that it went to a tune of the same type as the modern 'Ball of Kirriemuir':

> *Singing, go, girls, go,*
>   *And we'll hae anither tune,*
> *And we'll ne'er dance sae young again,*
>   *Gin ance this night were done.*

> There were three score o' maidens gaed,
>   ('Twas braw being there),
> But only ane come hame again;
>   Judge ye an' that was fair.

> There was twa into the barn,
>   And twa into the byre,
> And twa among the pease strae,
>   I think they'll never tire.

> There was twa ahint the pease stack,
>   And twa amang the pease;
> But ye could na see the barn-floor
>   For naked hips and thighs.

In came John Anderson,
    Says he to brother James,
'Will ye gang to the barn-floor,
    And kiss the wanton queens?'

In came John Tait, the factor's man,
    Says he, 'Well may ye thrive!'
But before he kissed his own true love,
    He play'd wi' ither five.

In came the minister's maid,
    And she was warst o' a';
For she tint her muslin apron
    Among the pease straw.

The lads they lost their knee-buckles,
    The lasses their bucklin-kames;
But three score o' maidenheads
    Play'd a' crack at ance.

Now ilka lad has ta'en his lass,
    And he's convoy'd her hame;
And ilka lass says to her lad,
    'Whan will ye do't again?'[20]

Those who enjoyed Penny Weddings — whether the orgy of 'The Kirriemuir Wedding' or the 'hirdum dirdum' of 'Muirland Willie' — were living examples of the 'passionate Desire' which Robert Wallace recognised as actuating the men and women of all classes. For the artistic expression of such a brutally insistent drive one has generally to go to the 'folk' end of the lyrical spectrum. Even here, songs of brutal and urgent desire are few in number — songs where a male protagonist says 'I want a woman, this is what it feels like to want a woman, and this is what I'm going to do to her when I get her'. The expression of the instinct is almost always distanced, in a miniature narrative framework, and shot through with comedy; in other words, the instinct — the appetite — can rarely be freed from the bawdy.

Thus the song of pure physical desire shades imperceptibly into a narrative dealing with the comedy of love and marriage.[21] The following expresses masculine desire at its simplest, with a barbaric sadism that is almost universal:

O gin I had her,
Ay gin I had her,
O gin I had her,
    Black altho' she be.

I wad lay her bale,
I'd gar her spew her kail,
She ne'er soud keep a mail
   Till she dandl'd it on her knee.[22]

And the same urgency, slightly less explicit, comes through in the folk fragment:

Lass, an I come near thee,
Lass, an I come near thee,
I'll gar a' your ribbons reel,
Lass, an I come near thee.[23]

When the poem is, grammatically speaking, in the first person, the 'I' of the song is generally a woman, even though we may feel certain that the real author was a man, and the song originally intoned at masculine convivial assemblies, as in the celebrated ' "Elibanks and Elibraes" so famous in baudy song to-day' mentioned by Burns in his *Journal of the Border Tour* for 14th May 1787. The woman in this song is not content to lie prone, in the 'missionary posture', but twines her thighs around her partner as if she were about to climb a rope or a tree;[24] and she boasts of her prowess in the first person. If the persona is not so much a real girl as the projection of a male wish-fulfilment dream, her very existence indicates that some Scotsmen had an ideal of active womankind that was poles apart from the pale lilies of polite society, however languorously these might deck their couches. In many a folk-song this ideal takes on flesh and blood to become a sexually proud and independent heroine of everyday life.

A woman of this sort appears in a late popular ballad fragment:

He look'd archly in her face
And blithely he did smile aye
Said let him do the warst he can
Still you'll be whore to Boyndlie.

She took him in her arms twa
And kissed him most kindly
Says I am whore to none but thee
And I'll die for thee my Boyndlie.[25]

The woman becomes 'whore' to Boyndlie after her father refuses to double her tocher so that she can be made Lady Boyndlie, and her repudiation of convention expresses her contempt for man-made property-based sexual morality. It is the contempt so characteristic of the independent heroine of folk and popular song, which makes her rather different from art-song's 'honest woman', the establishment's counterpart of the eighteenth century's 'noblest work of God', The following fragment from the St. Clair MS. conveys her overwhelming delight in getting the man she loves:

> I gotten the laddie that (I) liked sair
> I gotten &c.
> I gotten &c.
> And I'll never lie wi' my auld minny nae mair.
>
> The Har'est it is shorn the rigs they are bare
> The Har'est &c.
> The Har'est &c.
> And I'll never lie wi' my auld minny nae mair.[26]

Alternatively, folk-song may express her intention to put sexual pleasure 'abune a' thing':

> I'll hae a fiddler to my goodman
> I'll hae &c.
> If I dinnae get meat eneugh I'll get play
> And I'll get skeeg about a' the lang day.[27]

And she will venture all for love just as surely as the heroine of popular nineteenth-century novels:

> And for you Johnny Lad
> And &c.
> I'll sell the Buckles o' my shoon
> For you Johnny Lad.
>
> Johnny's no a gentleman
> And Johnny's no a Laird
> But I will marry Johnny Lad
> Altho he were a card.[28]

Visually, the independent heroine is Jenny Nettles:

> Saw ye Jenny Nettles,
>   Jenny Nettles, Jenny Nettles,
> Saw ye Jenny Nettles
>   Coming frae the market;
> Bag and baggage on her back,
>   Her fee and bountith in her lap;
> Bag and baggage on her back,
>   And a babie in her oxter.[29]

But only visually. The fully developed type is far removed from the
helpless figure of Ramsay's song; she does not need any Robin
Rattle to use her kindly, to

> Tak hame (her) wean, make Jenny fain,
> The leel and leesome gate o't.

On the contrary, the independent heroine is more often than not
liable herself to take the initiative. Nor is she to be found only in
Scotland. She is as much English or Irish as Scots, and the really
distinguishing thing about her is that she is a woman of the people.
She is the girl in Martin Parker's seventeenth-century 'The Wooing
Lasse and the Way-Ward Lad';[30] and some of her spirit turns up
in the town prostitute too, in 'The Ranting Wanton's Resolution;
Wherein you will find that her only Treasure Consisteth in being a
Lady of Pleasure. To the Tune of General Monk's March':

> Oh! fye upon Care,
> Why should we despair?
> Give me the lad that will frollick,
> There is no disease,
> But Musick will please,
> If it were the stone or the cholick.
> The lad that drinks Wine,
> Shall only be mine,
> He that calls for a Cup of Canary,
> That will tipple and sing,
> Kiss, caper, and spring,
> *And calls for his Mab, and his Mary.*[31]

She is of a piece with the lass in the compressed narratives and
broadsides who follows her lover to the wars dressed in man's
attire[32] and with many a heroine in the Child ballads.

It is such a lass, even, whose desires are intoned by the Crochallan Fencibles and other roisterers of the upper-class all-male
clubs of eighteenth-century Scotland. It is she who sings;

> O some delights in cuttie stoup,
> And some delights in cuttie-mun,
> But my delight's an a--elins coup,
> Wi' Andrew an his cuttie gun.
>
> *Blythe, blythe, blythe, was she,*
> *Blythe was she but and ben,*
> *An' weel she lo'ed it in her neive,*
> *But better when it slippit in.*[33]

When married, she is the protagonist in 'John Anderson my jo', a
plebeian beauty with insatiable demands:

> I'm backit like a salmon,
>   I'm breastit like a swan;
> My wame it is a down-cod,
>   My middle ye may span:
> Frae my tap-knot to my tae, John,
>   I'm like the new-fa'n snow;
> And it's a' for your convenience,
>   John Anderson, my jo . . .
>
> When ye come on before, John,
>   See that ye do your best;
> When ye begin to haud me,
>   See that ye grip me fast;
> See that ye grip me fast, John,
>   Until that I cry 'Oh'!
> Your back shall crack or I do that,
>   John Anderson, my jo.[34]

If these demands are not satisfied, the independent wife will give
him the 'cuckold's mallison' — or, as she says in st. vii of the *Scots
Nightingale* text, not printed in the Merry Muses version:

> I'll study my ain conveniency
> John Anderson, my jo.

St. iii of the anonymous 'John Anderson' ('I'm backit like a salmon')
is surely one of the finest renderings of nude beauty in British poetry.
Its excellence is a matter of vigour and precision of diction. Because
of their verbal force, the participial *backit* and *breastit* suggest action
that is not merely the movement of a woman's body, but includes a
shaping that resembles an artist's bending or moulding of a form in
clay. Furthermore, the alliterative pattern of *b*'s and *s*'s increases
our sensation of activity. The fish and animal similes place the
woman's beauty in a natural context, the 'down-cod' in a domestic
one: similarly, the warm whiteness of the feather pillow both
contrasts and harmonises with the chill of blinding snow. 'Convenience' is again warm, human, domestic — and is sung, one feels,
with a sad ironic tenderness that knows her threats of cuckolding
will all too probably come to pass.

   Strongly sensual courtships, then as now, often led to marriage
through pregnancy, as in 'Oxter my lassie', a stall song uniting
narrative and dialogue:

> When every lad had got his lass,
> To drink and dance their custom was;
> Into a dark room with my love I did creep,
> And there I did oxter my lassie sae sweet. . . .

When she came home late, her parents scolded her mercilessly, and

> The lassie she blushed like any rose,
> 'Tis for the ruffling to her cloth;
> The weeting of her docups in the dew,
> That caus'd my lassie so sair for to rue.

After nine months the narrator was 'discover'd to the public', mounted the stool of repentance in the parish Kirk, and finally married the girl:

> There's not a lad in this country side,
> That ever met with a bonnier bride.
> With her I got three thousand mark,
> For kissing my lassie in the dark,
> The same I received with heart and good will,
> And now boys I'll oxter my lassie still.
>   My lassie, still, &c.[35]

This doggerel song must reflect the reality of many a village courtship, as well as many a poor ploughman's dream of a large dowry.[36] Allan Ramsay's 'Corn rigs are bonny' from *The Gentle Shepherd*, in contrast, idealises and stylises the relationship, as befits the drama in which it occurs.[37]

Fergusson's 'The Lee-Rig', the original of Burns's of the same title, again celebrates an open-air wooing, this time on the 'meadow ridge':

> Will ye gang o'er the lee-rigg,
>   My ain kind deary O!
> And cuddle there sae kindly
>   Wi' me, my kind deary O?
>
> At thornie-dike and birken-tree
>   We'll daff, and ne'er be weary O;
> They'll scug ill een frae you and me,
>   Mine ain kind deary O.
>
> Nae herds wi' kent, or colly there,
>   Shall ever come to fear ye O;
> But lav'rocks, whistling in the air,
>   Shall woo, like me, their deary O!

> While others herd their lambs and ewes,
>   And toil for warld's gear, my jo,
> Upon the lee my pleasure grows,
>   Wi' you, my kind deary O ![38]

The pastoral convention can be felt in Fergusson's stanzas; and beside it, another convention — that of Scots bawdry, 'I'll lay (rowe) thee on the lea-rig, my ain kind dearie, O'.[39] No matter whether 'laying' or a simple rendezvous were in question, the open air was the commonest, almost the *necessary* venue — witness the fragment in the Herd MS. which is perhaps the original of all the 'Lea Rig' songs:

> Tho' the night were ne'er sae dark
> And I were ne'er sa weary,
> I'd meet on the ley-rig
> My ain kind deary.[40]

The songs of rural courtship express a greater variety of tone and situation than one might at first expect. There are, for example, merry meetings, like 'Jocky said to Jeany', marked by Allan Ramsay as an old song, and characterised by a delightful humorous repartee:

> Jeany said to Jocky, gin ye winna tell,
> Ye shall be the lad, I'll be the lass my sell.
> Ye're a bonny lad, and I'm a lassie free,
> Ye're welcomer to tak me than to let me be.[41]

A song whose author we know, from the last years of the century, converts a rural courtship comedy into a genre piece. It is Alexander Robertson's 'The lass that winna sit doun':[42]

> What think ye o' the scornfu' quine
>   'ill no sit doun by me.
> I'll see the day that she'll repine
>   Unless she does agree.
> O she did hoot, and toot and flout
>   'cause I bid her sit doun;
> But the next time that e'er I do't
>   I'll be whip't like a loon.
>   Wi a tirry, &c.

The girl's pride vanishes when she hears him sing, and at last she 'fairly' casts 'a sheep's ee' upon him. These lovers are members of a community; the song's action takes place in the middle of a crowd, and their language is that of looks and gestures — they are not much given to words. A single glance is enough:

> I ga'e the lass a lovin' squint,
>   That made her blush sae red,
> I saw she fairly took the hint,
>   Which made my heart fou glad.

In 'My Jo, Janet', the comedy is generated by the contrast between two 'lichtsome' personalities, between the girl's extravagant desires and the man's sarcastic canniness. It is an amorous flyting, a battle of gamesmanship between the sexes:

> Sweet Sir, for your courtesie,
>   When you come by the Bass then,
> For the love ye bear to me,
>   Buy me a keeking glass then.
> *Keek into the draw well,*
>   Janet, Janet,
> *And there ye'll see ye'r bonny sell,*
>   *My Jo* Janet.

The next stanza has an unforgettable reference to the solution taken by some pregnant girls in a Calvinist community:

> Keeking in the draw-well clear,
>   What if I shou'd fa' in
> Syne a' my kin will say and swear,
>   I drown'd mysell for sin.
> *Had better be the brae,*
>   Janet, Janet:
> *Had better be the brae*
>   *My Jo* Janet.

In st. iii, again for love, she asks him to buy a pair of shoes for her as he comes through Aberdeen, but he tells her to 'clout the auld, the new are dear'. The characterisation of Janet, though slight, is altogether delightful in its combination of energetic lighthearted-ness and keen sensitivity to public opinion:

> But what if dancing on the green,
> And skipping like a mawking,
> If they shou'd see my clouted shoon,
> Of me they will be tauking.
> *Dance ay laigh, and late at e'en,*
>   Janet, Janet,
> *Syne a' their faults will no be seen,*
>   *My Jo,* Janet.

When she next asks for a pacing-horse, she is firmly put in her place –
the home, and domestic industry:

> *Pace upo' your spinning-wheel,*
>   Janet, Janet;
> *Pace upo' your spinning-wheel,*
>   *My Jo,* Janet.

She makes her come-back by bringing in a potentially sexual
allusion; he ends up by making it explicit:

> My spinning-wheel is auld and stiff,
>   The rock o't winna stand, Sir,
> To keep the temper-pin in tiff,
>   Employs aft my hand, Sir.
> *Make the best o't that you can,*
>   Janet, Janet;
> *But like it never wale a man,*
>   *My Jo,* Janet;[43]

'Kind-hearted Nancy', in Herd's *Scots Songs* (1776), is another
effervescent flyting dialogue, this time between Nancy and 'Sla
cow'rdly Wilsy', which takes this sort of amorous folk comedy a
stage further. Here it is the girl that always gets the better of the
argument – the strongly independent heroine we have already met
with. In sts. i-iii she announces she will go to the green-wood;
Wilsy asks 'what an I come after you?'; and she replies 'and what
gif ye come back again?'. Sts. iv-vii, run as follows:

> But what gif I shou'd lay thee down?
>   Quo WILSY, quo' WILSY;
> What gif I should lay thee down?
>   Quo' sla cow'rdly WILSY.
>
> And what gif I can rise again?
>   Quo' NANCY, quo' NANCY;
> And what gif I can rise again?
>   Quo' kind hearted NANCY.
>
> O but what if I get you wi' bairn?
>   Quo' WILSY, etc.
> If you can get it I can bear't,
>   Quo' NANCY, etc.

In sts. viii-xi Wilsy asks where they'll get a cradle ('There's plenty
o' wood in Norway' is the answer), and a cradle-belt ('Your
garters and mine'); and the last stanzas, xii-xv, return to a course

which is parallel to another question-and-answer group, 'Dabbling in the Dew':

> Then whar'l I tye my beastie to?
> Quo' WILSY, etc.
>
> Tye him to my muckle tae,
> Quo' NANCY, etc.
>
> O what gif he should run awa'?
> Quo' WILSY, etc.
>
> Deil gae wi' you, steed an a',
> Quo' NANCY, etc.[44]

What could be more indigenous, more thoroughly Scottish in tone and spirit than this little interchange? Yet its analogues are not Scottish but English. The 'Dabbling in the Dew' songs are from south of the border, and 'sla cowardly Wilsy' has his forerunner in the English 'slow Willie Stenson'.[45] We are not here dealing with conscious faking, with turning a pseudo-Caledonian song like those manufactured in England by Thomas Durfey in the late seventeenth century into a genuine Scottish one, but with folk-borrowing within the oral tradition. Its import for our general argument is similar. Just as Allan Ramsay and other would-be artistic creators of Scottish 'national song'[46] sometimes quite consciously based their lyrics on Grub Street imitations, so, too, English folk-songs became Scottish through a natural process of diffusion. Scottish and English popular songs were closely connected at *every* level.

REFERENCES

1. More accurately, some members of these classes, especially women, increased in sophistication; but there is considerable evidence that heavy, brutal drinking was commoner amongst men towards the end of the century than at the beginning, while women tended to meet apart from the men.

2. A. D. Hope, *A Midsummer Eve's Dream* (London, 1971), presents some of the evidence for this.

3. *The Statistical Account of Scotland*, 21 vols. (1791-9), henceforth cited as *Stat. Account*, XV, 311.

4. W. Creech, *Edinburgh Fugitive Pieces: with Letters, containing a comparative view of the modes of living . . . manners &c. of Edinburgh, at different periods* (Edinburgh, 1815), henceforth cited as Creech, p. 177.

5. The MS. is in the Laing Collection of the University of Edinburgh Library (La. II.620), and was printed by Norah Smith in *Texas Studies in Literature and Language*, XV, 3 (Fall, 1973), 430-44.

6.   J. Ramsay (of Ochtertyre), *Scotland and Scotsmen in the Eighteenth Century*, ed. A. Allardyce, 2 vols. (Edinburgh, 1888), henceforth cited as Ramsay of Ochtertyre, II, 59.

7.   Note the assumption of the 'double standard', even in Wallace.

8.   A. Edgar, *Old Church Life in Scotland: Second Series* (Paisley and London, 1886), henceforth cited as Edgar, p. 194.

9.   As would also the other Irvine case of the old soldier who in 1769 wished to get married but was accused of being already a married man. He admitted that he had 'lived with another woman in the army for some time . . . but said that he was married to her no otherwise than by stepping over a sword' (Edgar, l.c.).

10.   Quoted in Edgar, p. 179.

11.   Milton, *The Doctrine and Discipline of Divorce*, Chapter XVI.

12.   Edgar, p. 179.

13.   Edgar, pp. 158-9.

14.   *Stat. Account*, IV, 86.

15.   Edgar, p. 156, n.

16.   *Stat. Account*, XII, 615.

17.   *The Bannatyne Manuscript* (1568), ed. W. Tod Ritchie, 4 vols. (S.T.S. 1928–34), III, 15-18.

18.   Comparison with the Bannatyne version at this point reveals the character of Ramsay's innovation:

> Fyive hundredth fleis now in a flok,
> Call ye nocht that an joly menȝe,
> To go to giddir, Jynny and Jok?

Ramsay's adjectives bring out the busy activity of the fleas: the MS. 'joly' is colloquially ironical. The Ramsay text is in *The Tea-Table Miscellany*, henceforth cited as *TTM*, II: (London, 1740), p. 166.

19.   'Harken and I will tell ye how', *TTM* I: (1740), p. 7.

20.   Sts. ii-ix, in *The Flower of Caledonia. . . .* Edinburgh. Printed by Sanderson & Co. No. 253, High Street. 1817: Glasgow University Library, Sp. Coll. 221. S. 1750 C (2).

21.   For a more detailed treatment of this topic, see below, Chapter VI.

22.   *The Merry Muses of Caledonia*, edd. James Barke and S. Goodsir Smith (Edinburgh, 1959), henceforth cited as *Merry Muses*, p. 155; *Love, Labour and Liberty*, ed. T. Crawford (Manchester, 1976), henceforth cited as *LLL*, 82.

23.   Cited in H. & H. III, 376; *LLL*, 83.

24.   Burns, *Merry Muses*, pp. 108-9, st. i, lines 5-8, sts. ii-iv.

25.   W. Motherwell, MS. *Ballad Book* (Glasgow University Library, MS. Murray 501), p. 471.

26.   St. Clair MS., p. 100; *LLL*, 103.

27.   *Ibid.*, p. 127; *LLL*, 104.

28.   *Ibid.*, p. 107.

29.   *TTM*, II: (1740), p. 177; *LLL*, 86.

30.   *The Roxburghe Ballads*, 9 vols. (London & Hertford, 1871–1902), henceforth cited as *Roxb. Bds.*, III, 296-301.

31.   *Amanda Group of Bagford Poems*, ed. Ebsworth (Hertford, 1880), I, *479-81, st. i.

32.   See below, p. 104.

33.   *Merry Muses*, p. 120, 'Andrew an' his Cuttie Gun'. Kinsley, *P. & S.*, p. 1249, suggests that in 1794 Burns may not have known this bawdy version of a bacchanalian song.

34.   *Merry Muses*, p. 114, sts. iii, v; *LLL*, 80. Versions in *Philomel* (London,

1744), p. 202; *The Masque* (London, 1762), p. 309; *The Scots Nightingale* (Edinburgh, 1778), p. 238.

35. BM, 1346 m. 7 (14), broadside dated 14th Sept. 1775.

36. T. C. Smout, in his treatment of population in *A History of the Scottish People 1560–1830*, estimates that the retained population of Scotland between 1755 and 1820 'increased by roughly two-thirds in sixty-five years', and notes that in 1755 both the birth-rate and the infant death-rate were extremely high. He speculates that economic conditions (increased production of farming and the introduction of the potato) may have diminished the fear of pregnancy, from which we may perhaps deduce an increase in sexual activity during the century. In any case the population was a very young one — 42 per cent under the age of 20 in 1755, 48 per cent under 20 in 1820: that is, there was a great increase in the love-making group during the century, i.e. in the numbers of those who would be most likely to sing or make love songs. What proportion of the increased births were conceived out of wedlock is uncertain, but it is likely to have been a high one. For a subjective judgement we may go to W. Alexander's *Notes and Sketches Illustrative of Northern Rural Life in the Eighteenth Century* (Edinburgh, 1877). Talking of the North-East of Scotland, he says that Kirk Session Records show there were just as many bastard births in the eighteenth century as in his own day, when the figure in some parishes was over 20 per cent of all live births. He laments the permissive attitude to sexual behaviour in this area and comments:

> Born into and nurtured from childhood in a pervasive social atmosphere of this sort it becomes readily intelligible how women whose characters otherwise one would be sorry to impugn in the least barely realise it as any permanent stain on their womanhood to have been the mother of a bastard. . . . Only this much must be said with truth that while the women who sadly fail in virgin modesty ordinarily prove true and faithful wives when married, even the men who join with them in wedlock do also as a rule act with conjugal fidelity thereafter. With them the vice as it exists is gross and open; we see it in its full extent, and may know its limits; and in this way the common people of the rural community probably suffer some considerable injustice when their sins in this respect are sought to be contrasted with those of certain other classes more highly civilised it may be, and enjoying far greater social advantage (p. 213).

This seems a shrewd comment on the *ethos* that lies behind the rural courtship lyrics of the eighteenth century.

37. 'My Patie is a lover gay', *Gentle Shepherd*, V, iii (Sang xxi).

38. *Scots Musical Museum*, 6 vols. (1787–1803), henceforth cited as *Museum*, 49; *Charmer* (Edinburgh, 1782), II, 191; *LLL*, 124.

39. Songs from David Herd's Manuscripts, ed. H. Hecht (Edinburgh, 1904), henceforth cited as Hecht-Hd., pp. 100, 281; Burns, *Notes on Scottish Song*, ed. J. C. Dick (London, 1908), henceforth cited as *Notes*, pp. 17-18.

40. Hecht-Hd., p. 101.

41. *TTM*, I: (1740), p. 70, st. iv. Ramsay incorporated this stanza into the first version of *The Gentle Shepherd* in 1725-6 (IV, i). The full text was printed in the editions subsequent to 1729, and is *LLL*, 115. See also below, p. 91.

42. *Museum*, 463 (1796).

43. *TTM*, I: (1740), p. 56.
44. Herd (1776), II, 176. For a fuller treatment of this group, see my article 'Jean Armour's Double and Adieu' in *Scottish Studies*, VII, Part 1 (1963), 37-46.
45. For a Scottish form, see [Peter Buchan, pseud.] Sir Oliver Orpheus, *Secret Songs of Silence* (1832), henceforth cited as *S.S.S.*, Harvard College Library MS. 25241.9, pp. 33-6.
46. See below, Chapters VIII, IX.

Chapter III

LOVE AND THE UPPER CLASSES

Where the independent heroine was not the fantasy-figure of all male drinking clubs, but a real girl convincingly presented, she often proved her independence against her parents or the husband chosen for her: the theme is found in many ballads and compressed narratives about elopement ('Then hey play up the rinaway bride,/ For she has ta'en the gee').[1] The conflict between love values and money and property values, felt by men and women of all classes, was particularly evident among the wealthy and the great. Robert Wallace[2] wrote at mid-century:

> According to our present manners few of the better sort &
> many of the poorer sort are not or do not think themselves
> in a condition to marry because they cannot support great
> families of children in the rank to which they think them
> intituled. Att least they cannot do it att that season of life
> when they have the greatest relish for Venery; therefore
> they do not marry till they are fourty or fifty years of age &
> have become rich. In the mean time they indulge themselves
> in debauchery, they debauch all the women of low rank who
> come their way & will suffer them; if they beget children,
> being uncertain about the issue, or even tho' they are certain,
> their children being bastards are miserably neglected.

Wallace's general observations are supported by Boswell's experiences as recorded in his Journals — for example, by his own adventures with prostitutes and other women of the lower classes. As an instance of neglect of bastards one may cite the case of Jeanie, a natural daughter of Lord Kinnaird, whom Boswell found in a close in the Luckenbooths. On 19th January 1768 he wrote:

> I was so happy with Jeanie Kinnaird that I very
> philosophically reasoned that there was to me so much
> virtue mixed with licentious love that perhaps I might be
> privileged. For it made me humane, polite, generous. But
> then lawful love with a woman I really like would make me
> still better. I forgot the risk I run with this girl.[3]

Most of the contradictions behind upper-class sexual behaviour are implied in these few brief lines from Boswell – male domination, the shameless double standard of morality, the conflict and inter-mingling of 'virtue' and licence, the horrors of prostitution, the pathetic desire for a deep and stable permanent union.

Marriage based on life-long love was certainly the ideal, and – in spite of all we have just noted – the Scots seemed to their neighbours to be a good deal more constant and less scandalous than the lovers of other nations, especially at the beginning of the century. No doubt the chastity of upper-class women was based on the whoredom of their poorer fallen sisters: a chastity, indeed, that went along with a freedom and spontaneity of manners that surprised the more formal English. Boswell noted it on his return from England, while Captain Topham observed in 1775 that 'the women are of a differ-ent nature and disposition from the men. They are all freedom, all affability, and breathe the very spirit of Gallantry. They have a certain vivacity and negligence in their behaviour, which has the most amiable appearance you can conceive'. Their menfolk were so dull in comparison that 'to rouse the latent spark, every assistance is necessary, so that it is in their interest to be perfect mistresses in the art of pleasing; and indeed, they are arrived at such perfection in it, as to be excelled by none in Europe'. And Topham goes on to say that, despite their womenfolk's 'appearance of levity and wantonness . . . no people are more constant, faithful and sincere in their amours'.[4]

There is some conflict of opinion about how free upper-class manners really were. Writing of an extensive period covering nearly two centuries, Charles Rodgers speaks of the 'lofty demeanour' of some gentlewomen and gentlemen, citing the very highest aristocracy – Charles II's Duke of Lauderdale, the ninth Earl of Abercorn, and the 'proud' Duke of Hamilton.[5] Elizabeth Mure of Caldwell, writing near 1790 and at the end of a long life, remembers that with the setting up of a weekly assembly for dancing in Edin-burgh about 1724, and the innovation of private balls carried on by subscription, women's society became more enlarged, and their conduct more refined, 'but it required time to have a proper effect'. She recollects that in the seventeen-twenties men's manners were more stiff and formal than 'the wemen's', who 'were undelicat in their conversation and vulgar in their manners'. She continues:

> As the awe and reverance for parents and elder friends wore off, they brought into company the freedom and romping they had acquired amongst their brothers and neer relations.

Many of them threw off all restrent. Were I to name the time when the Scotch Ladys went farthest wrong, it would be betwixt the 30 and 40. I'm at a loss to account for this, if it was not owing to our young noblemen bringing home Franch manners; and least they should be lead into marriges, made their addresses to those only that were in that state. No doubt the contrast betwixt the young men educated abroad and ours who were closs at home would be very great. Besides, the manners of the Ladys might lead the men to more freedom if they were so disposed, as they had not yet lairnd that restrent so necessary where society is inlarged. Yet this was far from being generall.[6]

In his Edinburgh visit of 1774 and 1775 Captain Topham failed to find 'that abandoned spirit for Intrigue' so common in England, and noted that 'the name of adultery is hardly known; it is a *rara avis*, a phoenix which exists only once in a hundred years'.[7] But Elizabeth Mure, in the passage quoted, obviously remembers *some* adultery from fifty years before. William Creech notes that in 1763 adultery was punished by fine, church censure and the ostracism of the women, but that in 1783:

> Although the law punishing adultery with death was unrepealed, yet church-censure was disused, and separations and divorces were become frequent, and have since increased. Women, who have been rendered infamous by public divorce, had been, by some people of fashion, again received into society. . . .[8]

It seems probable that Topham idealised present manners, Creech those of his youth, and that with the decline in Presbyterian strictness adulterers became less discreet and more numerous towards the end of the century.

Be that as it may, there would no doubt be some difference between the behaviour of the sons and daughters of country lairds, living on their own estates, and those of the Edinburgh establishment. Yet town *did* influence country. Elizabeth Mure notes that after the tea-table habit[9] took on in the seventeen-twenties:

> . . . the Teatables very soon interdused supping in private houses. When young people found themselves happy with one another they were loath to part, so that supping came to be the universal fashion in Edinr. . . . Those merry suppers made the young people find a want when they went to the country, and to supply the place of them was

introduced Colations after Supper; when the young people
met in some one of their bed chambers, and had either tea
or a posset, where they satt and made merry till far in the
morning. But this meeting was carefully consealed from the
Parents, who were all ennimys to these Collations.[10]

Despite the free manners of town and country adolescents, the
pressures of the marriage-property system cannot be gainsaid;
they left their traces in the diaries and memoirs of the time. At the
level of pure comedy, we may cite John Murray of Ochtertyre who
married Lucky Thom, a tavern-keeper, to clear a £4000 debt he
had contracted to her.[11] More seriously, we learn from the Rev.
Alexander Carlyle of the long engagement of his sister Margaret,
which could not be 'fulfilled for four years or more'. Margaret had
been brought up at Dumfries by her aunt Bell and her uncle,
George Bell, the Provost and political leader of the Town, 'who was
governed by his wife – who was swayed by her niece and Frank
Paton, Surveyor of the Customs, who was a very able man, and who,
with my sister were the secret springs of all the provost's conduct'.
Margaret's marriage to a Dr Thomas Dickson was opposed by the
Provost on financial grounds, and by Carlyle on other grounds –
that Dickson was not intelligent or lively enough for his sister. The
marriage did not take place till George Bell was dead, 'and Dickson
in better circumstances'.[12]

During his own long and unsuccessful courtship of his first
love, Carlyle used 'family politics', namely the esteem of her
uncle, to try to gain her affections.[13] He seems to have been attracted
by her personality rather than by her fortune, and complains with
some bitterness that 'with an air of haughty prudery, (she) had
enough of coquetry both to attract and retain her lovers, of whom
she had many'.[14] The search for a wife could be an expensive business,
as we learn from the case of the minister of Traquair, who got into
debt in 1729 and was asked by the Presbytery to give a complete
statement of his losses and in particular any unusual expenses he
had incurred. One of the items reads 'by courting during my widow-
hood, near eight years, considering the different persons I was in
quest of, and the distance of place, £1000'.[15] Then as now, the
marriage-property system was cut across by sheer infatuation –
sometimes quite mildly, as when the Rev. George Ridpath flirted
with Betty Pollock 'a very pretty, natural thing' in 1757. One of
Ridpath's entries reads 'still, I believe foolishly, conspired to fondle
the Naiad', and another – 'Spent the night somewhat wildly, as
usual excited by the sweet lassie, Bett Pollock'.[16] The case of Hugh,

3rd Earl of Marchmont shows an interesting blend of infatuation and male dominance. Alexander Carlyle comments: 'His second lady who was young and handsome, but a simple and quiet woman, and three daughters he had by his former lady, were all under due subjection, for his lordship kept a high command at home'.[17]

But the story of how the Earl acquired this suitably subdued 'second lady' is the classic one of love at first sight. It is told by David Hume in a letter to James Oswald of Dunnikier:

> [Lord Marchmont] has had the most extraordinary adventure in the world. About three weeks ago he was at the play, where he espied in one of the boxes a fair virgin, whose looks, air, & manner made such a powerful & wonderful effect upon him, as was visible to every beholder. His raptures were so undisguised: His looks so expressive of passion: His inquiries so earnest, that every body took notice of it. He soon was told her name was Crampton, a linen draper's daughter, that had been bankrupt last year & had not been able to pay above 5 shillings in the pound. The fair nymph herself was about 16 or 17, & being supported by some relations, appeared in every public place, & had fatigued every eye but that of his Lordship, which being entirely employed in the severer studies, had never till that fatal moment opened upon her charms. Such, & so powerful was their effect, as to be able to justify all the Pharamonds & Cyruses in their utmost extravagances. He wrote next morning to her father, desiring leave to visit his daughter on honourable terms, & in a few days, she will be Countess of Marchmont.[18]

How like an incident in a play or broadside ballad!

The most approved marriages in the eighteenth century, however, were those in which reason and good sense prevailed over passion. Alexander Carlyle married at the age of 38, when his wife was 17. The Rev. John Home, author of *The Douglas*, pointed her out to him as a 'proper object of suit', and he later felt a glow of proprietorial pride at the impression she made on the Edinburgh *literati* – 'the very superior men who were my closest and most discerning friends, such as Ferguson, Robertson, Blair and Bannatine' – which was conveyed not merely by words, 'but by the open, respectful, and confidential manner in which they conversed with her'. He esteemed her as 'the most valuable friend and companion a man ever had', excelling alike in 'understanding' and 'that lively and striking expression of feeling and sentiment which never failed to attract'.[19]

Most typical of all, perhaps, is James Boswell — the man who above all others embodied in himself the extremes of the century. When he finally married his cousin Margaret Montgomerie it was not for money, but for precisely those qualities of mind and character which would have commended themselves to Alexander Carlyle. When Boswell had previously paid court to the heiress, Miss Blair, he went through all the most ridiculous posturings and idealisations of the upper-class love-songs of the time. And when, later, he courted the Irish heiress, Mary Ann Boyd, he acted out the business as an upper-class pastoral, again aping attitudes found in many of the more artificial lyrics of the century. Frank Brady has categorised the relationship as 'Boswell's Horatian romance; she was an Arcadian shepherdess and he a "Sicilian swain". He carved her initial on a tree, and cut off a lock of her hair'. But with Margaret Montgomerie it was quite otherwise: to begin with, she was 'my lady' and 'my valuable friend', and long acquaintanceship ripened into a deep love based on a rational appreciation of her mind and character.[20] From the pages of Boswell's journals one can derive a record of every sort of love-emotion of which an eighteenth-century Scotsman was capable, from the most brutal and licentious through the extravagantly sentimental to the profound devotion of a 'reasonable' marriage and family life.

All these feelings are expressed in the songs of the period, with varying degrees of success. There are many lyrics which express the ideal of a life-long love based on reason and common sense. Allan Ramsay's 'I'll never leave thee' ('Tho' for seven years and mair, honour should reave me') is from one point of view just a simple elaboration of its refrain line. It is a dialogue between lovers; a song of parting — Johnny is about to go off to the wars; and a statement of the relationship supposed to exist between physical and mental attraction — the physical is the foundation, coming first in time. Couched in highly artificial language, its fusion of Scots and standard poetic diction is infelicitous in the extreme:

> For while my blood's warm, I'll kindly caress ye:
> Your blooming saft beauties first beeted love's fire,
> Your vertue and wit make it aye flame the higher.

But the final stanza, given to Johnny, manages to infuse some originality into the stock comparisons of the kind found in 'A red, red rose':

> Bid iceshogles hammer red gauds on the studdy,
> And fair simmer mornings nae mair appear ruddy,

Bid *Britons* think ae gate, and when they obey ye,
But never till that time, believe I'll betray ye.
Leave thee, leave thee, I'll never leave thee;
The stars shall gang withershins ere I deceive thee.[21]

Peggy's song in *The Gentle Shepherd*, 'Speak on — speak thus, and still my grief',[22] to the tune of 'Waes my heart that we should sunder', is a lyric of pastoral parting, —

Ah! I can die but never sunder,

(a line that looks forward to Burns's 'I can die — but canna part')[23] and an assertion of life-long devotion. It is followed by another song given to Peggy, on the theme of absence, which rather comically asserts the girl's intention to make herself worthy of her young man, now discovered to be of gentle birth:

Whilst thou wast a shepherd I priz'd
No higher degree in this life;
But now I'll endeavour to rise
To a height in becoming thy wife.

Beauty, she says, is only skin deep, unless it is inwardly rooted. Then:

Nor age, nor the changes of life,
Can quench the fair fire of love,
If virtue's ingrain'd in the wife,
And the husband has sense to approve.[24]

Peggy's lyric reflects the double standard of the approved upper-class and middle-class view of married love. The quality of 'virtue' is attributed to the wife, with the seventeenth- and eighteenth-century sense of 'chastity', whereas the contrasting husbandly quality is the social and mental quality of 'sense'.

In another Ramsay song, 'The last time I came o'er the moor', a casual meeting leads to lasting love. The stalest clichés of art lyric are once again linked with folk hyperbole:

In all my soul there's not one place
To let a rival enter:
Since she excels in every grace,
In her my love shall center.

Sooner the seas shall cease to flow,
Their waves the *Alps* shall cover,
On *Greenland* ice shall roses grow,
Before I cease to love her.

When he comes back, he will marry the lass he met on the moor.[25]
In the polite words set by Joseph Mitchell to the tune of 'Leave
kindred and friends, sweet Betty',[26] the word 'virtue' has a different
connotation from its meaning in the *Gentle Shepherd* song examined
above, 'Speak on—speak thus and still my grief'. Now virtue is
common to both sexes:

> The gifts of nature and fortune
>   May fly, by chance as they came;
> They're grounds the destinies sport on,
>   But virtue is ever the same.

For Mitchell, there is a strong sensual basis to a life-long 'virtuous'
attachment, which comes through the stilted style of his final
stanza:

> Oh! were I but once so blessed,
>   To grasp my love in my arms!
> By thee to be grasp'd and kissed!
>   And live on thy heaven of charms;
> I'd laugh at fortune's caprices,
>   Shou'd fortune capricious prove;
> Tho' death shou'd tear me to pieces,
>   I'd die a martyr to love.

Ramsay's 'Mary Scot' ('Happy's the love which meets return')[27]
celebrates reciprocated love 'when in soft flames souls equal burn'.
Although the lover has not yet made his declaration, and is by no
means certain of the flower of Yarrow's response, he is absolutely
sure that it is a lasting marriage that he wants:

> When *Mary Scot*'s become my marrow,
> We'll make a paradise on Yarrow.

Such pieces as this, among the most popular of all the tea-table
lyrics throughout the century, were favourites of the whole people.
This is indicated by the large number of chapbook and 'slip'
reprints, and by the almost legendary esteem in which the Flower
of Yarrow was held; to name her was to name a symbol. It follows,
then, that an entire class of popular songs helped to consolidate a
respect for virtue and 'decency' in sexual matters, and to spread
sentimental attitudes among all who heard and learned them,
whether they belonged to tea-table circles or not.

    The qualities of mind and heart which Alexander Carlyle and
James Boswell alike prized in a wife are often found in the lyrics.
In 'My Celia's neck more white than snow', directed to be sung to

the tune of 'Leith Wynd', the whole theme is the soul's superiority
to the body:

> Thus, while in Hymen's sacred bands,
>   By charms of person led,
> The vulgar join their plighted hands,
>   Of two one flesh is made.
>
> But us one common wish shall bound,
>   One mutual fear controul,
> And of two hearts the string shall sound
>   An unison of soul.[28]

The third stanza, lines 5-8, render the female counterpart of the
'honest man' of Alexander Pope and Robert Burns:

> But me the good, the chaste, yet kind,
>   Wound more than beauty's dart,
> Unbiass'd rectitude of mind,
>   And honesty of heart.

In exactly the same way 'Not on beauty's transient pleasure', in
The Charmer (1782), Vol. II, states that the lady's main attraction is
'not her form, the boast of nature', but 'her spotless mind', and
ends by stating:

> The virtuous mind alone possessing,
>   Will your lasting bliss secure.[29]

What did refined taste make of that honest lust whose expression
in folk and popular modes we examined in the last chapter? In the
tea-table lyrics of the upper classes it was reduced to a luxurious
sensuality with sentimental overtones. In art-song's rendering of
sentimental desire there is a noticeable lack of particularity, and
descriptions such as 'The Progress of Love' are common:

> Beneath the myrtle's secret shade
>   When Celia bless'd my eyes:
> At first I view'd the lovely maid,
>   In silent soft surprise.
> With trembling voice and anxious mind,
>   I softly whisper'd love;
> She blush'd and smiled so sweetly kind,
>   Bid all my fears remove.
>
> Her lovely-yielding form I press'd,
>   Sweet maddening kisses stole;
> As soon her swimming eyes confess'd
>   The wishes of her soul.

> In wild tumultuous bliss, I cry'd
>   O *Celia*, now be kind!
> She press'd me close, and with a sigh
>   To melting joys resign'd.[30]

When purely descriptive, such a style can produce only a catalogue
of items, each with its appropriate adjectives used a thousand times
before – soft pains, ambrosial kisses,[31] amorous flames.[32] fluttering
souls,[33] mould divine,[34] melting smiles, killing air,[35] matchless shape,
graceful mien[36] and all the rest of the repertoire of tea-table clichés.
It is only when there is some attempt to render action, even if this
is no more than a heaving bosom, that the languor is effectively
communicated:

> Who ever hears your short-breath'd sighs
>   Or sees your bosom pant;
> Who marks the languish of your eyes
>   Or the warm blushes as they rise,
>   Must see what 'tis you want.[37]

In these lyrics of cultivated sensuality much is made of the traditional association between love and death, as in the last stanza of
'Ye western climes where Peggy goes', in which 'Ye sylvan nymphs'
are addressed:

> Her golden locks with diamonds tye,
>   Her waste with care unlace;
> And loudly cry if danger's nigh,
>   Whilst she's in her undress.
>
> Defend my dearer self from death,
>   When on the deep she lies:
> If ought should sink her down beneath,
>   With her her lover dies.[38]

The essence of sentimental day dreaming – the dangerous prevalence
of 'imagination' in one of Johnson's senses of that word[39] – is
admirably expressed in a lyric attributed to Mrs Barbauld:

> If, when the darling maid is gone,
> Thou dost not seek to be alone,
> Wrapt in a pleasing trance of tender wo;
>   And muse, and fold thy languid arms,
>   Feeding thy fancy on her charms;
> Thou dost not love, for love is nourish'd so.[40]

In 'Delia's smile is wealth to me', however, there is a rather
pleasant deployment of thought-clichés in st. iii, followed by an un-

commonly vivid use of eighteenth-century cliché to render the
movement of a woman's breasts as she breathes and walks. The
image is sharp, the observer's interest not in the least prurient:

> The kiss, the sigh, the tender look,
> One language—all from nature's book!
> Our studies only to impart
> Mutual pleasures to the heart . . .

> The regions of her beauteous breast
> Seem of two gentle souls possest:
> Advancing now with fond desire
> They now with modesty retire.[41]

Ramsay's 'Bonny Jean' ('Love's goddess in a myrtle grove'), an
enormously popular song throughout the century, gives an artificial
but nevertheless vivid picture of a universal experience. The
recreation in 'fancy' of the woman's charms is inevitable, unwilled,
associated with feelings of boundless joy because she favours him.
It is noteworthy that the man described by Ramsay is a landed
gentleman:

> A thousand transports crowd his breast,
>   He moves as light as fleeting wind,
> His former sorrows seem a jest,
>   Now when his *Jeany* is turn'd kind:
> Riches he looks on with disdain,
>   The glorious fields of war look mean;
> The chearful hound and horn give pain,
>   If absent from his bonny *Jean*.

> The day he spends in am'rous gaze,
>   Which ev'n in summer shorten'd seems;
> When sunk in downs, with glad amaze,
>   He wonders at her in his dreams.
> All charms disclos'd, she looks more bright
>   Than *Troy*'s prize, the *Spartan* queen,
> With breaking day, he lifts his sight,
>   And pants to be with bonny *Jean*.[42]

Many of these drawing-room wooers love to contemplate the
sensual appearance of a cultivated woman as she yields to physical
desire. One of them sings 'I had rather enjoy a girl that is coy',
and goes on to describe how initial reluctance leads on to the 'joy of
a lover refin'd'.[43] Such critical moments are often located on the
honeymoon, when 'love sits laughing in her eyes, and betrays her

secret wishes', whereupon the order is given to 'spread the downy couch for love,/And lull us in your sweet embraces'.[44]

For sensuality outwith marriage one has to go to a survival of the Restoration style, the cosmopolitan Jacobite chieftain Alexander Robertson of Struan. It is he alone of the poets I have examined who celebrates homosexuality in a witty pastoral,[45] but he was equally proficient with more orthodox material. When in his exile he came to write a formal 'Pindarick Ode upon Celestia bathing in the Seine', he produced a minor poem of considerable charm. True, there is more than a trace of bathos intermingled with wit in this description of his sunburnt heroine:

> All day the beamy Monarch warms the Dame,
> And in the Ev'ning she returns his Flame.

But the following conceit — much further from the style of the singable lyric than most of our subject matter — is surely a pleasant enough rendering of nudity:

> Behold, in yonder shady Grove,
> The Pow'r and Immortality of Love,
> Her snowy Limbs and beauteous Face inspire
> A lasting Love and endless Fire;
> Her magick Chain is sure to tye
> The restless Thought, and the most wand'ring Eye.
>   But oh! beware t'approach the Shade,
>   While on the Moss she lyes,
>   She's coy as ever any Maid,
>   And if you stir she flyes;
> But, while you feed your longing Eyes, take Care
> To be invisible, and still like Morning Star:
>   And now she comes, behold her stand
>   Naked upon the yielding Sand;
> That Sand, which seems to ope itself, and meet
> The gentle touches of her tender Feet;
>
>   With what unusual Haste it takes
>   The well-proportioned Print she makes;
>   In vain it twines, in vain it tryes
>   To fix the lovely fleeting Joys,
> The neighbouring Flood will soon possess. . . .[46]

This seems the epitome of physical love in a neo-classic age. Celestia is not passive, but dominant, as she presses on the sand. Her nakedness is positive, the sand symbolises the malleability of non-human matter in the face of a reality as forceful as woman's beauty.

At the same time, the relation between her foot and the sand is an erotic one, for it 'seems to ope itself'; and the conceit serves to convey an extraordinarily concrete impression, both visual and tactile, of the grains pressing and sifting through the toes. The sand is shifting, unstable, and even more so is the Flood which will wash away the prints, however firmly made. Love is beautiful, and may also be precisely and classically shaped ('well-proportion'd'). Its enemy is the chaos, the flood which will remove all trace of love just as it destroys Celestia's footprint.

In 'Betty, 'tis foolish to deny',[47] Robertson has Strephon sing a well-turned request that Betty yield. She answers, as follows:

> My naked Beauty thus display'd
>   Unguarded from thy wanton Hand,
> May be sufficient to persuade,
>   I wish to be at thy Command.
>
> But, gentle STREPHON, pray forbear
>   To press the Argument so strong,
> And let me whisper in your Ear,
>   Why I refuse thy Joy so long.
>
> It is not to secure a Fame,
>   (That empty Purchase I give o'er)
> For, happy to deserve the Name,
>   I grudge not to be call'd thy Whore.
>
> But rather, as most Lovers are,
>   After Enjoyment you grow cold,
> And we poor wretches still must fear
>   To be abandon'd when we're old.[48]

The two lyrics (of which only the second is quoted here) — together form a pastoral love-dialogue. 'Strephon' and 'Betty' are not even an Arcadian Shepherd and Shepherdess, still less real country folk, but masks for a man and woman of the world about to become lovers; and 'Betty's Answer to Strephon' moves from a cool sensuality of situation to a lyric of character with an elegiac-pathetic conclusion. It is the successful expression of a real human predicament, of the emotions of a woman 'caught' in the elegant meshes which envelop her sex, that give this lyric its quality. Wit is indeed present, but subordinate to humanity.

A faintly masturbatory tendency is found in some of the more 'refined' lyrics of sensuality in this period. In 'He who presum'd to guide the Sun', Robertson of Struan seems to hint at it in the second-last stanza:

> He who presum'd to guide the Sun,
>   Was crown'd with bad Success,
> Tho' for his rash Attempt undone,
>   Had glory'd ne'er the less.
>
> Him you resemble, and aspire
>   To lead our brightest Fair;
> Like him too, tho' consum'd by Fire,
>   You boast because you dare.
>
> Yet not to disappoint you quite
>   Call Fancy to your Aid;
> Fancy may grant you the Delight,
>   Refus'd you by the Maid.
>
> A strong Conception of her Charms,
>   While you but CHLOE kiss,
> Then put her Image in your Arms,
>   To give you real Bliss.[49]

One suspects (without, however, possessing any real evidence) that masturbatory 'Fancy' was the concern of the middle classes, of the 'cits', rather than of the aristocracy or the farming community. For Robertson, the Highland but cosmopolitan aristocrat, the love-making that ends in mutual orgasm is a supreme value; and his lyric 'On two Reciprocal Lovers' is a celebration, not of brutal and urgent desire, but of a civilised union of the mind and body, united by wit:

> Thrice happy the Pair,
>   Whose mutual Graces
> Invite them to share
>   Of each others Embraces,
> When the Youth overboils
>   With an ardent Desire,
> And the Shepherdess toils
>   To extinguish his Fire!
>
> But if Wit and Discretion
>   In each of them shine
> How blessed their Station,
>   Their Love how divine!
> For PRIAPUS by Night
>   Will preside in his Way,
> And yield up his Right
>   To APOLLO by Day.[50]

Apart from lyrics directly embodying the ideals of upper-class marriage and the languorous sensuality of the tea-table, the sophisticated were drawn to songs that arose directly from their lives, or reflected their own traditions — personal pieces where the sentiment is especially refined, songs of artificial compliment, 'occasional' love verse, pastoral lyrics mingling landscape with sentiment.[51] Among the conventional themes beloved by the tea-table singers were the loved one's smile, a kiss, 'she delays too long' and 'she coquets'. Generally her smile is featured as merely one of her incidental attractions; we do not often find whole lyrics on this topic. One of the most artificial, Robert Crawford's 'To Mrs S. H. (Miss Anne Hamilton) on seeing her at a concert', begins with a smile that involves the cheeks and indeed the whole face, not just the lips:

> Look where my dear *Hamilla* smiles,
>> *Hamilla*! heavenly charmer;
> See how, with all their arts and wiles,
>> The *Loves* and *Graces* arm her.
>
> A blush dwells glowing on her cheeks,
>> Fair seats of youthful pleasures,
> There love in smiling language speaks,
>> There spreads his rosy Treasures.[52]

Although the Bettys and Nancys of pseudo-folk pastoral can be just as coquettish as any Sylvias or Clarindas,[53] the love-game is naturally commoner in the literature of the upper classes, who have more leisure for coyness.

Often the poems that seem most 'personal' are merely occasional. Ramsay's 'To Delia, on her drawing him to her Valentine' does not get beyond the conventions of 'her smile' and the wish to be in her breast:

> I came, and *Delia* smiling show'd,
> She smil'd, and show'd the happy name; . . .
> She drew the treasure from her breast,
>> That breast where love and graces play,
> O name beyond expression blest!
>> Thus lodg'd with all that's fair and gay.
> To be so lodg'd! the thought is extasy,
>> Who would not wish in paradise to ly?[54]

'Ah, Chloris, cou'd I now but sit', an English song often re-printed in Scotland throughout the century, successfully renders the feeling of an older man who suddenly finds himself in love with a young girl whose infant beauty he had casually observed a year or two before.[55] The somewhat similar 'Tell me, Hamilla, tell me why'[56] by Hamilton of Bangour and addressed apparently to a very young member of his own family, is an adaptation of Horace's 'Vitas hinnuleo me similis, Chloe' (*Odes*, I. 23), bearing some resemblance to a dialogue by his English predecessor, Etherege. In Etherege's 'The Forsaken Mistress', Phillis asks:

> Tell me gentle Strephon why
> You from my embraces fly . . .[57]

Hamilton's poem begins:

> Tell me, *Hamilla,* tell me why
>   Thou dost from him that loves thee run?
> Why from his soft embraces fly,
>   And all his kind endearments shun?

It ends, quite charmingly, in a stanza that reproduces the personal, family situation:

> Cease then, dear wildness, cease to toy,
>   But haste all rivals to outshine,
> And grown mature, and ripe for joy,
>   Leave *mama's* arms, and come to *mine.*

At no time during the century did any group relish only the artificial and sentimental pieces we have just discussed — not even the most genteel of Edinburgh ladies: the upper classes were always aware of genuinely popular, and even folk, songs and tunes. Young lairds were often educated alongside their tenantry in their earliest years, and would imbibe folk-songs and ballads from their playmates. Their sisters mixed with their maids and with farmers' daughters, and in their youth and later often travelled regularly between town and country. Not merely knowledge of popular songs, but even active composition of songs in the popular style, was part of the very texture of daily life in upper-class households, just as was dancing to Scottish tunes and playing or listening to music with a strong popular or folk flavour.[58] It is hardly surprising, then, that the most interesting of all the love lyrics are not those whose content is the preserve of one class alone, but those whose attitudes are shared by town and country, rich and poor alike.

REFERENCES

1.   Herd (1776), II, 87.
2.   EUL, MS. La. II. 620: N. Smith, 'Robert Wallace's "Of Venery",' *Texas Studies in Literature and Language,* XV. 3 (Fall, 1973).

3. *Boswell in Search of a Wife 1766–69*, ed. F. Brady and F. A. Pottle (London, 1957), pp. 129-30. One feature of the changing manners of eighteenth-century Edinburgh was the increase in prostitution. According to Creech, in 1763 'there were five or six brothels . . . and a very few of the lowest and most ignorant order of females sculked about the streets at night', but by 1783 'the number of brothels had increased twenty-fold, and the women of the town more than a hundred-fold' (*Edinburgh Fugitive Pieces*, p. 105). These are no doubt highly imaginative estimates.

4. F. Topham, *Letters from Edinburgh* (London, 1776), henceforth cited as Topham, pp. 285-6.

5. C. Rogers, *Social Life in Scotland from early to recent times*, 3 vols. (Edinburgh, 1884), henceforth cited as Rogers, I, 100-1.

6. Elizabeth Mure, 'Some Observations of the Change of Manners in My Own Time, 1700–1790' in *Scottish Diaries and Memoirs 1746–1843*, ed. J. G. Fyfe (Stirling, 1942), henceforth cited as Fyfe, p. 73.

7. Topham, pp. 255-6.

8. Creech, pp. 103-4.

9. Tea-table society encouraged the singing and writing of lyrics — witness the very title of Ramsay's *Tea-Table Miscellany*.

10. Fyfe, pp. 79-80.

11. *The Autobiography of Dr. Alexander Carlyle of Inveresk 1722–1805*, ed. J. H. Burton (London and Edinburgh, 1910), henceforth cited as Carlyle, pp. 223-4.

12. *Ibid.*, p. 215.

13. *Ibid.*, p. 216.

14. *Ibid.*, p. 421.

15. Quoted in Edgar, p. 154, *n.*

16. G. Ridpath, *Diary*, in Fyfe, pp. 122-3.

17. Carlyle, p. 275.

18. Hume, *Letters*, ed. J. Y. T. Greig, 2 vols. (Oxford, 1932), I, 110.

19. Carlyle, pp. 421-2, 430.

20. *In Search of a Wife*, Intro., pp. xx-xxi.

21. *TTM*, I: (1740), p. 54, st. iii, lines 2-4; st. v.

22. *TTM*, II: (1740), p. 206; *Museum*, 131.

23. 'Ca the yowes', set 2, st. v; Kinsley, 456; *LLL*, 125.

24. *TTM*, II: (1740), p. 207. For a fuller discussion of *The Gentle Shepherd*, see Chapter V, below.

25. *TTM*, I: (1740), p. 39; sts. v, vi.

26. *TTM*, I: (1740), p. 28. Signed M.

27. *Ibid.*, p. 62; *Museum*, 73; *LLL*, 125.

28. *Charmer* (Edinburgh, 1749), I, 345, final st.

29. P. 142.

30. *Caledonian Weekly Magazine, or Edinburgh Intelligencer* (1773), I, 179.

31. 'What beauties does Flora disclose', *TTM*, I: (1740), p. 4.

32. 'Hear me ye nymphs and every swain', *Ibid.*, p. 2.

33. 'Celestial Muses, tune your lyres', *Ibid.*, p. 29.

34. 'Ye watchful guardians of the fair', *Ibid.*, p. 41.

35. 'When absent from the nymph I love' (Ramsay), *TTM*, II: (1740), p. 116.

36. 'No more my song shall be ye swains', *The Lark* (Edinburgh, 1765), p. 212.

37. 'To Delia', st. ii, in *Caledonian Weekly Magazine*, I.

38. *Charmer* (Edinburgh, 1749), I, 57. This song is in *Scots Magazine*, I (1739), 275, where it is initialled 'A. B. at Bl.-Drum-d.' It contains some Scotticisms.

39.   *Rasselas*, Chap. xliv.

40.   'Come here, fond youth, whoe'er thou be', st. vi, in *Charmer* (Edinburgh, 1782), II, 14.

41.   Sts. iii, v, in *Ibid.*, II, 113.

42.   *TTM*, I: (1740), p. 43, sts. iii-iv. 'Bony Jean' was printed in at least seventeen Scottish song-books throughout the century.

43.   *Collection of Songs* (Edinburgh), 1762, p. 204.

44.   'Is Hamilla then my own?', sts. iii-iv, in *TTM*, I: (1740), p. 5.

45.   'An Ode inscribed to King William', *LLL*, 88.

46.   A. Robertson of Struan, *Poems on Various Subjects and Occasions* (Edinburgh, n.d.-?1751), henceforth cited as Robertson, *Poems*, pp. 168-74, lines 47-48, 15-35.

47.   *Ibid.*, p. 199.

48.   'Betty's Answer to Strephon' in *Ibid.*, p. 200; *LLL*, 79.

49.   *Ibid.*, pp. 223-4.

50.   *Ibid.*, pp. 109-10. Robertson describes his lyric as 'An Ode'.

51.   For convenience of presentation, songs mingling landscape and sentiment are discussed in the next chapter along with other pastorals.

52.   *TTM*, I: (1740), p. 18.

53.   'Slighted Nansy', in *Ibid.*, p. 21 (line 1, 'Tis I have seven braw new goons'); 'Scornfu' Nansy', in *Ibid.*, p. 19 (line 1, 'Nansy's to the greenwood gane').

54.   'Ye Pow'rs! was Damon then so blest', *TTM*, I: (1740), p. 10, st. ii, lines 1-2; st. iii.

55.   *TTM*, I: (1740), p. 46. *Museum*, 66. This piece, sung in Sir Charles Sedley's 'The Mulberry Tree', was wrongly attributed to Duncan Forbes of Culloden.

56.   *TTM*, I: (1740), p. 30.

57.   G. Etherege, *Poems*, ed. J. Thorpe (Princeton, 1963), p. 3. The poem was reprinted during the eighteenth century in song-books published in Scotland.

58.   For some of the evidence for this, see Chapter IX below.

Chapter IV

THE COMMON PURSUIT

In their songs all classes of society praise the lover's charms, write about kissing, wish to be some object near or around the loved one, bring love and flowers and birds into the same context, lament her (or his) delay, feel love-longing, anguish and despair; all, except of course monarchs themselves, imagine they are 'as happy as a king' when the affair is going well; all, even townsmen, like to make love in the country and in springtime; all, that is to say, are influenced by modes which can loosely be described as pastoral.

To judge from their songs, Scots (high and low) were more attracted by a girl's legs, or by her middle 'jimp and sma', than by her eyes, to which traditional aristocratic and courtly love-poetry often gave pride of place. Yet one should perhaps beware of first impressions. It is true that Captain Topham says this about the amatory taste of Scotsmen: 'Large women please them most, and they pay little regard to a just symmetry of parts, complexion or colour'. But he goes on: 'The eyes are the charm which attracts them most, and whose language they best understand'.[1] And the first thing that struck Boswell about a woman was, almost always, her eyes.[2] There are, however, more songs about kissing than about eyes. Lingering kisses feature more in upper-class pastoral, and therefore, perhaps, in upper-class wooing, than in genuine country songs. In 'Fair Iris and her swain', in the *Tea-Table Miscellany*, Thirsis first asks her to kiss him longer, 'longer yet, and longer', and then:

> Oh *Iris*! kiss me kindly,
>   In pity of my fate,
> Fair *Iris*, kiss me kindly,
>   Kindly still, and kindly,
> Before it be too late.[3]

Two stanzas end with the proverbial 'But never kiss and tell'. 'If a kiss you would gain' from the English cantata *The Rose*, by Samuel Webbe, is printed in at least three song-books published in Scotland during the period. It is of six lines only:

> If a kiss you would gain,
>   Am I bound to explain?
> Ah! could you not guess by my eyes?
>   When they without guile
>   So twinkle and smile,
> A glance is enough to the wise.[4]

In Scottish song, kissing may be seen, like all love, in the context of the Kirk and its prohibitions, which were felt by the men and women of every class. There is a song in Herd's *Scots Songs* (1769), 'Some say kissing's a sin', with st. ii of one text as follows:

> If it were a transgression,
>   The ministers it would reprove;
> But they their elders and session,
>   Can do it as weel as the lave.[5]

Or else, it is merely a part of other rituals, the prelude to afterwards:

> Kissin is the key o' love,
> An' clappin' is the lock,
>   An' makin o's the best thing
> That ere a young thing got.[6]

There is a no-nonsense air about another fragment in Herd, the basis of Burns's 'O John, come kiss me now':[7]

> JOHN, *come kiss me now, now, now,*
>   O John, *come kiss me now,*
> JOHN, *come kiss me by and by,*
>   *And make nae mair ado.*
>
> Some will court and compliment
>   And make a great ado,
> Some will make of their goodman,
>   And sae will I of you —

a song with a long history, in Scotland and England.[8]

The most interesting song on a kiss to be printed in the song-books of eighteenth-century Scotland is 'The Parting Kiss', by Robert Dodsley, an Englishman, simply because it is the source of Burns's 'Ae Fond Kiss':

> One kind kiss before we part,
>   Drop a tear, and bid adieu:
> Tho' we sever, my fond heart,
>   Till we meet, shall pant for you.

> Yet, yet weep not so, my love,
>   Let me kiss that falling tear;
> Tho' my body must remove,
>   All my soul will still be here.
>
> All my soul, and all my heart,
>   And ev'ry wish shall pant for you:
> One kind kiss before we part,
>   Drop a tear, then bid adieu.[9]

The emotions in Dodsley's poem are those a drawing-room miss or 'woman of a certain age' might hope her hero would feel, and they are conveyed by the connotations implied by the diction of sentimental art-song. How different from the directness of this folk-song on a kiss:

> There was a pretty maiden & she was dress'd in satin
> And she was dress'd in satin,
> And she sat down upon the ground
> Cried kiss me Jacky Latin.
>
> Kiss me Jacky, kiss me Jacky,
> Kiss me Jacky Latin
> Won't you kiss your pretty maid,
> Altho' she's dress'd in satin.[10]

Yet 'Jacky Latin' is in reality more complex that Dodsley's insipid piece. Although it is on the border-line between children's verse and a song of teen-age desire, it is very near to a singing-game, and also instinct with drama and character: is Jacky Latin a poor tutor in a noble family where the young minx is the daughter of the house — or is he the lad o' pairts in a village school whom the lasses cluster around because he is different from the ruck of farmers' sons?

A theme already mentioned in Chapter III is the lover's conventional wish to live in his mistress's breast. This is expressed in st. ii of the somewhat artificial 'Rose in Yarrow' (' 'Twas summer, and the day was fair'),[11] and is followed by the rejection of worldly ambition so characteristic of one eighteenth-century notion of 'The Happy Man':[12]

> There would I live or die with pleasure,
> Nor spare this world one moment's leisure. . . .
> My joy complete on such a marrow,
> I'd dwell with her, and live on Yarrow.

But the most beautiful expression of the fantasy of living between breasts is in vernacular Scots, in a fragment in Herd (1776)

> O gin my love were yon red rose,
> That grows upon the castle wa'!
> And I mysell a drap of dew,
> Into her bonny breast to fa'!
>
> Oh, there beyond expression blest,
> I'd feast on beauty a' the night;
> Seal'd on her silk-saft falds to rest,
> Till flyed awa by Phoebus light.[13]

'At the close of the day on the banks of the Tweed', in *The Union Song Book* (Berwick, 1781),[14] makes much play with the symbolism of flowers, and with the posy as an emblem of frail beauty and eternal virtue. Although 'the language of flowers', where each species had its traditional meaning (Ophelia's 'there's pansies, that's for thoughts') formed part of the texture of eighteenth-century art-song, it was also found in genuinely popular songs, through which it was transmitted to the folk-singers of a later day.[15]

Despite the artificiality of many eighteenth-century English lyrics on this floral theme, reprinted in some Scottish song-books, the whole tradition has genuinely popular roots. Common-sense suggests that the same is likely to be true of the 'Bonie Doon' group of lyrics, of those songs in which the singer addresses a bird —either one with a melancholy song, such as a nightingale, or one with a cheerful song, like a lark—and expresses his sadness or despair: after all, peasants are just as liable as landowners to observe apparent contrasts between men and birds. Yet in Scotland at any rate, apostrophised birds seem to occur mainly in art song, and it is therefore peculiarly appropriate that Burns's Clarinda—Mrs Agnes McLehose, whom he loved briefly in Edinburgh and for whom he wrote 'Ae fond kiss'—should have composed a lyric which is the epitome of the whole class. It is 'To a Blackbird', and it contains this for its second stanza:

> Go on, sweet bird, and soothe my care,
> Thy cheerful notes will hush despair:
> Thy tuneful warblings, void of art,
> Thrill sweetly through my aching heart.[16]

The best-known lyric of this kind is Burns's own 'O, Stay, sweet warbling wood-lark, stay',[17] where the lark's notes, far from being regarded as cheerful, are invested with the melancholy more traditionally associated with Philomel.

The contrast between a cheerful bird and a despairing lover that forms part of the pathos of 'Bonie Doon' appears much earlier in English than in Scottish *popular* literature, whatever may be true of the *art* literature of medieval times. St. iii of the seventeenth-century 'Sad Marshall to the Singing Lark', ends:

> Whilst I with care am thus opprest,
> Thou chant'st a chearfull note.

In the broadside the lark's song cheers up Marshall; the whole thing ends on a note of piety; and from the internal evidence of rhyme one might suspect that the ballad came from a Scottish or at any rate Northern hand.[18] Finally, 'When absent from the nymph I love',[19] printed in a number of Scottish song-books throughout the century, has these lines at the beginning of the second stanza:

> All day I wander through the groves,
> And sighing hear from ev'ry tree
> The happy birds chirping their loves,
> Happy compar'd with lonely me.

Another very common purely conventional theme found in both lower- and upper-class lyrics is 'She delays too long'. The theme is of course found in many art songs which are translations or adaptations of 'carpe diem' or 'gather ye rosebuds' – songs where the language is generally English. A rather attractive specimen, more original than most, is Allan Ramsay's 'The Bob of Dumblane', where merely by writing in the vernacular the poet has given the sentiment an inimitably popular colouring. The little Perthshire town of Dunblane, like Kirriemuir in a later century,[20] seems to have gathered bawdy associations around it. Thus 'The Bob of Dumblane' has an equivocal sense: in the song, it refers to both the marriage festivity with its accompanying high jinks, and the sexual act itself. 'Leading of monkies' is leading apes in Hell, the fate reserved for old maids:

> Lassie, lend me your braw hemp heckle,
>   And I'll lend you my thripling kame;
> For fainness, deary, I'll gar ye keckle,
>   If ye'll go dance the *Bob of Dumblane*.
>
> Haste ye, gang to the ground of ye'r trunkies,
>   Busk ye braw, and dinna think shame;
> Consider in time, if leading of monkies
>   Be better than dancing the *Bob of Dumblane*.

> Be frank, my lassie, lest I grow fickle,
>   And take my word and offer again,
> Syne ye may chance to repent it mickle,
>   Ye did nae accept of the *Bob of Dumblane*.

> The dinner, the piper and priest shall be ready,
>   And I'm grown dowy with lying my lane,
> Away then leave baith minny and dady,
>   And try with me the *Bob of Dumblane*.[21]

It is perfectly clear that for Ramsay in this lyric there is no question of 'The Bob of Dumblane' taking place outside of marriage. 'She delays too long' and 'carpe diem' are not merely private emotions in folk and popular song — they always have their social aspects, whereas in upper-class forms they are more likely to be entirely personal.

Love-melancholy and despair, perhaps the commonest feelings expressed in the love-lyric, are natural rather than purely conventional, and of course they are not confined to any single social class. Yet when decked in the trappings of the degenerate pastoral mode they may seem nauseous in their artificiality,[22] in complete contrast to the intense pathos which results when the stark tragedy of a ballad situation is adapted to a lyrical end:

> It's open the door, some pity to show,
> It's open the door to me, oh!
> Tho' you have been false, I'll always prove true,
> So open the door to me, oh!

> Cold is the blast upon my pale cheek,
> But colder your love unto me, oh!
> Though you have, etc.

> She's open'd the door, she's open'd it wide,
> She sees his pale corps on the ground! oh!
> Though you have, etc.

> My true love she cry'd, then fell down by his side,
> Never, never to rise again, oh!
> Though you have, etc.[23]

'It's open the door' is a compressed narrative, the lyrical concentrate of the *Liebestod* situation, but it may also be thought of as the lyrical expansion of such an intense emotional cry as the chorus of 'Oh on O chri oh':

> O was not I a weary wight!
>   Oh on, O chri oh!
> Maid, wife and widow in one night,
>   Oh on, O chri oh![24]

The love-cry of grief or anguish is sharply distinguishable from the more long drawn out and wistful sigh, expressed in such a reproachful line as 'Heh, how, Johny lad, ye're no so kind's ye sud ha been',[25] or Burns's 'Somebody' and its sources.[26] The sigh breathes *Sehnsucht* or love-longing, nowhere more exquisitely caught than in 'Dunt, dunt, pittie pattie':

> On Whitsunday morning
>   I went to the fair,
> My yellow hair'd laddie
>   Was selling his ware;
> He gied me sic a blyth blink
>   With his bonny black eye,
> And a dear blink, and a sair blink
>   It was unto me.
>
> I wist not what ail'd me
>   When my laddie came in,
> The little wee starnies
>   Flew ay frae my een;
> And the sweat it dropt down
>   Frae my very eye-brie,
> And my heart play'd ay
> Dunt, dunt, dunt, pittie, pattie.
>
> I wist not what ail'd me,
>   When I went to my bed,
> I tossed and tumbled,
>   And sleep frae me fled.
> Now its sleeping and waking
>   He is ay in my eye,
> And my heart play'd ay
> Dunt, dunt, dunt, pittie pattie.[27]

The same emotion is caught in 'Ay waukin, O', both in Burns's arrangement and its antecedents, such as the following fragment from the Herd MS:

> O wat, wat – O wat and weary!
> Sleep I can get nane
> For thinking on my deary.
> A' the night I wak,
> A' the day I weary,
> Sleep I can get nane,
> For thinking on my dearie.[28]

And 'My daddy forbad, my minny forbad' in the *Tea-Table Miscellany*
has these lines, reminiscent of the Herd fragment:

> When I think on my lad,
>   I sigh and am sad,
> For now he is far frae me.[29]

What could be simpler, more direct, more universal — or, indeed
more like the in-breathing and out-breathing of a sigh itself?

The songs of this group are often the overheard complaints of
young girls, and are concerned with parting. For example, 'A
lass that was laden'd wi' care' looks back to a lover's parting in
the past:

> Sae merry as we twa hae been,
>   Sae merry as we twa hae been,
> My heart it is like for to break,
>   As I think on the days we have seen. . . .
>
> At eve when the rest of the folk
>   Were merrily seated to spin,
> I set myself under an oak,
>   And heartily sighed for him.[30]

The piece just quoted is a popular song of the stall-sheet type. A
more artistic lyric is Ramsay's version of 'The lass o' Livingston'
where Jamie (a Scots laird, as his name implies) is led, incredibly,
'by some god' to overhear her self-criticism:

> Why took I pleasure to torment,
>   And seem too coy — and seem too coy?
> Which makes me now alas lament
>   My slighted joy — my slighted joy.[31]

Jamie rushes forward, and all ends well: the song is indeed a happy
mingling of popular and pastoral. The black and white letter
broadsides are full of hopeless swains eavesdropping upon their
nymphs as they bewail their own cruelty, just as here; and the song
also presents us with another trick of the Common Muse in her
pastoral habit — she often chooses to round off a plaint by a happy
ending when sheer stark tragedy would be artistically more
appropriate.

What of the sister muse of Polite Letters in *her* pastoral mood?
That most tenacious of all upper-class lyrical conventions, orthodox
pastoral, did more than just linger on during the century. The
Chloes and Damons of Queen Anne's England were charming

disguises for the sophisticated attitudes of the glittering Beau
Monde, so exquisitely and wittily displayed in Congreve's 'Amoret':

> Fair Amoret is gone astray;
>   Pursue and seek her, ev'ry Lover;
> I'll tell the Signs, by which you may
>   The wandring Shepherdess discover.
>
> Coquet and Coy at once her Air,
>   Both study'd, tho' both seem neglected;
> Careless she is with artful Care,
>   Affecting to seem unaffected.[32]

In the Scotland of the great country families, 'The Shepherd
Adonis' manipulates the stock ideas with considerable skill, delicately
flavouring them with a faint tincture of Scots. Adonis resorts to the
woods 'for a retirement', far from the business, legal, political or
military activity of his class; drinks of the burn and eats of the tree;
is free from ambition and love until he hears Amynta singing of
the sweet passion in a 'shady green neighbouring grove', which
makes him her prisoner and slave.[33] As the century wore on the
song, felt as completely Scottish, gradually became a standard part
of the national lyric tradition, as is indicated by its being printed in
chapbooks[34] and its inclusion in *The Scots Musical Museum* (No. 159).

In the Scottish song-books of the century there were lyrics
where, despite the happy season, nymphs disdained;[35] light songs
about amorous tactics[36] or amorous hide-and-seek;[37] sentimental
pastorals where both lovers expire;[38] songs where the swain says he
will die if he does not get the nymph;[39] songs, indeed, conveying
every emotion which had ever been attributed to masquerade
shepherds and shepherdesses, and every stereotyped situation in
which it had been customary to place them. Yet personal emotion
and the socially acceptable feelings of the time can be poured into
the most unlikely vessels. In 'Beneath a beech's grateful shade'
(*Colin's complaint to young Peggy*),[40] Robert Crawford's despairing
persona says he will love her for ever though she despises him – a
sentiment known to the faithful Dobbins of every period; while
later in the century, in 'Come here, fond youth, who e'er thou be',[41]
Mrs Barbauld gives vent to the varying symptoms and 'tender
sorrows' of men and women of feeling in the age of Sterne and
Henry Mackenzie. Kane O'Hara's 'The forsaken nymph'[42] (though
not by a Scot, it appeared in at least seventeen Scottish song-books
and was sung in his 'burletta' *The Golden Pippin*, 1773) is pastoral in
form, but presents a common-sense solution to a problem of everyday life – the nymph will seek out some lowly care, some task of

responsibility in order to make life bearable now that her swain has abandoned her.

The pastoral lyrics cannot forbear shading over towards realism, taking into themselves what Raymond Williams has taught us to call the dominant 'social character' and the contemporary 'structure of feeling'.[43] Of course it is the non-pastoral lyrics without shepherds and shepherdesses which exhibit these features most clearly—like the social ideal of the perfect husband depicted in 'Gentle in personage, conduct and equipage',[44] the lyrics centred on the perennial strife between love and reason,[45] the few 'double standard' lyrics opposing marriage and preaching promiscuity,[46] and the many more propounding the orthodox position,[47] praising love matches and relationships where mind is more important than beauty[48] or promising 'mutual pleasures to the heart'.[49] Yet even the more narrowly pastoral lyrics celebrate both social reality and social ideals. In some, moderation is praised, for pastoral contentment eschews excess,[50] and there is enthusiasm for a rational if sensuous love, as in Thomson's 'Come gentle god of soft desire'[51] which puts undisciplined passion firmly at a distance. And others set forth a thoroughly respectable moralism, like the dialogue 'Damon and Laura' in the *Goldfinch* group of song-books, where nymphs are advised not to yield until marriage, and swains not to 'betray the sweet creatures you are born to defend'.[52] Certain postures, too, even imply social criticism, but of a sort that could be accommodated within the conventions of the age, like the following, which today we think of as peculiarly Burnsian:

> He threw by his club,
>   And he laid himself down;
> He envy'd no monarch,
>   Nor wish'd for a crown.[53]

Yet the stanza just quoted was printed in *The Tea-Table Miscellany* half a century before Burns wrote. And in 'The Rose in Yarrow' already quoted, the singer, just like Burns, asks to lie in Mary's breast:

> Despising kings and all that's great,
> I'd smile at courts and courtiers' fate.[54]

The idea is again a hoary commonplace, found in the work of English and Irish poetasters as well as in lyrics by Scotsmen. Thus stanzas iii and iv of 'How oft, Louisa, hast thou said',[55] printed in Vol. II of *The Charmer* (1782), are remarkably similar in tone, if not in quality, to 'Mary Morison', 'O wert thou in the cauld blast', and to such a sentiment as 'I'd reign in Jeanie's bosom':

> Then how, my soul, can we be poor,
>   Who owns what kingdoms cou'd not buy?
> Of this true heart thou shall be queen;
>   And serving thee, a monarch I.

> Thus uncontrou'ld in mutual bliss
>   And rich in love's exhaustless mine,
> Do thou snatch treasures from my lips,
>   And I'll take kingdoms back from thine.

Similar sentiments are expressed in 'Katherine Ogie', a Durfey-type song going back to the late seventeenth century and Scottified by the inclusion of a few vernacular words.[56] The 'happier than kings' idea was thoroughly naturalised by Ramsay himself in st. iv of 'O'er Bogie':

> There blythly will I rant and sing,
>   While o'er her sweets I range,
> I'll cry, Your Humble servant, King,
>   Shame fa' them that wa'd change
> A kiss of Betty, and a smile,
>   Albeit ye wad lay down
> The right ye hae to *Britain's* isle
>   And offer me ye'r crown.[57]

Thereafter the sentiment—often expressed before Ramsay in the English broadsides of the seventeenth century—became standard in the Scottish popular lyric; it is recorded even in the twentieth century.[58]

Orthodox pastoral likes to set love emotions in the (generally idealised) countryside. According to Gavin Greig, that great collector of the early twentieth century, when it mingles landscape with sentiment art-song makes far too much of landscape 'accessories', whereas in folk-song 'human interest is paramount, and what of scene and setting may be needed is introduced quite naturally and so as never to divert attention from the main interest'. As an example of good landscape folk-song Greig quotes 'Nairn's River Banks', which goes back to the Napoleonic Wars:

> Her fleecy flocks around her
>   All on the grass they fed,
> As she lay sore lamenting
>   Upon her primrose bed:

> And as she issued forth her grief
> The little birds they sang
> Upon a tree whose branches
> Out o'er the river hang.[59]

We may agree that this is poetically simpler and more affecting than many eighteenth-century art-lyrics. But it is surely *not* better than the classic illustration of this situation to which I have already referred, Burns's 'Bonie Doon',[60] and may even have been influenced by it. In Robert Crawford's art-song 'Tweedside'[61] dating from the early years of the eighteenth century, the landscape is not individualised in the least, and daisies, roses, linnets, larks, thrushes, blackbirds, the river Tweed and the arbitrarily named Tay are simply decorative elements in a pleasant tapestry. Nor are 'The Birks of Invermay' particularised in the song with that title.[62] Its theme is a vague 'carpe diem' in a setting of hills and vales, bees and 'the reptile kind', where pleasure dissolves in the 'soft raptures' of a gentlemanly passion and there is not the slightest hint of the 'rough strife' expressed in the finest poems on this subject.

Spring settings are ten a penny, as one might expect. Ramsay's 'To Mrs E. C.' begins on a faintly novel note — the lambs know the steps of specifically northern dance-measures!

> Now *Phoebus* advances on high,
> Nae footsteps of winter are seen;
> The birds carrol sweet in the sky,
> And lambkins dance reels on the green.[63]

Rather amusingly, the stanza does not forbear to mention the utilitarian value of gentle exercise and the profitability of plantations. This is a far cry from Congreve's courtly Amoret! It is the Scotland of rural improvement, where the landscape is economically as well as erotically important, that we are presented with:

> Thro' plantings, by burnies sae clear,
> We wander for pleasure and health,
> Where buddings and blossoms appear,
> Giving prospects of joy and wealth.

These lines, however, exhaust the slender measure of originality with which the song is endowed. When the lover goes on to state that nothing in this scene is 'sae perfect' as Eliza, he very soon thrusts material profit aside — her charms alone absorb his attentions:

Thy een the clear fountains excell,
   Thy locks they out-rival the grove;
When zephyres thus pleasingly swell,
   Ilk wave makes a captive to love.[64]

In singing such songs the upper classes of Ramsay's day were lending a peculiarly Scottish piquancy to the aristocratic game of indulging their refined emotions in the garb of shepherds and peasants. They themselves knew the English originals — the minutely carved art-lyrics of Dryden, Congreve, Etherege, Gay, Lord Lansdowne, Sedley, Oldham and the Earl of Mulgrave; the witty colloquialism of Prior; the rival non-lyrical pastoral schools of Pope and Ambrose Philips; and even, behind the English, the French and the Italians, the Greek and Latin originals in Theocritus and Virgil. English neo-classic lyrics were popularised in Scotland above all by the third volume of *The Tea-Table Miscellany*, which printed no Scottish pieces, and it is surely significant that an ancestral classic, Marlowe's 'Come live with me and be my love', was reprinted in no less that fifteen Scottish song-books before 1786. The best of the Scots efforts in English, or in English with a thin sprinkling of Scots, displayed the very same quality which has been attributed to the finest southern neo-classic lyrics: 'the power of manipulating words with such lightness and surety of touch that the result is as finely wrought as the most exquisite Dresden China statuette'.[65] But that quality was mixed with others peculiar to Scotland, and even more difficult to define. A fairly late example is the remarkably cosmopolitan 'Beneath a green shade a lovely young swain', by Thomas Blacklock,[66] which the renowned Signor Tenducci used to sing in Edinburgh to the tune 'The Braes of Ballendine':

How happy, he cried, my moments once flew,
Ere Chloe's bright charms first flash'd on my view!
Those eyes then with pleasure the dawn could survey;
Nor smiled the fair morning more cheerful than they.
Now scenes of distress please only my sight;
I'm tortured in pleasure, and languish in light.

                  (st. ii)

The exquisiteness of such a song can be relished only by the antiquarian imagination, for it would require performance, and probably Tenducci himself, for it to make much of an impression; by themselves, the words on the page achieve only a pale insipid charm. But the texture of most Anglo-Scottish pastoral songs was often coarser, their details less delicately moulded, their emotions more robust than their purely English counterparts. For example, Sir Gilbert Elliot of Minto's 'My sheep I neglected, I lost my sheep-hook'[67] has the sensibility of those who enjoyed such novels as Richardson's *Pamela* or Fielding's *Amelia*; it is not too fanciful, surely, to discern, beneath its surface, a kind of realism:

> My sheep I neglected, I lost my sheep-hook,
> And all the gay haunts of my youth I forsook,
> Nae mair for Amynta fresh garlands I wove,
> For ambition, I said, would soon cure me of love.
> > *O what had my youth with ambition to do?*
> > *Why left I Amynta? why broke I my vow?*
> > *O gi' me my sheep, and my sheep-hook restore,*
> > *I'll wander frae love and Amynta no more.*
>
> Through regions remote in vain do I rove,
> And bid the wild ocean secure me from love!
> O fool! to imagine that ought can subdue
> A love so well-founded, a passion so true.
> > *O what had my youth,* etc.
>
> Alas! 'tis o'er late at thy fate to repine;
> Poor shepherd, Amynta nae mair can be thine:
> Thy tears are a' fruitless, thy wishes are vain,
> The moments neglected return nae again.
> > *O what had my youth,* etc.

The text I have followed here, that of Herd's *Scots Songs* (1776), has specifically Scots features which presumably reflect the way the words were actually pronounced when sung to the traditional 'My apron, dearie', and the song's enormous popularity can be gauged from the large number of printings.[68] Sir Gilbert's pastoral is closer to contemporary reality than any we have so far cited; his shepherd's 'roving' could be paralleled equally with a poor borderer's emigration or enlistment, or with a laird off on the Grand Tour, or embarked on a diplomatic or military career overseas.

It was in Scotland rather than England that pastoral succeeded in converting the limitations of a provincial way of feeling into something significantly new. That achievement was the work principally of one man, Allan Ramsay, in one pastoral drama — *The Gentle Shepherd.*

REFERENCES

1. Topham, p. 255.
2. E.g. *In Search of a Wife*, p. 72 ('Not yet firm against fine eyes').
3. *TTM*, III: (1740), p. 252.
4. *Chearful Companion* (Edinburgh, 1780), p. 16.
5. P. 13; *LLL*, 72. The earliest version printed in Scotland seems to be in *Charmer* II (Edinburgh, 1751), 231.
6. Burns, *Letters*, I, 76; *LLL*, 73.
7. Kinsley, 343.
8. Herd (1769), p. 315.
9. *Charmer* I, (Edinburgh, 1749), 354. See also O. Ritter, 'Burnsiana', *Anglia*, XXXII (1909), 230. Dodsley's song was set by Oswald, a Scotsman.
10. St. Clair MS., p. 14; *LLL*, 10.
11. *TTM*, I: (1740), p. 37.
12. See M. Røstvig, *The Happy Man*, 2 vols. (2nd edn., Oslo, 1971), II, *passim*.
13. Herd (1776), II, 4; *Museum*, 594.
14. P. 286.
15. Cp. 'The Monthly Rose', collected by Gavin Greig, *Folk-Song of the North-East* (1909–14), henceforth cited as *FSNE*, Ser. II, Art. clxvii, st. iii: 'I would crown him all with roses/Sweet-william, thyme, and rue'.
16. *The Life and Works of Robert Burns*, ed. R. Chambers, revised W. Wallace, henceforth cited as C. & W., 4 vols. (Edinburgh, 1896), II, 261, 290; Anders, *Archiv für das Studium der neueren Sprachen*, CXIX, 64.
17. Kinsley, 495.
18. *Roxb. Bds.* ed. Chappell, III, 190-3.
19. *TTM*, II: (1740), p. 116; *Museum*, 53. The song comes from T. Southerne (1659–1746), *The Disappointment: or The Mother of Fashion*, acted as late as 1784.
20. See 'The Kirriemuir Wedding', discussed above, pp. 21-2.
21. *TTM*, I: (1740), p. 34; *LLL*, 123.
22. See Mrs Barbauld's 'As near a weeping spring reclined', where a shepherd advises a despairing nymph that death is her only remedy, *Charmer* (Edinburgh, 1782), II, 14.
23. *New & Complete Collection of the Most Favourite Scots Songs* (Edinburgh, [1782]), II, 30. This seems to be the first publication. The same text, substantially, is in the St. Clair MS., pp. 313-4, and it is of course the source of one of the most beautiful of Burns's songs. It is *LLL*, 90.
24. *Museum*, 89; *LLL*, 91.
25. Hecht-Hd., p. 128; *LLL*, 136.
26. Kinsley, 566; H. & H., III, 416.
27. *TTM*, IV: (1740), p. 429; *LLL*, 67.
28. Hecht-Hd., p. 240; *LLL*, 68.
29. *TTM*, I: (1740), p. 93; st. iii, lines 1-3 (not in 1723–4 edn.).
30. *The Lark* (London, 1740); Herd (1769), p. 173, *Museum*, 59; chorus and st. iii, lines 5-8.
31. 'Pain'd with her slighting Jamie's love', st. iii, lines 5-8, *TTM*, I: (1740), p. 51. For a further treatment of songs of parting, see below, Chapter VI.
32. In eighteenth-century Scotland, printed in *TTM*, III: (1740), p. 305 and *Charmer* II (Edinburgh, 1751), 138.
33. *TTM*, II: (1740), p. 114.
34. E.g. 'Five excellent new Songs', Edinburgh, Printed and sold by William Forrest, 1766, 12mo, 8 pp. It even became transformed into a broadside

of twenty stanzas rhyming *aa, bb*, in contrast to the original's six stanzas rhyming *ab cb de fe*: an excellent example of how quickly upper-class pastoral could be accommodated to the urban popular mode.

35. 'Behold the sweet flowers around' (J. Miller: sung to 'Tweedside', set by Arne), *Charmer* I (Edinburgh, 1749), 348.

36. 'Be wary, my Celia, when Celadon sues', *TTM*, II: (1740), p. 235.

37. 'As Damon and Phyllis were feeding their sheep', *Goldfinch* (Edinburgh, 1777), p. 7.

38. 'By a murmuring stream a fair shepherdess lay', *TTM*, I: (1740), p. 17; with music in *Orpheus Caledonius* (1725).

39. 'Fond Echo forbear the light strain', sung to 'Tweedside', *Charmer* II (Edinburgh, 1751), 243.

40. *TTM*, I: (1740), p. 71.

41. *Charmer* (Edinburgh, 1782), II, 13.

42. 'Guardian angels now protect me', *Charmer* II (Edinburgh, 1751), 92.

43. For these concepts, see Raymond Williams, *The Long Revolution* (London, 1961) and *The Country and the City* (London, 1973), *passim*.

44. *Charmer* II (Edinburgh, 1751), 93.

45. 'Hence painful pleasure, pleasing pain', *Lark* (Edinburgh, 1765), p. 253.

46. 'Free from confinement and strife', *Scots Nightingale* (Edinburgh, 1778), p. 78.

47. 'Defend my heart, ye virgin pow'rs', *Charmer* (Edinburgh, 1782), II, 212; 'Deign, tuneful nine, to aid my lay', *Ibid.*, II, 213.

48. 'Fly no more, cruel fair, but be kind and relenting', *Charmer* II (Edinburgh, 1751), 267.

49. 'Delia's smile is wealth to see', *Charmer* (Edinburgh, 1782), II, 113.

50. 'Come haste to the wedding ye friends and ye neighbours', *Nightingale* (Edinburgh, 1776), p. 43.

51. *Charmer* (Edinburgh, 1782), II, 203.

52. *Goldfinch* (Edinburgh, 1777), p. 25; also in *Goldfinch* (Edinburgh, 1782) and *Goldfinch* (Glasgow, 1782).

53. 'The shepherd Adonis', st. i, lines 5-8, *TTM*, II: (1740), p. 114.

54. *TTM*, I: (1740), p. 37, st. iii, lines 5-6 (line 1, ''Twas summer and the day was fair').

55. P. 119; attributed to Sheridan.

56. *TTM*, I: (1740), p. 66 (line 1, 'As walking forth to view the plain').

57. *TTM*, I: (1740), p. 63; *Museum*, 168 (line 1, 'I will awa wi' my love').

58. *Roxb. Bds.*, *passim*, esp. Vol. VI; Greig, *FSNE*, lxxxii, 'The Gloamin Star': and *FSNE*, xc, 'The Lawyer's Bonie Peggy', st. xix.

59. Greig, *FSNE*, xxviii, st. iii.

60. Kinsley, 328.

61. *TTM*, I: (1740), p. 4; *Museum*, 36 (line 1, 'What beauties does Flora disclose?').

62. *TTM*, IV: (1740), p. 318; *Museum*, 72 (line 1, 'The smiling morn, the breathing spring').

63. *TTM*, I: (1740), p. 92.

64. *Ibid.*, st. ii.

65. C. W. Peltz, 'The neo-classic lyric 1660–1725', *English Literary History*, XI (1944), 112. Miss Peltz cites fifty-five English neo-classic lyrics in the course of her article. Seventeen of these were printed in Scottish song-books before 1786.

66. *Charmer* II (Edinburgh, 1751), 99. Blacklock's song was printed by so

militant a Scot as David Herd in his *Scots Songs* (1769 and 1776), and in so patriotic an undertaking as *The Scots Musical Museum* (1787), 92.

67.   *Charmer* I (Edinburgh, 1749), 309.
68.   Herd (1769), p. 4; (1776), I, 174. I have found nineteen printings between 1749 and 1785, apart from magazines, chapbooks and broadsides.

Chapter V

THE GENTLE SHEPHERD

At least two literary historians have seen in Allan Ramsay a figure of considerable, indeed of revolutionary, significance. For J. W. Mackail in 1924 it was Ramsay who gave 'the first clearly assignable impulse to the romantic movement of the eighteenth century',[1] transmitted primarily by the Preface to his *Ever-Green* (1724) and by *The Gentle Shepherd*: an opinion which was echoed and developed at some length by J. E. Congleton in 1952.[2] Now if romanticism is one of the great and irreversible upheavals in cultural history, if the basis for the whole European movement was laid in Britain, if Allan Ramsay (a Scot) provided the 'first clearly assignable impulse', and if that impulse came mainly from his pastoral drama, then it would seem to follow that in *The Gentle Shepherd* we have an un-recognised masterpiece crying out for revaluation. Yet both Mackail and Congleton were of the opinion that the play, despite its historic importance, fails as a whole. 'What defeated Ramsay and made the amorphous structure of *The Gentle Shepherd* so absurd is that he tried to embody the idyllic sketches in the cumbrous frame-work of a regular drama constructed by rule' (Congleton), and it is only in a few of the individual songs, abstracted from the drama and considered as things in themselves, that the revolutionary potential resides — songs which, as Mackail put it, 'give perfect expression to the native quality of the North, the "delicate spare soil", the "slender and austere landscape" where "through the thin trees the skies appear" '.[3]

The inescapable conclusion is that Ramsay was an innovator by accident, in marginal details rather than in his main design; and a similarly qualified verdict is reached by A. M. Kinghorn in what is probably the fullest examination of the drama to date, when he says that the play's 'merit as a dramatic work of art is slight'. Apart from its historical importance 'in other respects it is a little-read curiosity, too superficial and lacking in emotional force to bear more than a rare revival on the stage . . . no strong sentiments of any kind are evoked by the situations of the shepherds, who have no conflicts to resolve'.[4] These judgments must now be tested against a careful scrutiny of the text.

Behind that text there lies not only the contemporary crisis of Scottish culture and the lowland nation, but also the great debate about pastoral in England of the previous twenty-five years, with its antecedents in seventeenth-century France; and behind these again is the long tradition of the genre, stretching back through Virgil to Theocritus. There would have been no pastoral tradition as we know it without that agonising, necessary and immensely fruitful opposition between town and country which has been one of the main causes of social and cultural change from at least Hellenistic times down to the present day. Hesiod's *Works and Days* (eighth century B.C.) is pre-pastoral, arising out of a total agricultural society, 'the practice of agriculture and trading within a way of life in which prudence and effort are seen as primary virtues'.[5] What is put forward for our admiration in Hesiod is not an absurdly false consciousness, an escapist dream, but the slightly idealised image of a real society. The first truly pastoral poems, the idylls of Theocritus, written in the third century B.C., already spring from the contradiction between town and country—as Sir Walter Greg put it over seventy years ago, 'the earliest pastoral poetry with which we are acquainted, whatever half articulate experiments may have preceded it, was itself directly born of the contrast between the recollections of a childhood spent among the Sicilian uplands and the crowded social and intellectual life of Alexandria'.[6] That is, the nostalgia was based upon a real country childhood (just as with Wordsworth or Edwin Muir), and the idealisation upon circumstances which the author had actually observed: sometimes Theocritus's shepherds quarrelled, or 'plotted to annex their neighbour's gear'.[7] Like Hesiod, Theocritus was aware of a real 'social character'; his idylls are an idealisation but not an utterly false one because there is a sense of 'a simple community, living on narrow margins and experiencing the delights of summer and fertility the more intensely because they also know winter and barrenness and accident'. In Roman times and at the Renaissance, the celebration of fertility and summer could be seen—in Raymond Williams' phrase, 'by false extraction'—as 'the essence, the only essence, of pastoral'. But even for Virgil, who is almost always considered the source and prime exemplar of false idealisation, 'the rural disturbance of his own Italy often breaks through', and in Eclogue IX 'the pastoral singing is directly related to the hopes and fears of the small farmers under threat of confiscation of their land'[8]—hopes and fears of the very same sort as those which, nearly eighteen hundred years later, inspired Burns in 'The Twa Dogs', in 'The Address of Beelzebub' and, within the convention of animal poetry, in 'To a Mouse'.[9] The main tension within Virgilian pastoral is that 'between the pleasures of rural settlement and the threat of loss and eviction',[10] existing in the interplay between the feelings of particular men and their economic lives. In Renaissance pastoral it is less easy to discern a single dominant conflict around which the other oppositions group themselves; there are, on the contrary, several conflicts of almost equal importance — cultural (civilised society epitomised in the artificiality and the corruption of the Court set over against a communistic Golden Age inherited from Virgil); conceptual (between the description of actual landscapes and characters, however conventional, and the growing tendency to allegorise — seen in England most obviously in Spenser); linguistic (Spenser's attempt to create a special 'rusticall language' in his *Shepheardes Calendar* out of Chaucerian archaisms and dialect words from disparate areas); and, lastly, generic (the narrative side of the genre expands into pastoral romances, like Sidney's *Arcadia*, in which refined sentiments are sophisticated at some length, while the eclogue develops into the pastoral drama, masque, and opera, with the emphasis more and more upon stylised nature and romantic love). But even so reality keeps breaking through, as in 'When icicles hang by the wall' at the end of *Love's Labour's Lost*, or in the Forest of Arden, where Corin is a rural proletarian in an arcadia strangely subject to the stresses of a market economy:

> But I am shepherd to another man
> And do not shear the fleeces that I graze.
> My master is of churlish disposition
> And little recks to find the way to heaven
> By doing deeds of hospitality.
> Besides, his cote, his flocks, and bounds of feed
> Are now on sale. . . .[11]

These lines from *As You Like It* express the same contrast between exploitation and the pleasures of a country life that we have noted in Virgil and in Burns. When the descripiton of landscape separates out into the country-house poems of the seventeenth century and later, another kind of reality appears, but one-sided, specialised, even *maimed* — the detached observation of the gentleman of scientific interests or the landscape painter who contemplates, rather than the small owner or tenant who works the land himself.

In the late seventeenth century the great English debate about pastoral began, stimulated by French experience, as an offshoot of the European quarrel between the Ancients and the Moderns. Rapin (1659)[12] takes his stand on the Ancients, Good Sense and

Decorum. Philosophy should be banned from pastoral because common-sense tells us that weighty 'sentences' are not fit for a shepherd's mouth;[13] there are rules for the genre, borrowed from the ancients, which he codifies; and on the matter of diction he involves himself in an interesting paradox when he says that the expression should be 'the purest which the language will afford' while at the same time approving the Greeks' use of 'dialect peculiar to the country'.[14] Because of the way the English language and the English class-system had developed, it was difficult if not impossible for these ideals to be realised south of the Tweed. The Scots vernacular revival of the eighteenth century, in contrast, enabled a poet to modulate at will from a fully colloquial dialect to what looks like standard poetic language on the printed page. Fontenelle (1688)[15] produced a psychological theory where the Idea is all in all—the idea of 'a quiet life, with no other business but Love'—rather than the imitation of a concrete social reality where people work and fight and pray. The function of pastoral, indeed, is to produce pleasing half-truths: 'the Illusion and at the same time the pleasingness of pastoral therefore consists in exposing to the Eye only the Tranquility of a Shepherd's Life, and in dissembling or concealing its meanness, as also in showing only its Innocence and hiding its Miseries'. Ideally, shepherds should be 'free from pressing want; and their minds ought to be refin'd, through a long use of Civil Society', which should make their doings an admirable front for the emotions and the dreams of the cultivated classes: this follows from the fact that the country is not in the last analysis necessary for exciting the pastoral emotions, since all that is essential is the quiet life.[16] The language of pastoral, too, should be such as fits in with civil society—inherited comparisons are in order but they should be used sparingly simply because they are so well known, and the poet should avoid 'those clownish proverbial sayings, which real Shepherds use almost continually'.[17]

In England as in France theoretical debate went step by step with the practical writing of pastorals. Interestingly enough, the English followers of Rapin (Walsh, Pope and Gay) and of Fontenelle (Addison, Ambrose Philips, Tickell and Purney), though in opposite camps, share a certain amount of common ground: thus Pope, in the realm of theory, contends that the 'nature' which Fontenelle discovered by his reason is the very same nature that Rapin found in Virgil, so that to obey one's reason is automatically to follow in Virgil's footsteps, and *vice versa*, while in the realm of practice, although the settings of his own pastorals are highly generalised, yet the particulars of a real locality, the indefinable atmosphere of the landscape and the river banks 'is vividly present to his mind'.[18] In the pastorals of Pope's enemy, Ambrose Philips, what strikes a modern reader as real is—exactly as in Pope—his changing river scenery[19] and his beautiful impressions of an English summer;[20] and (quite otherwise than with Pope) his expression of a new, sensuous tearfulness. In the first editions of Philips's pastorals the Spenserian archaisms derided by Pope seem relatively few in number, though they are repeated fairly often ('weladay', 'whilome', 'make mock of', 'whitless younglings' for 'simple lambs'), but there is no serious attempt to reproduce a full rural dialect. The names of his characters are rustic, and he goes in for the occasional sentimental simplicity; but these are more than adequately counterbalanced by Augustan poetic diction and an almost reflex antithesis. The closest he comes to true rustic language is in passages such as the following from the Sixth Pastoral:

HOBBINOL
When Locusts in the fearny Bushes cry,
When Ravens pant, and Snakes in Caverns lye;
Then graze in Woods, and quit the burning Plain,
Else shall ye press the Spungy Teat in vain.

(lines 29-32)

Yet all the 'homely' words in this passage are (and were!) standard; the contrast is between two levels of diction within a common language and not between centre and region. There is thus very little basis for Gay's parodic exaggeration of Philips's timorous flirtation with dialect.

But before Gay wrote his *Shepherd's Week*, theory intervened. Following the publication of both Philips's and Pope's pastorals in a single volume, Tottel's *Miscellany* (1709), there appeared a notable series of articles in *The Guardian* of 1713—nos. 22, 23, 28, 30, 32 and 40;[21] the first four are generally ascribed to Thomas Tickell, the last (no. 40) is indubitably Pope's. Tickell's papers restate and develop Fontenelle's position to fit English conditions. A few isolated points deserve comment. We like pastoral because we all love ease; we have a 'secret approbation of innocence and simplicity', we all love the country[22]—that is, our aesthetic response comes from an innate quality of human nature. In our writings, rustic characters need not be boors and bumpkins: 'we may . . . introduce shepherds with good sense and even with wit, provided their manner of thinking be not too gallant or refined'.[23] Does not this sentence sum up in advance the patriarchs of 'The Farmer's Ingle' and 'The Cotter's Saturday Night'—and even, in its reference to wit, anticipate

the character of Burns himself? Pastoral writers should use proverbial
sayings; just as Virgil and Theocritus have 'left-handed ravens,
blasted oaks, witch-crafts, evil eyes', so English pastoral should
make use of native superstition.[24] Of the 'theology' of ancient
pastoral, we should retain only 'that part . . . which is universally
known, and the rest to be made up out of our own rustical superstition of hobthrushes, fairies, goblins and witches'.[25] Germany apart,
it was in Scotland that this precept was carried out to the full—by
Ramsay ('Up in the Air/Wi' my bonny gray mare'),[26] by Burns in
Tam o' Shanter, the *Address to the Deil* and *Death and Dr Hornbook*, by
Scott (the goblin page, Gilpin Horner, in *The Lay of the Last Minstrel*)
and, supremely, by James Hogg ('king of the Mountain and the
Fairy School', as his contemporaries called him), in both verse and
prose. Finally, in Tickell's *Guardian* papers, the linguistic experiments of both Spenser and Philips were approved. Both writers have
'copied and improved the beauties of the ancients. . . . As far as our
language would allow them they have formed a pastoral style
according to the Doric of Theocritus in which I dare not say they
have excelled Virgil! but I may be allowed, for the honour of our
language, to suppose it more capable of that pretty rusticity than
the Latin'.[27] It is at this point in the argument that the English
disciples of Fontenelle make contact with the powerful currents of
national feeling, and provide an obvious inspiration for Scottish poets
to cultivate a rusticity that, potentially, was far from merely 'pretty'.

Pope's *Guardian 40* sought to annihilate this school, whose own
inner logic led inevitably towards the exploitation of dialect, by
what he considered the *reductio ad absurdum* that would finish off
Philips's defenders for good and all:

> . . . I should think it proper for the several writers of
> pastoral, to confine themselves to their several counties:
> Spenser seems to have been of this opinion; for he hath laid
> the scene of one of his pastorals in Wales, where, with all
> the simplicity natural to that part of our island, one shepherd
> bids the other good-morrow in an unusual and elegant
> manner.
>
> > 'Diggon Davey, I bid hur God-day;
> > Or Diggon hur is, or I mis-say.'
>
> Diggon answers,
>
> > 'Hur was hur while it was day-light:
> > But now hur is a most wretched wight.' etc.
>
> But the most beautiful example of this kind that I ever
> met with, is a very valuable piece which I chanced to find

among some old manuscripts, entituled, A Pastoral Ballad:
which I think, for its nature and simplicity, may
(notwithstanding the modesty of the title) be allowed a
perfect pastoral. It is composed in the Somersetshire dialect,
and the names such as are proper to the country people.
It may be observed, as a farther beauty of this pastoral, the
words Nymph, Dryad, Naiad, Faun, Cupid, or Satyr, are
not once mentioned through the whole. I shall make no
apology for inserting some few lines of this excellent piece.
Cicily breaks thus into the subject, as she is going a milking:

'Cicily.   Rager go vetch tha kee, or else tha zun
           Will quite be go, bevore c'have half a don.
Roger.   Thou shouldst not ax ma tweece, but I've a be
           To dreave our bull to bull tha parson's kee.'

It is to be observed, that this whole dialogue is formed
upon the passion of jealousy; and his mentioning the
parson's kine naturally revives the jealousy of the
shepherdess Cicily, which she expresses as follows:

'Cicily.   Ah Rager, Rager, chez was zore avraid
           When in yond vield you kiss'd tha parson's maid:
           Is this the love that once to me you zed
           When from tha wake thou broughtst me ginger-
                           bread?
Roger.   Cicily thou charg'st me false — I'll zwear to thee,
           Tha parson's maid is still a maid for me.'

In which answer of his are expressed at once that 'spirit of
religion', and that 'innocence of the golden age', so necessary
to be observed by all writers of pastoral.

As to the conclusion of this piece, the author reconciles
the lovers, and ends the eclogue the most simply in the world:

        'So Rager parted vor to vetch tha kee,
        And vor her bucket in went Cicily.'

I am loth to show my fondness for antiquity so far as to
prefer this ancient British author to our present English
writers of pastoral; but I cannot avoid making this obvious
remark, that both Spenser and Philips have hit into the
same road with this old west country bard of ours.[28]

Gay carried such ridicule much further in the burlesque
Shepherd's Week (1714), a curiously double-edged work which
succeeded against its author's intention in showing that realistic

poems and plays about countrymen and women who speak and sing in a rural dialect and work productively rather than 'pipe idly on oaten reeds', were an exciting and creative possibility.[29] That Gay 'writ no language' and lived 'in a sort of half-way house, not wholly given over either to travesty, or realism'[30] does not matter; what concerns us are the possibilities of his form. These were developed by Thomas Purney in 1716–17, some years before Allan Ramsay turned to the eclogue. When Purney's *Pastorals in the Simple Manner of Theocritus* were advertised in *The Post Boy* for Nov. 15, 1716, it was stated that they aimed to 'introduce into our Language a Dialect entirely Pastoral; having at once Rusticity, Softness and Simplicity; being what Rapin, Dacier and the French Criticks allow their Language uncapable of'.[31] Purney's language was a poetical creation based on Spenser and mingling archaisms with dialect words taken from different parts of England. Philips had given his characters names sometimes English, sometimes borrowed indirectly from the pastoral heritage – Lobbin, Thenot, Colinet, Albino, Angelot, Palin, Mico, Argol, Cuddy (from Spenser), Geron (an older man), Hobbinol and Lanquet. Gay's burlesque nomenclature included Lobbin Clout, Cuddy, Cloddipole, Sparabella, Bumkinet, Clumsilis, Hobnelia, Lubberkin, Boobyclod, Grubbinol, while Purney, quite seriously, had Paplet, Soflin, Cubbinet, Collikin, Fauney, Lallet, Floreynet, Cuddleit, and Dillin. On the debit side, we must say that Purney is too often a candidate for the Right Worshipful Fraternity and Honourable Order of the Stuffed Owl; he can be more mawkish than Philips and at greater length, without Philips's talent for poetry. On the credit side, he is good at conveying adolescent sexuality – particularly in young girls as they appeal to a youth's imagination: the quality of feeling here is almost precisely that of the lyrics of sensual desire cited in the last chapter.[32] And his impressions of nature are far more individualised than anything in either Philips or Pope:

> The easy-faring Fish sweet wandered
> All in the wet, and sweetly plai'd.
> He! He! the tender-tongued *Paplet*, cry's;
> To see the little Fish catch Flys.
> So merry lookt they, whenso came in sight;
> You'd said they were asham'd of light!
> To see 'em fled the Mew and Diedapper,
> And thought themselves so happy there!
> Glist'ring in th' Sun, they skim the top all-fair;
> Then scowr away ev'n flit as Air.[33]

Following Gay, and anticipating Ramsay, Purney puts songs into his Eclogues; his Pastorals are divided into scenes, with such locales as 'A Blea and open Heath, with Bushes', 'The Corner of a Meadow; made by the Eden's running into the Medway', and 'A Bushy Brake, on this side of a small running Water', which look forward to Ramsay's precise setting in the Pentland Hills. As in Spenser, the word 'gentle' runs through these poems like a motif: 'A Gentle Swain in Kentish mead'; 'Say me, ye gentle striplings, say', 'Sure gentle Paplet 'tis I see'. The closely associated 'tender' is equally common, and the second pastoral, 'Lallet', is sub-titled '*The Tender Shepherdess*'. Quite clearly, one of the contexts of *The Gentle Shepherd* is the line that comes from Rapin and Fontenelle via Pope, Philips and Gay to Purney.

But not the only context. True, the germ of *The Gentle Shepherd* is to be found in Ramsay's two eclogues 'Patie and Roger' and 'Jenny and Meggy', which the S.T.S. editors conclude were written in 1720 and 1723 respectively,[34] and which stem directly from Gay and Philips, perhaps also from Purney. The newly awakening tradition of the vernacular revival, begun by Sempill of Beltrees in the mid-seventeenth century and continued by the publication of Watson's *Select Collection* in 1706–11, by Ramsay himself and Hamilton of Gilbertfield, meant that the linguistic ideal of Philips and Purney was much more likely to succeed in Scotland than in England. All the conditions were ripe for such a fusion of the colloquial and the consciously archaic, and they had even been put forward as a theoretical possibility by an Englishman, Basil Kennet, at least as early as 1713, when referring to Theocritus's rustic style: 'As for our selves, the *Scotch-Songs*, which pass with so much applause, show that it is not impossible to revive this old Conduct among Us with Success'.[35] *The Gentle Shepherd* extended 'Patie and Roger' and 'Jenny and Meggy' first towards drama and then towards the musical play: and the influences here, directly or indirectly, were the European and English pastoral plays and masques of the sixteenth and seventeenth centuries. From one point of view it was 'belated', the 'swan-song' of pastoral drama; from another, the precursor of a sensibility altogether new.

According to Ramsay's own statement *The Gentle Shepherd* was written in the years 1724 and 1725. When the first edition came out in 1725 there were only four songs, 'Peggy, now the King's come', II, iii; the duet between Patie and Peggy, 'By the delicious warmness of thy mouth', II, iv; Bauldy's snatch of song, 'Jenny said to Jocky, "Gin ye winna tell" ', IV, i; and the conclusion to the whole work, Peggy's 'My Patie is a lover gay'. Although it is most unlikely, as is sometimes claimed, that the first edition, containing a mere handful of songs, had any influence on *The Beggars' Opera*, it is nevertheless certain that there was at first some interaction between these almost opposite works. Gay's ballad opera was performed in Edinburgh by Tony Aston's company in October 1728 and seen by the pupils of Haddington Grammar School, who thereupon asked Ramsay to do the same with his drama; the upshot was a 'public performance of *The Gentle Shepherd*, with musical accompaniment, given on 22 January, 1729 "in Taylor's Hall, by a *Set of Young Gentlemen*" ', in which the four songs were expanded to twenty-one. The 1734 printed edition describes itself as 'the sixth edition with the songs'. A manuscript life of the poet, ascribed to his son, Allan Ramsay the painter, claims that he soon became unhappy with the expanded form and wished the songs away, but 'comforted himself with the thought that the contagion had not infected his second Volume in Quarto, where *The Gentle Shepherd* is still to be found in its original purity'.[36] Nevertheless, it was in its ballad opera form that it was widely known, in both Scotland and England, until the early nineteenth century; and it was through the reprints of the songs in the later editions of *The Tea-Table Miscellany*, other song-books, and chapbooks that it most influenced the popular lyrical tradition.

The Gentle Shepherd is set at the time of the Restoration of 1660, and its plot is of the slightest. In a village at the foot of the Pentland Hills, near Edinburgh, the poor but independent Patie is in love with Peggy, who requites his passion; his rich friend Roger dotes on Jenny, who slights him. The foundling Peggy, brought up by a shepherd called Glaud, is actually a laird's daughter; and Patie, reared in his turn by Symon, is the son of Sir William Worthy, exiled during the Cromwellian interregnum. Sir William returns disguised as a fortune-teller, reveals himself to Symon and covertly observes young Patie, with whom he is well pleased. The shepherd's real identity is disclosed to him; he is truly 'gentle' (i.e. one of the upper classes), and it behoves him, now that his restored father is about to enjoy his own again, to give up the low-born Peggy. This is the cue for Mause, who had at one time been Peggy's nurse, to reveal the truth about the heroine. All this time the action has been counterpointed by a sub-plot. In her flouting of Roger, Jenny coquettishly appears to favour the boorish Bauldy. But Bauldy (who once courted Neps) now wants Peggy; believing that Mause is a witch he asks her to use her eldritch skills to make Peggy dote on him and transfer Patie's affections to his own former sweetheart, Neps. In IV, i Madge (Glaud's sister) accuses Bauldy of being a heartless jilt and drives him off the stage in the style of crude popular farce, while Mause and Madge plot to scare Bauldy out of his wits, and his unseemly passion, by dressing up as ghosts. At the end Patie and Peggy are betrothed, as are Roger and Jenny while the sadder and wiser Bauldy goes back to Neps, and there is general rejoicing.

The plot is so trite and conventional that, as A. M. Kinghorn has put it, 'direct ancestry is untraceable . . . the pattern of lovers, the foundling complications, and the device of disguise are all stylised descendants of classical comedy': it goes right back through the Renaissance to Roman comedy and Attic new comedy.[37] But the structure of the action, deriving so obviously from written, even learned forms, and couched in the form of a regular neo-classic drama observing the unities[38], nevertheless manages to preserve some of the responses aroused by the folk-tale. After a minute examination of a hundred Russian fairy tales, Vladimir Propp concluded that the total number of 'structural functions' never exceeded thirty-one, and that whatever the number of such functions in a given tale, they always appear in the same order. Examples of such structural functions are Propp's nos. 21, 22 and 23 — 'the hero is pursued', 'rescue of the hero from pursuit' and 'the hero, unrecognised, arrives home from another country'.[39] No less than twenty-one of Propp's functions appear in *The Gentle Shepherd*, only they are not always assigned to a single hero, but are split between Patie and his father, and they do not always appear in the same order as in narrative folk-tale. When *The Gentle Shepherd* is scrutinised with Propp's categories in mind, some of the functions which in a simple Fairy Tale are given to hero or villain, are in Ramsay embodied in the historic process itself: for example, 'the hero acquires the use of a magical agent'. Because History is on the side of Sir William's return and therefore, unknown to him, of Patie, History usurps the function of a magical agent. I shall come back to this point in a moment. In the meantime, it is worth observing that at the level of structure Ramsay's pastoral attempts to synthesise different traditions; and that it does exactly the same at the level of texture.

This is exemplified in the first four lines of the piece, in the six-lined Prologue which sets the scene:

> Beneath the south side of a craigy beild,
> Where crystal springs the halesome waters yield,
> Twa youthful shepherds on the gowans lay,
> Tenting their flocks ae bonny morn of May.

Not only is the plain directness of the first line, moving from the neutral 'south side' to the downright Scots of 'craigy beild', contrasted with the Augustan balance of the second, but the counterpointing within the figure is heightened by the way the Scots 'halesome' offsets the English 'crystal', at the same time as Scots and English are linked between the lines by the cross alliteration of '*cr*aigy' and '*cr*ystal'. In the ballad-opera the Prologue is followed immediately by one of Ramsay's best pastoral lyrics, 'My Peggy is a young thing', sung by Patie, and first printed in the 1729 edition of the *Tea-Table Miscellany*. This lyric shows exactly the same contrasts as the Prologue. Its thin sprinkling of Scots is dramatically appropriate for Patie, one of nature's gentlemen who also happens to be socially a gentleman, although he does not yet know it; and a Scots expression in the second stanza, 'To a' the lave I'm cauld' is paralleled in the last stanza by its English translation, no doubt to provide the medial rhyme: 'By a' the rest, it is confest/By a' the rest that she sings best'. In this first song, too, we are presented with a genuine contemporary ideal that is one of the positives of the play. The songs Peggy sings best are informed 'With innocence the wale o' sense'; she is loved for her own personal qualities which are those of nature's gentlewoman; she excels others not only in singing but in true womanly qualities, as a Scots lady should. In the whole of the following eclogue, which does duty for Act I, sc. i, the movement is at first from the contrast between Patie's joyous mood, perfectly in tune with the sunny morning, and Roger's despair at Jenny's scorn, towards the more permanent difference between their inherent characters. Patie, cheerful but impoverished, is popular with all; Roger, despairing though wealthy, is unpopular — especially with the girls. The notions of innate excellence, of its opposite, innate meanness, and of 'Slow rises Worth, by poverty depressed', are brought out by the rhetoric of Roger's very first couplet:

> I'm born, O Patie! to a thrawart fate;
> I'm born to strive with hardships sad and great.
>
> (I, i, 15-16)

The stars and his forbears have given Patie a slow, solid, stoical common-sense that can be found in all classes, but is particularly suitable in a landowner or community leader:

> The bees shall loath the flower, and quit the hive,
> The saughs on boggie-ground shall cease to thrive,
> Ere scornful queans, or loss of warldly gear,
> Shall spoil my rest, or ever force a tear.
>
> (I, i, 21-4)

The transition to the second part of the scene, where the topic is Jenny's coquettishness, is made by means of superstition, a subsidiary theme of the whole work; as we have seen, such folk-beliefs were a debating point in the theoretical discussions over pastoral.[40] Roger says:

> I dream'd a dreary dream this hinder night,
> That gars my flesh a' creep yet with the fright
>
> (lines 63-4)

which Patie counters with 'Daft are your dreams' (line 67) — the very voice of common-sense and the Enlightenment; but when Roger begins to tell how badly Jenny has treated him, he uses another allusion to rural superstition — 'she fled as frae a shellycoat (spectre clad in a rattling coat) or kow (goblin)' (line 78), thus consolidating the difference between the character-types of the two men. Patie advises him to give over his 'silly whinging way' (line 103) and use amorous tactics, seeming to forsake her. After all, it worked for him with Peggy:

> Blythsome, I cry'd, my bonny Meg, come here,
> I ferly wherefore ye're sae soon asteer;
> But I can guess, ye're gawn to gather dew:
> She scoured awa, and said, 'What's that to you?'
> 'Then fare ye well, Meg Dorts, and e'en's ye like',
> I careless cry'd, and lap in o'er the dike.
> I trow, when that she saw, within a crack,
> She came with a right thievless errand back;
> Misca'd me first, — then bade me hound my dog
> To wear up three waff ews stray'd on the bog.
> I leugh, and sae did she; then with great haste
> I clasp'd my arms about her neck and waste,
> About her yielding waste, and took a fouth
> Of sweetest kisses frae her glowing mouth.
>
> (lines 121-34)

This is a completely new voice in British poetry. The pentameter couplet is now naturalised in Scotland and has become something quite different in the process. It has acquired a colloquial vigour not found in Purney or Philips, let alone in Pope's Pastorals: and the passage quoted, so admirably conveying the cut and thrust of everyday flyting ('What's that to you?', 'Fare ye well, Meg Dorts, and e'en's ye like'), and so full of action-verbs, is preceded by a beautifully sensuous description that is again far more effective than any similar passage from Ramsay's southern predecessors:

I saw my Meg come linkan o'er the lee;
I saw my Meg, but Meggy saw na me:
For yet the sun was wading thro' the mist,
And she was close upon me ere she wist;
Her coats were kiltit, and did sweetly shaw
Her straight bare legs that whiter were than snaw;
Her cockernony snooded up fou sleek,
Her haffet-locks hang waving on her cheek;
Her cheek sae ruddy, and her een sae clear;
And O! Her mouth's like ony hinny pear.

(lines 109-18)

In the ballad-opera, Patie expands his advice given in the following couplet

Seem to forsake her, soon she'll change her mood;
Gae woo anither, and she'll gang clean wood

into the song 'Dear Roger if your Jenny geck', which quite charmingly embroiders the meaning of the preceding couplets: unlike some of the later songs, though it may be superfluous, it still manages to be effective as decoration. The first scene — the eclogue — is resolved in a new friendship and understanding between Roger and Patie. Roger agrees to follow the advice of his natural superior (Patie) and will celebrate the change in their relationship with the gift of a tartan plaid of his mother's making. Patie caps this with the offer of his own greatest treasure, his new flute, in a marvellous couplet that triumphantly blends the idiomatic with the concise:

My flute's be your's, and she too that's sae nice
Shall come a will, gif ye'll tak my advice.

(lines 157-8)

In an equally fine and simple couplet, Roger refuses the flute —

As ye advise, I'll promise to observ't;
But ye maun keep the flute, ye best deserv't.

(lines 159-60)

The scene ends with an anticipation of breakfast which gives Ramsay an opportunity to restate in Scots the old pastoral preference for homely fare and the traditional condemnation of luxurious dishes:

Be that time bannocks, and a shave of cheese,
Will make a breakfast that a laird might please;
Might please the daintiest gabs, were they sae wise,
To season meat with health instead of spice.

(lines 165-8)

The contrast and linking of Scots and English language, of the simple with the sophisticated, which we noted in the Prologue, are again present here, and aptly synthesised in the last line quoted, balancing 'health' against 'spice': an abstract noun standing for a whole way of life against the concrete symbol of an opposite complex of values. A Scots colouring is delicately imparted by the pronunciation; the normally voiced 'wise' becomes voiceless to rhyme with 'spice'.

The second scene—and it too, we remember, was originally a separate eclogue—is formally parallel to the first. It is a debate between Peggy and Jenny where

> . . . Jenny what she wishes discommends,
> And Meg with better sense true love defends
> (lines 7-8)

to such effect that, just like Pate in the preceding scene, she converts her friend to her own view. Their friendship is re-established under the dominance of the natural leader, Peggy: she is as superior in her feminine sphere as Patie is in his masculine one.

For the girls, any debate about love is automatically a debate about marriage. Jenny scorns her own lover out of fear because of what she has seen and heard of the 'perils' of marriage, but Peggy utterly rejects her suggestion that Pate will tire of her after a fortnight, 'And think he's tint his freedom for your sake' (line 85). His innate male superiority is her guarantee that he will respect her type of female superiority for life: 'His better sense will lang his love secure' (line 106). Jenny next paints a grim picture of the trouble of family life—'whindging getts about your ingle-side,/Yelping for this or that with fasheous din', toiling and spinning from morn to night, and the inevitable sick and fractious children:

> The deel gaes o'er John Wobster, hame grows hell,
> When Pate misca's ye war than tongue can tell.
> (lines 116-17)

We have come a long way from the deliberate idealisation demanded by Fontenelle, or the contention in *Guardian* 22 that true pastoral writing represents only the simplicity and hides the misery of country life.[41] In her next statement, Jenny gives a stark picture of rural poverty in a period of general economic crisis:

> Gif o'er your heads ill chance shou'd beggary draw:
> But little love, or canty chear can come,
> Frae duddy doublets, and a pantry toom.

Your nowt may die – the spate may bear away
Frae aff the howms your dainty rucks of hay. . . .
A dyvour buys your butter, woo and cheese,
But, or the day of payment, breaks and flees.
With glooman brow the laird seeks in his rent:
'Tis no to gi'e; your merchant's to the bent;
His Honour mauna want, he poinds your gear:
Syne, driven frae house and hald, where will ye steer?
(lines 129-33, 136-41)

In reply, Peggy avers that Jenny's mistake has been to ignore the *mental* aspects of love (line 190) and she wins the minx over in a beautiful, if traditional, extended simile:

Bairns, and their bairns, make sure a firmer try,
Than ought in love the like of us can spy.
See yon twa elms that grow up side by side,
Suppose them, some years syne, bridegroom and bride;
Nearer and nearer ilka year they've prest,
Till wide their spreading branches are increast,
And in their mixture now are fully blest.
This shields the other frae the eastlin blast,
That in return defends it frae the west.
Sic as stand single, – a state sae liked by you!
Beneath ilk storm, frae ev'ry airth, maun bow.
(lines 191-201)

Ramsay does not just set a glib idealism over against a brutal 'real world' of battered babies, battered wives and unfaithful husbands. His vision of married happiness is far from idyllic; he well knows the storms of life are fierce; but it is a matter of simple observation that the friendship and companionship of a happy marriage are the surest safeguards against such storms. The values in this scene are the highest point in the drama, and they are precisely those which Burns was later to express in four of his most hackneyed lines:

To make a happy fireside clime
    To weans and wife,
That's the true *Pathos* and *Sublime*
Of Human Life.[42]

The extended, musical version has three songs summing up the girls' respective positions in the debate: Sang iii, given to Peggy ('The dorty will repent/If lover's heart grows cauld'); Sang iv, given to Jenny ('O dear Peggy, love's beguiling'); and Sang v, which is again Peggy's ('How shall I be sad when a husband I hae/ That has better sense then any o' thae'). In Sang vi ('I yield, dear lassie, ye have won'), Jenny acknowledges her defeat. While all are lyric expansions of what is more pithily expressed in the dialogue, only the third and the sixth songs are completely mechanical: the fourth and the fifth add some nuances of emotional tone to what is said in the preceding passages.

One function of the two eclogues which Ramsay put together to form Act I is to set the pastoral firmly in *place*. We only gradually become aware of its exact locale, and this arouses in us a distinct sense of movement inwards towards a centre. When Patie tells us he has bought a new flute in the West-port, we deduce, if we are watching a performance without a printed programme, that the action probably takes place near Edinburgh (I, i, 56). And it is only in the second scene, when Peggy says 'Go farer up the burn to Habby's How', that we know the little community is situated in a particular corner of the Pentland Hills (I, ii, 13).

The parallel function of II, i, where Glaud and Symon crack about politics, is to fix the play solidly in *time*, using the Scots reductive idiom to bring national politics within the compass of a rustic mind. Symon brings the news:

> Now Cromwell's gane to Nick; and ane ca'd Monk
> Has play'd the Rumple a right slee begunk,
> Restor'd King Charles, and ilka thing's in tune. . . .
> > (II, i, 29-31)

The two main political themes of the scene, that political revenge is sweet and that the ideal landlord, epitomised in the character of Sir William Worthy, does not 'stent' his tenants in a 'racket rent', are singled out by the seventh and eighth songs in the opera version:

> (1)   Cauld be the rebels cast, —
> >   Oppressors base and bloody;
> > I hope we'll see them at the last
> >   Strung a' up in a woody.
> > > (Sang vii, 1-4, Tune 'Cauld Kail in Aberdeen')
>
> (2)   The laird who in riches and honour
> >   Wad thrive, should be kindly and free,
> > Nor rack the poor tenants who labour
> >   To rise above poverty. . . .
> > > (Sang viii, 1-4, Tune 'Mucking o' Geordy's byre')

The social paternalism of the last lines is no isolated observation but connects with Peggy's conviction that a tenant's first duty is to his landlord:

> A flock of lambs, cheese, butter, and some woo,
> Shall first be sald to pay the laird his due;
> Syne a' behind's our ain.

$$\text{(I, ii, 157-9)}$$

II, ii and II, iii develop the sub-plot and prepare the way for the discomfiture of the wretched Bauldy. Mause's fine song 'Peggy, now the King's come' to the tune of 'Carle and the king come', one of the four lyrics in the original drama, allows the audience to anticipate the final resolution by informing them that Peggy is herself 'gentle', at the same time as it relates Mause to the main plot.

These scenes connect obviously and even obtrusively with Burns. Ramsay's Enlightenment condemnation of witch-beliefs and also much of his detail are taken over bodily into 'Tam o' Shanter'. In II, iv the action shifts to a lovers' meeting between Patie and Peggy, and lines 57-68 of the original, describing how they became acquainted, are in the opera expanded into a courtship dialogue-song of three stanzas in anapaestic couplets to the tune of 'Winter was cauld, and my claithing was thin'. The first two stanzas are surely as good as the corresponding couplets, and the whole song is aesthetically pleasing in itself:

PEGGY

> When first my dear laddie gaed to the green hill,
> And I at ewe-milking first sey'd my young skill,
> To bear the milk bowie no pain was to me,
> When I at the bughting forgather'd with thee.

PATIE

> When corn-riggs wav'd yellow, and blue heather-bells
> Bloom'd bonny on moorland and sweet rising fells,
> Nae birns, brier, or breckens, gave trouble to me,
> If I found the berries right ripen'd for thee.

$$\text{(Sts. i, ii)}$$

It is a lyric community that surrounds Patie and Peggy, where songs are sung at work and at evening ceilidhs, forming part of the very texture of daily life:

Pat.   Jenny sings saft *The Broom of Cowden-knows*,
And Rosie lilts *The Milking of the Ews*;
There's nane like Nansie, *Jenny Nettles* sings;
At turns in *Maggy Lauder*, Marion dings:

> But when my Peggy sings, with sweeter skill,
> *The Boat-man*, or *The Lass of Patie's Mill*;
> It is a thousand times mair sweet to me:
> Tho' they sing well, they canna sing like thee.
>   (II, iv, 69-76)

At the end of the scene there is a duet, 'By the delicious warmness of thy mouth', sung 'to its own tune', that ends with a kiss upon the stage. The lyric puts forward once again the official ideal of this society—long devotion and no sex before marriage, though some sensuality is permitted:

> *Sung by both*
> Sun, gallop down the westlin skies,
> Gang soon to bed, and quickly rise;
> O lash your steeds, post time away,
> And haste about our bridal day:
> And if ye're wearied, honest light,
> Sleep, gin ye like, a week that night.
>   (II, iv, 120-5)

This song at least, which was in the text from the start, is dramatically appropriate.

Since III, i introduces Sir William Worthy, who speaks English as a matter of social decorum, except when disguised, the prologue is in Scots-English with a modicum of Scots vocabulary, the pronunciation being indicated by the orthography. Sir William's English couplets are not the sign of a split national consciousness but a matter of realism and decorum. His long soliloquy of fifty-two lines, taking up the entire scene, presents the stock 'happier than kings' ideal, the simple life to which he has consigned his son during exile; in the opera, these ideas are repeated in the nondescript Sang xii. The scene as a whole connects what the audience has come to accept as a real community of homely peasants with an almost mythic ideal; it presents the little hamlet or village as a microcosm of the Golden Age *within* a society menaced by the 'dinsome town', revolutionaries like Cromwell, and corrupt self-seeking money-grubbers. The conclusion, not stated directly but implicit in the feeling-tone of the drama as a whole, is that the closest we can come to realising the pastoral ideal is when the worthy, epitomised by Sir William, enjoy their own—when the best rule, and the entire country is governed by a natural aristocracy who are in practice identical with the traditional aristocracy of property and blood.

In the next scene (III, ii) the hint that Peggy is a natural aristocrat, given in II, iii by Mause's song 'Peggy, now the King's come', is strengthened by Symon, when he repeats the rumour that Peggy was a foundling. We are now in the second part of the play, which A. M. Kinghorn finds decidedly less attractive than the first: 'the action dominates the background and there is only a limited appeal in the conventional gathering of the threads. The manipulations in the interests of a standard *dénouement* are not particularly ingenious, nor is there much attempt on Ramsay's part to make the principal characters individual.'[43] Surely Dr Kinghorn is less than fair to Ramsay. Surpassing ingenuity is not required by the genre and truly realistic character-presentation would necessitate a kind of historical drama nowhere produced in early eighteenth-century Europe. Although it is true, as Dr Kinghorn says, that *The Gentle Shepherd* 'was not intended as a mask for political allegory',[44] its great achievement was to give expression to both the social and national character of early eighteenth-century Scotland: an achievement of which Ramsay was partly conscious, and partly unconscious. In the remainder of III, ii, disguised as a spaeman peddlar, Sir William offers to tell fortunes — and does so, in good vernacular Scots. When the strange 'warlock' prophesies that Patie will be a laird, Patie is the identical stalwart sceptic of Act I:

> A laird of twa good whistles, and a kent,
> Twa curs, my trusty tenants, on the bent,
> Is all my great estate — and like to be:
> Sae, cunning carle, ne'er break your jokes on me.
>
> (lines 94-7)

The rationality of the natural aristocrat is identical with the shrewd common-sense of the more solid and experienced peasants, for both Glaud and Symon are sceptical of spaemen. There is some simple but effective stage-business. Sir William 'looks a little at Patie's hand, then counterfeits falling into a trance, while they endeavour to lay him right'; when he 'starts up and speaks' it is to foretell his own return and Patie's transformation into 'Mr Patrick', *via* an allegorical tale about 'A knight that for a Lyon fought,/ Against a herd of bears' (III, ii, 112-24). In a strongly contrasting love scene, Jenny — despite her decision to accept love and its obligations — repeats a real fear to Roger, the tyranny of a soul-destroying domestic drudgery:

> When prison'd in four waws, a wife right tame,
> Altho' the first, the greatest drudge at hame.
>
> (lines 38-9)

Roger retorts that woman's slavery is caused by money and arranged marriages: it is different in a love-match. Love—as in a hundred lyrics of 'the common pursuit'—is supreme, and—should Jenny's father deny,

> ...I carena by,
> He'd contradict in vain;
> Tho' a' my kin had said and sworn,
> But thee I will have nane.
>
> (Sang xiv, lines 9-12, tune 'O'er Bogie')[45]

In III, iv, the recognition scene between Sir William and Symon, Symon praises Pate to his father. As befits a natural aristocrat, he is the acknowledged leader of the other shepherds, and studious too, buying books every time he goes to Edinburgh. To say, as A. M. Kinghorn does, that the laird's 'sententious observations about the elevating value of education for peasants as well as for gentlemen read rather quaintly nowadays', and that his 'ponderous moral statements delivered in his rôle as patron of the rustics'[46] are equally uninteresting, is to give less than due attention to *The Gentle Shepherd* in its historical context. When we are told that Roger reads Shakespeare, Ben Jonson, Drummond, William Alexander, and Cowley (lines 73-6), we are being told what sort of *traditions* ought to mould Scottish culture: Anglo-Scottish ones, uniting the best from both countries. And when (lines 84-5), Sir William says

> Reading such books can raise a peasant's mind
> Above a lord that is not thus inclin'd

he is in fact expressing a national ideal, the 'social character' of the Good Scotsman implicit in John Knox's free school in every parish, looking forward to the later myth of the 'lad o' pairts'. In the opera, the only song from this scene (Sang xv), to the tune 'Wat ye wha I met yestreen', which occurs at the end of the act just before the curtain falls, no more than paraphrases the soliloquy that precedes it, where Sir William says that 'Mister Patrick' must now forget his 'rustic business and love' and go abroad to improve his 'soul' in 'courts and camps'. In other words, the leading classes must be not just Scottish; they must be *international*, experiencing the practical introduction to European culture and manners, which only the grand tour can give.

In IV, i, when Maud and Madge tell us how the community rejoiced at Sir William's restoration, there is one highly significant line which 'nationalises' the values of pastoral, identifying them with the heroic age of the War of Independence. Without giving away anything about Peggy's birth, Mause hints that she may, after all, be able to marry 'Mr Patrick':

> Even kings have tane a queen out of the plain:
> And what has been before, may be again.
>
> (lines 36-7)

To which Madge retorts:

> Sic fashions in King Bruce's days might be;
> But siccan ferlies now we never see.
>
> (lines 40-1)

The artificial plot, by ensuring that this 'ferly' takes place after all, identifies Sir William's restoration, and therefore, by extension, the restoration of the Stuarts in 1660, with 'King Bruce's days'. When Bauldy comes on, singing the magnificent 'Jocky said to Jenny, Jenny wilt thou do't',[47] of which only four lines were printed in the 1728 text, there follows a vigorous vernacular flyting between Madge and Bauldy, leading on to the slapstick already mentioned, where Madge bloods his nose and drives him off the stage.

The hero's dilemma when he is expected to give up Peggy, is the subject of IV, ii, formally organised in two dialogues — the first between Roger and Patie, the second between Patie and Peggy — separated by a brief soliloquy in which Patie beautifully sums up her conflicting emotions and, by implication, his own:

> With what a struggle must I now impart
> My father's will to her that hads my heart!
> I ken she loves, and her saft saul will sink,
> While it stands trembling on the hated brink
> Of disappointment. — Heaven! support my fair,
> And let her comfort claim your tender care.
> Her eyes are red!
>
> (lines 106-12)

At the purely formal level the scene parallels both the first eclogue (I, i) between the two shepherds, and the first love-meeting of Peggy and Pate (II, iv). And at the level of meaning the two halves of the scene set before us (1) ideological tensions which run through the whole drama — love against duty, rural simplicity against the 'monkey-tricks' of aristocrats in capital cities where Mammon rules, and (2) the concepts we are to see as 'positives' — inborn uncomplicated innocence, the improving power of education and book-learning (lines 91-4) and life-long sincere love whose centre is marriage and the family. The first part of the scene is a debate in which Roger, though in a muted and subordinate manner, as befits one of the 'lower orders', shows exactly the same solid common-sense as Patie did in I, i; the second is an emotional dialogue about parting, full of contrasting satirical thrusts at the affectations of upper-class life (lines 178-85). In the opera text four songs are added, which merely embellish crucial parts of this dialogue, and give the actress who plays Peggy a chance to captivate the audience still further with her singing. They are set to such popular tunes as 'Wae's my heart that we should sunder', 'Tweedside' and 'Bush aboon Traquair'; the second of these, quoted in Chapter III above,[48] is a ludicrously naïve expression of female submissiveness. Peggy has no doubts whatever about her rôle: the husband is superior, the upper classes are superior, 'virtue' and common-sense are woman's highest qualities. The best of the three (Sang xix) has one delightful quatrain:

> I'll visit aft the birken bush
>   Where first thou kindly told me
> Sweet tales of love, and hid my blush
>   Whilst round thou didst enfold me.
>   (lines 5-8)

In the fifth act two recognition scenes flank an interchange between Glaud, Jenny, Peggy and Madge that concludes on a note both stoical and fatalistic:

> Gif I the daughter of some laird had been,
> I ne'er had notic'd Patie on the green:
> Now since he rises, why should I repine?
> If he's made for another, he'll ne'er be mine:
> And then, the like has been, if the decree
> Designs him mine, I yet his wife may be.
>   (V, ii, 71-6)

The first recognition (V, i, continued at the beginning of V, iii) sees folk-superstition firmly vanquished by civilised reason, and Sir William's sophisticated ridicule finds an echo in Glaud's peasant common-sense:

> 'Tis true enough, we ne'er heard that a witch
> Had either meikle sense, or yet was rich.
>   (V, i, 76-8)

The lyric which ends V, i in the opera is the once popular 'The bonny grey-ey'd morn begins to peep', given to Sir William, expressing the Horatian ideal of 'health and quietness of mind' in country retirement 'plac'd at a due distance from parties and state', untroubled by either ambition or avarice blind, and (in lines 3-4) anticipating some of the language of Gray's *Elegy*:

> The hearty hynd starts from his lazy sleep,
> To follow healthfu' labours of the day.

In V, iii, when Peggy is revealed as Sir William's niece, she and Pate embrace and kneel to him in a visual emblem of the play's utterly orthodox values. Reunion is to be followed by social reconstruction: pastoral is now subsumed in the improvements and rational planning of enlightened landlords:

> I never from these fields again will stray:
> Masons and wrights shall soon my house repair,
> And bussy gardners shall new planting rear. . . .
> (V, iii, 163-5)

Dynastic restoration of the Stuarts and political Toryism are identical with 'building' and 'planting'; the magical agent of fairy-tale, the Warlock, is identified with the social class and the ethic of sober reason which will dominate the next hundred years, and therefore with the historic process itself. The last word is *almost* left to Sir William:

> My friends, I'm satisfied you'll all behave,
> Each in his station, as I'd wish or crave.
> Be ever virtuous, soon or late you'll find
> Reward, and satisfaction to your mind.
> (V, iii, 222-5)

But not quite. The final note, in both play and opera, is lyrical, a song on the supreme value of 'virtuous love' from the lips of an attractive singer, to the tune of 'Corn rigs are bonny':

> Let lasses of a silly mind
>   Refuse what maist they're wanting:
> Since we for yielding were design'd,
>   We chastly should be granting.
> Then I'll comply, and marry Pate,
>   And syne my cockernonny,
> He's free to touzel air or late,
>   Where corn-riggs are bonny.
> (st. iii)

The song is yet another instance of the formal balance of the whole work; it is the counterpart of Pate's 'My Peggy is a young thing' which begins the operatic version. But thematically it by no means negates Sir William's adjuration. 'Each in his station' and 'chaste granting' are of equal value, and it is towards the effect achieved by putting them so closely together that the entire play has been moving.

How, then, does Ramsay's drama fit in with the early eighteenth-century debate about pastoral which is part of its background? It must be seen as 'practical criticism' of the more nostalgic forms of pastoral idealisation. Symon, Glaud, Bauldy, Madge, Elspa, Roger and Jenny are not courtiers in masquerade, with ladies' and gentlemen's feelings below their shepherds' clothing: and when Pate and Peggy turn out to be from the upper classes, this is acceptable because their 'natural aristocracy' is an extension and embellishment of peasant virtues and peasant common-sense. If *The Gentle Shepherd* does not idealise, as the *fêtes galantes* of Watteau idealise, it nevertheless presents a model to be imitated – a simplified silhouette of the type of man Ramsay admired. Although there are passages which unmask bad landlords and urban affectation as well as oafish superstition, its main effect is not *socially* critical but a bodying forth of the social character of early eighteenth-century Scotland. It reveals and builds on some of the main tensions of contemporary society – between, for example, man and woman in a money-economy, between realistic and idealistic views of marriage, between superstition and sceptical common-sense, between the urge for refinement and the brutal inheritance of the past: thus Bauldy is punished by Mause, not because he is a fool, but because he broke good-breeding's laws (V, iii, Prologue). The social character, which produces its ideal man and woman for innumerable citizens to emulate, is manifest above all in Sir William Worthy, restored royalist and ancestral Tory; in Pate, the man of independent, rational common-sense who may be found in any social class; and in his female counterpart, Peggy. These idealised embodiments are transitional between upper-class Augustan paradigms of 'the happy and the good' man or woman, and Burns's man of independent mind, perhaps self-educated, who 'looks and laughs at a' that'. The Burnsian ideal is a democratisation of the image held up by Ramsay for our approval; in the following century he formed a pattern for innumerable lowlanders to imitate – self-made men, godly fathers of families, radical Chartists, pioneer settlers in Canada and Middle America, in Brisbane and Otago and the African veldt. Kipling's Macandrew and Conrad's McWhirr in *Typhoon* were among his descendants, and countless non-Scots – humble artisans, democrats, evangelical Christians, radicals and socialists of every persuasion,

identified themselves with the archetypal figure behind the
'*Marseillaise* of Equality'.[49]

Not for nothing does the statue of Burns in Canberra bear as its
inscription Pope's line 'An honest man's the noblest work of God',
quoted in *The Cotter's Saturday Night* (line 166) and, on the statue,
wrongly ascribed to Burns himself. For there is a direct line of
evolution between the enlightened hard-headedness of a Pope or a
Swift, the ideology of the Scottish Vernacular Revival, and
colonial democracy.

REFERENCES

1. 'Allan Ramsay and the Romantic Revival', *Essays and Studies by Members of
    the English Association* (1924), IX, 138.
2. In *Theories of Pastoral Poetry in England 1684–1798* (University of Florida
    Press, repr. 1968), pp. 113-14 and *passim*.
3. Congleton, p. 113, where the phrases from Mackail are quoted.
4. *The Works of Allan Ramsay*, S.T.S. edn., IV (1970), 102.
5. Raymond Williams, *The Country and the City*, Paladin edn. (1975), p. 24.
6. *Pastoral Poetry and Pastoral Drama* (London, 1906), henceforth cited as
    Greg, p. 5.
7. Greg, p. 9.
8. Williams, pp. 25-7.
9. See my *Burns*, pp. 169-74, 160-8.
10. Williams, *loc. cit.*
11. *As you like it*, II, iv, 76-82.
12. Preface to his *Eclogae Sacrae*; translated into English in 1684 and printed
    with Thomas Creech's translation of Theocritus' *Idylliums*.
13. Creech (Oxford, 1684), p. 67; quoted Congleton, p. 61.
14. Second edn., 1713, pp. 27-8.
15. 'Discours sur la nature de l'eclogue': translated into English as *Of Pastorals*
    by P. A. Motteux (1695).
16. *Ibid.*, pp. 282-4; Congleton, pp. 67-8.
17. *Ibid.*, p. 293; Congleton, p. 69.
18. The phrase is C. V. Deane's in *Aspects of Eighteenth-Century Nature Poetry*
    (London, 1935: repr. 1967), p. 116.
19. *Third Pastoral*, lines 57-8, 93-4 (1708 edn.).
20. E.g. *Fourth Pastoral* (1708 edn.), lines 19-20:
            The Fields breath sweet; and now the gentle Breez
            Moves ev'ry Leaf, and trembles thro' the Trees,
    and lines 115-18:
            But see; the Hills increasing Shadows cast:
            The sun, I ween, is leaving us in haste:
            His weakly Rays but glimmer thro' the Wood,
            And blueish Mists arise from yonder Flood.
21. Reprinted in *The British Essayists*, ed. James Fergusson, 45 vols. (London,
    1819), XVI. All references are to this edition.
22. *Guardian*, No. 22, pp. 118-19.

23. No. 23, p. 120.
24. No. 23, pp. 122-3. Allan Ramsay was so steeped in these that he compiled a collection of *Scots Proverbs*.
25. No. 30, p. 157.
26. *TTM*, I: (1740), p. 73 (line 1: 'Now the sun's gone out o' sight').
27. *Guardian*, No. 30, p. 158.
28. No. 40, pp. 211-12.
29. *The Shepherd's Week*, 'Proeme to the Courteous Reader'.
30. *The Works of Thomas Purney*, ed. H. O. White (Oxford, 1933), p. xxv.
31. Quoted in *ibid.*, p. xxviii.
32. Above, pp. 45-6.
33. The Second Pastoral: 'Beauty and Simplicity', Scene i, in *Works*, ed. White, p. 76.
34. *Works*, S.T.S. edn., IV, 91, 106.
35. *The Idylliums of Theocritus with Rapin's Discourse upon Pastoral, made English by Mr. Creech. . . . To which is prefix'd the Life of Theocritus*, by Basil Kennet (London, 1713), p. 57.
36. *Works*, S.T.S. edn., IV, 92-3; VI, 96-7.
37. *Ibid.*, IV, 99.
38. After 'The Persons', the following is printed in the 1725 edition:
    First Act *begins at Eight in the Morning.*
    Second Act *begins at Eleven Forenoon.*
    Third Act *begins at Four afternoon.*
    Fourth Act *begins at Nine-a-clock at Night.*
    Fifth Act *begins at Day-light next Morning.*
39. Propp, *Morphology of the Folktale* (Austin, Texas, 1970), pp. 21 ff., summarised in Robert Scholes, *Structuralism in Literature* (New Haven and London, 1974), pp. 63-5.
40. Above, p. 75.
41. *British Essayists*, XVI, 117.
42. 'To Dr Blacklock', lines 51-4 (Kinsley, 273B).
43. S.T.S. edn., IV, 99.
44. *Ibid.*, IV, 101.
45. Although Sang xiii in the opera version (a duet) merely repeats the essence of the previous dialogue, the lines quoted from Sang xiv are an addition to the content, as are lines 13-14:
    Then never range nor learn to change,
    Like those in high degree.
46. S.T.S. edn., IV, 99-100.
47. The full text, from the MS. and the 1725 edition, is printed in S.T.S., VI, 101; *TTM* (1740) and *TTM* (14th edn., *repr.* Glasgow 1876); and *LLL*, 115, the most readily available source. It was also (with music) in *Museum*, 61.
48. P. 41.
49. The phrase is from Auguste Angellier, *Robert Burns: la vie, les oeuvres*, 2 vols. (Paris, 1893), II, 216.

Chapter VI

PARTING, ELOPEMENT, LOVE'S COMEDY

The Gentle Shepherd was the most complete treatment of 'straight' pastoral in the eighteenth century, and it appeared at the end of the third decade. But that did not mean that the song-culture, or even the pastoral genre marked time from then on. Far from it; their greatest triumphs, in point of quality, were yet to come, and there are many expressions of the Common Pursuit in both pastoral and non-pastoral modes which we have not yet considered.

The best-known songs of parting, like Dodsley's 'The Parting Kiss' already discussed, or Burns's 'Ae fond Kiss' derived from it, are in art and sentimental style, while elopement is more commonly featured in folk- and broadside-song. When they do treat of parting, folk and popular narratives often depict dramatic reunions after travel. *Four Excellent New Songs* printed at Edinburgh by J. Morren, Canongate (n.d.)[1] includes 'Bleak was the morn when William left his Nancy', a tale of a sailor's separation and return, and there are several such compressed narratives in the Aberdeen broadsheets of the 1770's.[2] 'The Sailor Bold', printed 12th March 1776, is a dialogue between Johnny and Nancy in which Johnny goes off to 'rifle' the Indies in order to 'bring you treasure here. . . . Enough for to maintain us both together here on shore'. The stock clichés are typical of broadside partings:

> Then kissing of her ruby lips, young Johnny took his leave
> And left his charming Nancy his absence to grieve.

In next to no time Johnny is on his way home, and the balladeer's McGonagalese encompasses a distorted classical reference, creating its own poetic diction in the process:

> The wind with gentle breezes did blow from crystal skies,
> The costly ship like Neptune did on the billows rise,
> Each wind did bring the vessel unto the happy shore,
> At Plymouth he arrived with gold and riches store.

He bestows his gold and silver on Nancy, they are married with great ceremony, and live happily ever after.[3] Another sheet in this series, dated 20th March 1776, contains 'Down by a Riverside; Or, Two true and constant Lovers: being the valiant Seaman's happy Return to his dearest Love, after long Absence from her: or a pleasant sweet Conference between these two Lovers at their first meeting',[4] a white letter reprint in eighteenth-century Scotland of a seventeenth-century English broadside in the rhythm of 'I'll never leave thee' and 'Jamie come try me':

> I stept unto her straight,
>   dearest what grieves thee?
> She answered me and said
>   none can relieve me.

Exactly as in the nineteenth-century 'Bleacher Lassie of Kelvin-haugh',[5] the woman has been parted from her lover for seven years. The young man shows her a token which he says he took from her lover after his 'brains were broken maintaining England's right', and he further asserts that the dead man commissioned him to deliver it with instructions that she should henceforth love the bearer. In a lament, the woman says she will take her own life, thus proving herself more constant than Leander, and will hide herself in the Elysian Shades until she finds the dead hero. He tries her further, and she rages 'like one distracted', employing further classical references more accurate than those in 'The Sailor Bold':

> The chaste Penelope
>   mourn'd for Ulysses,
> I have more grief than she
>   robb'd of such blisses.

She will 'slight him with disdain' if he comes near her. As is usual in such stories, he slips off his disguise, and she unburdens her passion in a spate of allusions to Hero, Leander, Dido, Aeneas, Venus and Adonis. One wonders how many Aberdonians who bought the broadside understood the allusions, and how many of them actually tried to sing it!

But the best song making use of this broadside theme is Burns's 'When wild War's deadly blast was blawn'; it makes the test far more convincing and realistic.[6] With altered voice, the soldier asks the girl to 'take pity on a sodger'. She says he is welcome to share 'our humble cot and hamely fare' for the sake of the man she once loved. The recognition scene is vividly and dramatically presented, and not just reported, as in so many of the broadsides:

> She gaz'd — she redden'd like a rose,
>> Syne pale like ony lily,
> She sank within my arms, and cried,
>> 'Art thou my ain dear Willie?'

In contrast, Allan Ramsay's earlier art-lyric on this topic, 'Beneath a green shade I fand a fair maid', is humorous, not serious.[7] Set to the tune of 'The Mill Mill, O', it shares something of the sexual associations of the *Merry Muses* words for this melody. A swain loves a sleeping girl who does not waken. While he is away fighting in Flanders she bears him a child and mounts the stool of repentance, 'nor kend wha had done her the ill O'. On his return he tells her that he was the man, and

> My bonny sweet lass, on the gowany grass,
>> Beneath the *shilling hill* — O,
> If I did offence, I'se make ye amends
>> Before I leave *Peggy's* mill — O.
>
> *O the mill-mill O, and the kill-kill O*
>> *And the cogging of the wheel — O;*
> *The sack and the sieve, a' that ye maun leave,*
>> *And round with a sodger reel — O.*
>
>> (st. iv. and chorus)

In the St. Clair Manuscript a folk dialogue is preserved which embodies the essence of the situation in a form that may well indicate oral transmission, with a broadside somewhere in the background. Its stark understatement is poetically superior to any thing in the Burns or Ramsay lyrics just quoted:

> O fair maid whase aught that bonny Bairn
> O fair maid, &c.
> It is a sodgers son she said
> That's lately gone to Spain
> Te dilly dan te tilly dan te dilly dilly dan
>
> O fair maid what was the sodgers name
> O fair, &c.
> In troth I't will never speak
> The mair I was to blame
> Te dilly, &c.
>
> O fair maid what had that sodger on
> O fair, &c.
> A scarlet coat laid o'er wi' gold
> A waistcoat o' the same
> Te dilly, &c.

O fair maid what if he should be slain
O fair, &c.
The King would lose a brave sodger
And I a pretty man
Te dilly, &c.

O fair maid what if he should come hame
O fair, &c.
The parish priest should marry us
The Clerk should say amen
Te dilly, &c.

O fair maid would ye that sodger ken
O fair, &c.
In troth I't well and that I wad
Amang ten thousand men
Te dilly, &c.

O fair maid what if I be the man
O fair, &c.
In troth I't well it may be sae
I'se had ye for the same
Te dilly, &c.[8]

The ultimate ancestor is the *chanson de toile* of the Middle Ages or a remoter antiquity where a warrior has returned to a deserted woman who is with child.[9]

What is common to many 'popular' songs of parting is the element of 'All for Love'. In another subtype of the 'All for Love' Group, the man urges the woman to 'Come in her coatie',[10] or states that if she *were* poor (which she isn't), like the wooer in Ramsay's 'Highland Lassie':

> Than ony lass in borrows-toun,
> Wha mak their cheeks with patches motie,
> I'd tak my *Katie* but a goun,
> Bare-footed in her little coatie.[11]

An English ballad of the seventeenth century, 'The Young-Man's hard shift for a Maiden-Head',[12] shows (if, indeed, any demonstration were needed) that the 'Come in thy Coatie '*motif* is by no means confined to Scotland, for in one line the young man declares 'you shall be welcome to me in your smock'.[13] This ballad combines various traditional elements: thus, each stanza of the first part ends with the burden 'Come away pretty Betty and open the door',[14] and when she finally accedes to this request, the natural result forms the subject of Pt. ii. Betty goes, pregnant, to 'pretty William's' house and asks *him* to open the door, but he bars it up instead and leaves her to her fate. Then the ballad moves over to the equally popular topic of the seduced maiden's plight.[15]

All classes are attracted by such stories — as we have seen, to marry for love was part of the protestant ethic, and the upper classes were as protestant as the lower. The classic 'all for love' plot involves elopement ('Jock o' Hazledean'): in upper class stories the hero, though poor, is usually a gentleman, but in plebeian tales the rich heroine is almost always carried off by a virile outsider. The Child ballad 'Johnny Faa' belongs to this type — a pastoral with both romantic and realistic overtones, which in all probability goes back to the seventeenth century, quite soon after the execution of the 'real' Johnny Faa in 1624. In many versions (e.g. Allan Ramsay's 'The Gypsy Laddie' in Vol. IV of *The Tea-Table Miscellany*)[16] there is often the suggestion of a supernatural and baleful influence behind the lady's decision to go off with the raggle-taggle. The magic of the gipsies' song, however, is mainly a dramatic device to justify her unnatural resolve:

> I'll make a hap to my Johnny Faa,
>   And I'll mak a hap to my deary,
> And he's get a' the coat gaes round,
>   And my Lord shall nae mair come near me.[17]

Nor is 'Johnny Faa' the only Child ballad to be built on this wish-fulfilment dream: 'The Famous Flower of Serving-Men' (Child 106) tells how a fair lady, after her husband is robbed and murdered, then travels as a serving man, becomes a King's chamberlain and is discovered, whereupon the King dresses her up in glamorous clothes, puts a crown on her head, and marries her:

> The likes before was never seen
> A serving-man to be a queen.

And in 'Tom Potts' (Child 109) a serving man loves the Earl of Arundel's daughter, while in the Scottish 'Richie Story' one of the daughters of the Earl of Wigtown follows her 'footman-laddie' for love — in some versions she ends up by mucking the byre with Richie, in others he turns out to be a nobleman in disguise.

Lyrics (rather than ballads) on the Lady Chatterley theme often have a hero who is a footman, a beggar or a tinker. In 'Geordie Downie' in the C. K. Sharpe MSS.:

> Downie melts the brass, the brass,
> An' Downie melts the tin, O;
> An' happy happy is the town
> That Downie enters in, O.
>
> My bonny love joe, my dearie you know
> My bonny love, Geordy Downie;
> I'll sell my hose and drink my sheen
> An follow Geordy Downie.[18]

'I'll tell thee the true reason', which William Motherwell obtained from a traditional singer in the early nineteenth century, features a lad of low degree who justifies himself in egalitarian terms:

> From Adam I'm descended
> My Dear as well as thee.[19]

Peter Buchan's version of 'Clout the Cauldron',[20] which appears to relate to the eighteenth-century chapbook form quoted below, uses the theme for popular bawdry. The lady does not elope with the disguised Johnny Sinclair (Willy Sinclair in the chapbook) but continues in an adulterous relationship, and there is the usual ambiguity of popular bawdy correspondence:

> She took him to the higher room,
> His work for to show,
> He took her by the middle small,
> And laid her body low. . . .
>
> There's not a nail that he's ca'ed in,
> But's well worth half a merk,
>
> The laird he then went down the gate,
> A dollor for to change;
> But long or he came back again,
> His cauldron got a range,
>
> It's tinker as for your wark,
> I think ye need no sending;
> For if ye bide our lang awa,
> My kettle will take mending.[21]

In the much older 'The Jolly Beggar', worth discussing here because it was constantly reprinted throughout the century, the goodman's daughter does not realise that the splendidly dressed man standing behind the door had previously visited the house in beggar's clothes:

> I took ye for some gentleman, at least the Laird of Brodie;
> O dool for the doing o't! are ye the poor bodie,
> *And we'll gang nae mair a roving,* &c.[22]

But the 'beggar' was in reality a more exalted personage still – the King himself!

> He took the lassie in his arms, and gae her kisses three,
> And four-and-twenty hunder mark to pay the nurice fee.
> *And we'll gang nae mair,* &c.

> He took a horn frae his side, and blew baith loud and shrill,
> And four-and-twenty belted knights came skipping o'er the hill.
> *And we'll gang nae mair,* &c.

> And he took out his little knife, loot a' his duddies fa',
> And he was the brawest gentleman that was amang them a'.

> *And we'll gang nae mair a-roving,*
>   *Sae late into the night,*
> *And we'll gang nae mair a-roving,*
>   *Let the moon shine ne'er sae bright,*
> *And we'll gang nae mair a-roving.*[23]

In the English broadside of 'The Jovial Tinker and Farmers Daughter', reprinted in Scotland during the century,[24] a noble lord disguises himself as a tinker to woo a farmer's daughter; he gets his will of her in the barn, where she has gone to make his bed. In the Scottish text, he says his name is Davie Faa, lies with her a second night, and leaves her fifty guineas for the 'nourice fee'. When the son is born the father sends a hundred pounds with a promise of 'as much again when he should come of age' in remembrance of the joyful night 'at the barring of the door'.

> If any will this damsel wed,
>   he'll give them a farm free,
> With horses, cows, harrow and ploughs
>   all fit for husbandry:
> Also a handsome fortune
>   of gold and white money;
> Altho' she's lost her maidenhead,
>   pray what the worse is she;
> But now we hear this dame is wed
>   to a farmer's son hard by;
> And when the goodman wants a hand,
>   the tinker does supply;
> And for to please the comely maid
>   as he had done before.

In Ramsay's text of 'The Gaberlunzie Man', the beggar is no king
or nobleman but a genuine outcast, and the good-wife's daughter
goes off with him to the simple life. Because she has not yet learned
'the beggar's tongue' and therefore cannot beg or sell trinkets, he
promises:

> Wi cauk and keel I'll win your bread,
> And spindles and whorles for them wha need,
> Whilk is a gentle trade indeed,
>   To carry the Gaberlunzie on.
>
> I'll bow my leg, and crook my knee,
> And draw a black clout o'er my eye,
> A cripple or blind they will ca' me,
>   While we shall be merry and sing.[25]

We shall return later, in Chapter X, to this highly significant attitude, with its unique blend of pastoral and anti-pastoral elements.

The most characteristically Scottish of 'Lady Chatterley' songs
are those in which the hero is a highlander. One eighteenth-century
song 'Down in yon shady grove, one day I chanced to wander'
quite typically unites, when dealing with this theme, the feeling-tone
of middle-class art song with two of the conventions of broadside
balladry — the girl who wanders abroad in man's attire and gives up
her parents for her lover:

> Oh! if I knew but where to find my dearest dear,
>   I would range the wide world all o'er;
> To sea I would repair, dressed in man's attire,
>   To find out the youth I adore,
> Thro' lonely woods I'll stray, and flow'ry meadows gay,
>   I will leave my mammy and dad,
> And never will return, but always sigh and mourn,
>   For my bonny Highland Lad.[26]

In a note to *Rob Roy*, Walter Scott quotes from Jamieson's version of
'Bonny Babby Livingstone', who is spirited away by the Highlander
Glen Lyon, and from a ballad about Rob Roy the younger (Robin
Oig) concerning his abduction of Jean Key, or Wright:

> Saying, be content, be content,
>   Be content wi' me, Lady:
> Where will ye find in Lennox land
>   Sae braw a man as me, Lady?[27]

The events of these ballads partake rather of marriage by capture.

In the text of 'Lizae Baillie' in the *Scots Nightingale*,[28] however, the lowland girl gives her consent:

> She wadna ha'e a Lowland laird
>   Nor be an English Lady:
> But she's awa' wi' Duncan Grahame,
>   He's row'd her in his plaidy.

And Allan Ramsay's 'The Highland Laddie' expresses the essentials of all these songs:

> O'er benty hill with him I'll run,
>   And leave my lawland kin and dady,
> Frae winter's cauld, and summer's sun,
>   He'll screen me with his highland plaidy.
>
> A painted room, and silken bed,
>   May please a lawland laird and lady;
> But I can kiss, and be as glad,
>   Behind a bush in's highland plaidy.[29]

The Highlander as active amorist, whose rôle in the popular consciousness was replaced in later centuries by the Italian, the Frenchman, the Spaniard, and the Pole, is depicted in these jeering lines from the streets:

> Where hae ye been a day
> Bonny Laddie Highland Laddie
> Up the Bank and down the brae
> Seeking Maggie, seeking Maggie.
>
> Where hae ye been a day
> Bonny Laddie Highland Laddie
> Down the back o' Bells Wynd
> Courting Maggie courting Maggie.[30]

The difference from the other lyrics lies in this, that in 'Where hae ye been' we have to do not with a laird, or with a plaidy-rolling Duncan Grahame, but with an ordinary clansman, first of all in the countryside (perhaps during the Jacobite campaigns) then in the city as one of the army of occupation or perhaps even as a member of the 'black banditti' of the City Guard. The Highland Laddie's activities on bank and brae are spelled out more precisely still in 'Comin o'er the Hills o' Couper':

> Kate Mackie cam frae Parlon craigs,
>   The road was foul twixt that and Couper;
> She show'd a pair o' handsome legs,
>   When Highland Donald he o'ertook her.

> Comin o'er the moor o' Couper,
> Comin o'er the moor o' Couper,
> Donald fell in love wi' her
> An' row'd his Highland plaid about her.[31]

And they are depicted from the lowland lass's point of view in a song often attributed to Burns (e.g. by Henley and Henderson):

> Put butter in my Donald's brose,
>   For weel does Donald fa' that;
> I loe my Donald's tartans weel
>   His naked a--e and a' that.
> For a' that and a' that,
>   And twice as meikle's a' that,
> The lassie got a skelpit doup
>   But wan the day for a' that.[32]

'Lady Chatterley' songs and ballads, where an upper-class woman or just an ordinary farmer's daughter goes off with a poor man or an outcast, whether beggar, serving-man, gipsy or highland marauder, connect one aspect of the Common Pursuit — the dreams of the unsatisfied, of the victims of a society where love was too often sacrificed to money — with the most artificial of amatory modes, the pastoral, extolling the loves of simple people out on the bent or under the greenwood tree. In all such songs the couples have to overcome social barriers to their love; and since comedy, more than any other genre, depends on surmounting obstacles to love, it is only natural that Lady 'Chatterley' pastoral should shade off into comedy. Nor should it be thought that the only side of love which popular songs find funny is the crudely sexual — the literary equivalent of the dirty joke. On the contrary, much of their comedy is transmuted into a rich strain of fantastic humour which is particularly evident in songs continuing the medieval anti-woman tradition. In the following instance, it grows out of a humorously realistic treatment of an unfortunate marriage which also happens to be a marriage for money:

> I married my wife in the light o' the moon,
> Fy! fy on her money!
> I rued what I did as soon as't was done,
> O what a bad luck had I![33]

The best Scots song of this type, Burns's 'Willie Wastle',[34] is apparently based on an older song 'Crooked Shoulder', to be found in the *Nightingale* (Edinburgh, 1776).[35] The love-money antagonism is at the centre of its comic reversal:

> My wicked friends did work the change,
>   Full sore against my own affection;
> Constrained me to wed for means;
>   I never chus'd her by election.
> I've got a wife, I'm cross'd with strife,
>   And find no way for to exclude her;
> I wish that I had lost my life,
>   First when I saw her crooked shoulder,
>   (st. vi)

and the song ends didactically, in true broadside manner, with the advice never to marry for money.

Alexander Ross's 'I am a bachelor winsom' features a man who is willing to take anyone, even if she is a cripple. But the girl who answers him in this 1779 text is not a complete cripple:

> But, cripple I am not, forsta' me,
>   What though bou'd-footed I be;
> Nor blind have you reason to ca' me,
>   What though I see but wi' one eye:
> These forty years I've been neglected,
>   As you the truth o't may see,
> Such offers should not be rejected,
>   Of what kind so ever they be.
>
> In Edinburgh speir for Jean Bladen,
>   A little below the Cross-Key,
> And at the sign of the Old Maiden,
>   There you will be sure to find me.
> Bring wi' you the priest o' the weddin
>   That a' things just finish'd may be,
> And I'll sing a sang to the beddin'
>   And wha'll be sae merry as we.[36]

The crooked-shoulder theme is here united to that staple of love-comedy, the desperate old maid. In the early nineteenth century M. Randall of Stirling reissued seventeenth-century stallsongs and ballads in chapbook form. One of his many reprints of this type, 'The Humours of Gravel-Lane, or the Cobler's Daughter's Wedding', fits into the context of 'Willie Wastle':

> To view the bride she was quite handsome,
>   Was you to see her in the dark;
> She was hump-backed, and bandy-legged,
>   And her mouth as wide as a barrel's bung. . . .[37]

And there have been many similar songs orally circulating in Scotland up to the present day, some of the best of which were noted by Gavin Greig in *Folk-Song of the North-East*.[38] It may be doubted, however, if either the realism or the fantasy of this comedy are specifically Scottish: rather, they are specifically *popular*, as can be demonstrated from the many analogues in the earlier literature of England, of which 'The Humours of Gravel Lane' is only one example.

Other related topics are those of the drunken wife cured by violent means, the folk tale of the Dumb Wife, and such reversals of nature as husband-beating ('My auld wife she bangs me').[39] It would indeed seem that the majority of Scots songs on these topics show English influence. As a test case, let us take the themes of the young man wedded to an old woman, and *vice versa*. In Ramsay's 'Lucky Nansy' the singer is not even married: he thinks that he is being uproariously funny when he praises her charms, and that she is the most fortunate of creatures to be the heroine of his song:

> Now ken, my reverend sonsy fair,
> Thy runkled cheeks and lyart hair,
> Thy haff-shut een and hodling air,
>   Are a' my passions fewel.
> Nae skyring gowk, my dear, can see,
> Or love, or grace, or heaven in thee;
> Yet thou hast charms anew for me:
>   Then smile, and be na cruel.
>
> *Leez me on thy snowy pow,*
> *Lucky* Nansy, *lucky* Nansy
> *Driest wood will eithest low*
> *And* Nansy *sae will ye now*.[40]

And the point is a satirical one, to reverse the conventions of upper-class love which Ramsay, when in serious mood, was only too keen to emulate. In another item in *The Tea-Table Miscellany*, 'Auld Rob Morris', the girl is merely the object of an old man's courtship, and she has no intention of marrying him, but the essence of the January-May contrast is starkly and simply presented in a dialogue between mother and daughter employing terms that occur also in 'Crooked Shoulder' and later songs where the two *are* married:

MITHER

Auld *Rob Morris* that wins in yon glen,
He's the king of good fellows, and wale of auld men,
Has fourscore of black sheep, and fourscore white too;
Auld Rob Morris is the man ye maun loo.

DOUGHTER

Had your tongue, mither, and let that abee,
For his eild and my eild can never agree;
They'll never agree, and that will be seen!
For he is fourscore, and I'm but fifteen.

MITHER

Had your tongue doghter, and lay by your pride,
For he's be the bridegroom, and ye's be the bride;
He shall ly by your side, and kiss ye too;
Auld *Rob Morris* is the man ye maun loo.

DOUGHTER

Auld *Rob Morris* I ken him fou weel,
His a--- it sticks out like ony peat-creel,
He's out-shinn'd, in-knee'd, and ringle-ey'd too;
Auld *Rob Morris* is the man I'll never loo.

MITHER

Though auld *Rob Morris* be an elderly man,
Yet his auld brass it will buy a new pan;
Then, doughter, ye shouldna be so ill to shoo,
For auld *Rob Morris* is the man you maun loo.

DOUGHTER

But auld *Rob Morris* I never will hae,
His back is sae stiff, and his beard is grown gray:
I had titter die than live wi' him a year;
Sae mair of *Rob Morris* I never will hear.[41]

The theme of the young man married to an old woman is also
found in the traditional folk ballads, for example in 'The Rigwoodie
Carlin' ('O faer ye gaun ye carlin, carlin') which C. K. Sharpe
obtained from Peter Buchan.[42] In alternate question and answer
stanzas the carlin tells the 'laddie' that she has just buried her man,
and asks him to fee with her (i.e. become her hired ploughman) —
first for two placks, which he rejects as 'but a herd's fee', then for
five merks, plus milk and bread, in its turn dismissed as 'bairns'
meat'.[43] Finally he is to get bread and meat, and when he turns
down the idea of lying with her bairns:

> I'll lay ye wi mysell, Will Boy, Will Boy,
> I'll lay ye wi mysell, my heart and my joy
> I'll lay ye wi mysell for now and for aye;
> Was e'er a young widdow sae happy as I!

> We'll gree about that, ye carlin, carlin,
> We'll gree about that, ye rigwoodie carlin,
> We'll gree about that, for now and for aye,
> Was there e'er a young laddie sae waddie as I?

These two final stanzas contain the comic peripety of the action, for in the previous stanzas the widow has been 'weary'. Now she is happy, but Will Boy is still 'waddie', as he has been from the beginning. The indications are, however, that the situation of the young girl married to a rich dotard is primary, and the reverse type a derivative, indeed a parody of the original genre. 'In the land of Fife there lived a wicked wife' manages to combine features of both, for its heroine, after being married to an old man whom she starves to death instead of giving him wholesome invalid fare, proceeds to marry a young wastrel 'who drank at the wine, and tippled at the beer, and spent mair gear than he wan'. When her substance is consumed she declares 'I wish I had my silly auld man!'[44]

And of course being married to an old man may cause a woman to take the Chatterley path, as in 'Whirlie Wha', one text of which is in Peter Buchan's 'Secret Songs of Silence',[45] prefixed by an explanatory anecdote. 'This song was written by Mary Hay, daughter of one of the Earls of Errol, after she was married to General Scott, from whom she eloped for want of . . .' A text, which G. Legman thinks is based on a lost holograph of Burns's, is in the Cunningham MS. in the British Museum:

> The last braw wedding that I was at
>   Was on a Hallow day
> An' there was meikle meikle fun
>   An' there was meikle play.
> The bells they rang the auld wives sang
>   An' to the kirk went they a'
> The bride's to bed wi' the silly bride-groom
>   To play wi' his whirlie-wha.
>
> First she turn't her back to him
>   An' syne she turn't her wame
> Lang she leuk't for kin'ness
>   But kin'ness she gat nane. —
> At length she's tae'n him in her arms
>   Flung him again' the wa'
> Says lie ye there ye fumblin devil
>   Ye've lost yir whirlie-wha.

> O wae light on my kith an' kin
>   They've done me meikle [ill]
> They've married me to an auld man
>   Fou sair again my will.
> But I'll dress myself in my ribbons sae green
>   Nae lassie will be sae braw
> An I'll hire a bonny young lad o' my ain
>   To play wi' his whirlie-wha.[46]

In Scottish bawdry, it is the woman whose desire is insatiable. After marriage the man, generally older, may lose interest in intercourse, with the result that his wife turns into a shrew in self defence:

> She took him to the cellar then,
>   Ha, ha, the girdin o't,
> To see gif he could do't again,
>   Ha, ha, ha, the girdin o't;
> He kiss'd her ance, he kiss'd her twice,
> An' by the bye he kiss'd her thrice
> Till deil a mair the thing wad rise
>   To gie her the long girdin' o't.
>
> But Duncan took her to his wife,
>   Ha, ha, the girdin' o't,
> To be the comfort o' his life,
>   Ha, ha, ha, the girdin' o't;
> An' now she scauls baith night an' day,
> Except when Duncan's at the play;
> An' that's as seldom as he may,
>   He's weary o' the girdin' o't.[47]

The predicament, which 'the folk' often see as comic, is that of 'The Bride-groom grat'[48] – a reversal of that other traditional situation where it is the bride who weeps. It is not always humorously treated, as can be seen from sts. i and ii of 'John Anderson', when these are sung to its melancholy tune:

> John Anderson, my jo, John,
>   I wonder what ye mean,
> To lie sae lang i' the mornin',
>   And sit sae late at e'en?
> Ye'll bleer a' your een, John,
>   And why do ye so?
> Come sooner to your bed at een,
>   John Anderson, my jo.

John Anderson my jo, John,
    When first that ye began,
Ye had as good a tail-tree,
    As ony ither man;
But now its waxen wan, John,
    And wrinkles to and fro;
I've twa gae-ups for ae gae-down,
    John Anderson, my jo.[49]

The humour of these *mal mariée* ditties and broadsides is often of a peculiarly unpleasant and inhumane type. It is a kind of humour to which Burns himself gave expression, on occasion, in poems as well as songs — 'Hallowe'en', for example, has some traces of it: humour that laughs at deformity, at sexual weakness, at ugliness, at everything that is 'against nature' when nature is defined in terms of the biological success of the species. Now the very existence of old maids negates that biological success, and it is therefore not surprising that an old maid's longing for marriage at all costs, the contradiction between her actual position and her desires, should feature in many comic songs of courtship. An eighteenth-century song of this sort, 'The Three Nuns in the Cowgate', features three old maids who are so desperate they will take anything in breeks or kilts, even fiddlers, pipers or drummers:

> *An auld maid and a hantle o' siller,*
> *An auld maid and a hantle o' siller,*
> *Gin she hadna' haen that, fient ane wad gane till her,*
> *An auld maid and a hantle o' siller. . . .*
>
> Some auld women gang mad for to marry,
> Some auld women gang mad for to marry;
> In the shape of a man they would jump at Auld Harry,
> Some auld women gang mad for to marry.
>
> (Chorus; st. v)[50]

'An Old Maid's Advice' ('Ye young maids so sprightly') is a character-lyric which dwells on the pathos of one who ruins her life because she disdains 'the humours of glen' — a euphemism for physical love. The insensitivity behind other treatments of this theme and its basis in the cruelties of everyday life are realistically expressed in the last stanza quoted:

> When I was a young one,
>   I flounced, I bounced,
> Disdained the offers of several young men;

> I thought it so airy,
>   My head high to carry;
> And never to marry for humours of glen.
>
>   But now in my turn,
>   Grown old and infirm,
> I'm held in great scorn by all jolly young men;
>   And there goes old aunty,
>   They jeeringly taunt me,
> Who never would harken to humours of glen;
>
>   Her grey hair all borrow'd,
>   Her cheeks thin and furrow'd,
> Her wan lips discolour'd invite no young men,
>   Her breast flat and wither'd
>   Love's flame there long smother'd,
> Retains no more moisture for humours of glen.[51]

'An Old Maid's Advice' ends moralistically: when young girls see their faces in the glass full of the humours of glen, then is the time to 'jump at the offers of worthy young men'. It has parallels in many earlier songs, including pseudo-Scottish Durfey types.[52] As the nineteenth century advanced, the figure of the Old Maid became less grotesque and was quite often invested with sentiment, even with sentimentality. As early as July 1802 a piece called 'The Neglectit Lassie' (line 1 'As Bessy sat down wi' her seam at the fire') was published in *The Scots Magazine*, beginning comically (e.g. she would rather die than marry lawyer Geordie, 'a wee stumpin' body'), but ending on a note of pathos:

> It's hard to take shelter ahint a laigh dyke,
> It's hard to take that we dinna well like,
> It's hard to forsake ane we fain wad be wi',
> It's harder that a'body's married but me.

Slightly later, there is J. Burt's variation on an old theme, where humour and sentiment mingle in a way that looks forward to the kail-yard school:

> Lasses that nae lad ha'e got,
>   But live in garrets lane and lorn,
> Let ilk be carefu' o' her cat —
>   Ne'er thinks o' heuks — your hairst is shorn.[53]

And a comic approach to old maids prevails in Scottish song right up to the present.[54]

We have already glanced briefly at merry wooings when we

dealt with courtship dialogues in relation to rural customs at the end of Chapter II,[55] and it is in the songs that deal with these meetings that the most light-hearted lyrical comedy is found. Lyrics that delight in the ups and downs of courtship, in the girl's coyness and the man's response to the game[56] are found in aristocratic and tea-table circles as well as among the folk. As an example of a tea-table merry wooing, let us take 'How easy was Colin, how blithe and how gay', where the fair Chloris behaves just like the Jennies and Maggies of vernacular song:

> With ardour he press'd her to think him sincere;
> But, alas! she redoubled each hope and each fear:
> She wou'd not deny, nor she wou'd not approve;
> And she neither refus'd him, nor gave him her love.

When he accepts Thirsis's advice to forsake her, Colin is cured of his own passion, while Chloris's love for him increases and she is left 'in vain/To sigh for a heart she could never regain'.[57] Such reversals are of course traditional in pastoral, the best-known Scottish example being Henryson's 'Robene and Makyne'.

Allan Ramsay is particularly attracted to the comedy of naysay. The reversal of 'Norland Jocky and Southland Jenny'[58] in the *Tea-Table Miscellany* involves a test: the northerner is a bashful wooer 'till blinks of her beauty and hopes of her siller,/Forc'd him at last to tell his mind till her'. When she says that all she has for him is beauty, and no 'gowd or money', he hypocritically produces good social reasons for his change of mind:

> Ye lasses of the south, ye're a' for dressing;
> Lasses of the north, mind milking and threshing;
> My minny wad be angry, and sae wad my dady,
> Shou'd I marry ane as dink as a lady.
> For I maun hae a wife that will rise in the morning,
> Crudle a' the milk, and keep the house a sculding,
> Toolie wi' her nibors, and learn at my minny,
> A norland *Jocky* maun hae a norland *Jenny*.

By rejecting the leaden casket, as it were, like the conventional suitors in *The Merchant of Venice*, he has failed the test:

> My father's only daughter, and twenty thousand pound,
> Shall never be bestow'd on sic a silly clown;
> For a' that I said was to try what was in ye,
> Gae home, ye norland *Jock*, and court your norland *Jenny*.

'A Cock Laird fou cadgie', one of Ramsay's very best songs, unites
spirited dialogue with a realistic sketch of the small landowner who
cultivates his own estate:

> Wilt thou gae alang
>   Wi' me, *Jenny, Jenny*?
> Thouse be my ain lemmane
>   Jo *Jenny*, quoth he.

Jenny will go, but on condition that she is feasted with 'caddels
[spiced drink] and good hacket-kail' and perpetually supplied with
the latest fashions. When he says he can't keep her in such luxuries,
she has the classic spendthrift's answer:

> The borrowstoun merchants
>   Will sell ye on tick,
> For we maun hae braw things,
>   Albeit they soud break.
> When broken, frae care
>   The fools are set free,
> When we make them lairds
>   In the abbey, quoth she.[59]

Another of Allan Ramsay's songs, 'Smirky Nan', is a borderline
case, half-way between realism and artificial pastoralism. The
names, it is true, are from ordinary life, but poor Willy is wasted to
a span like any Corydon, and the similitudes are drawn from
threshing and baking for quite conscious comic effect:

> I'm grown so weak, a gentle breeze
>   Of dusty *Roger's* winnowing fan
> Would blow me o'er yon beechy trees,
>   And all for thee, my smirky *Nan*.
>
> The alewife misses me of late,
>   I us'd to take a hearty can;
> But I can neither drink nor eat,
>   Unless 'tis brewed and baked by *Nan*,
> The baker makes the best of bread,
>   The flour he takes, and leaves the bran;
> The bran is every other maid,
>   Compar'd with thee, my smirky *Nan*.
>
> But *Dick* o' the green, that nasty lown
>   Last *Sunday* to my mistress ran,
> He snatch'd a kiss; I knock'd him down,
>   Which hugely pleased my smirky *Nan*.

But hark! the roaring soger comes,
And rattles *Tantara, Tarran*,
She leaves her cows for noisy drums,
Woes me, I've lost my smirky *Nan*.[60]

The puppet, Petroushka-like actions in the last stanza, particularly those of the stylised 'roaring soger', lift the lyric from the realistic plane into the realm of humorous fantasy, and despite the Scots-English diction the style is as easily colloquial as in many a vernacular Scots song.

Throughout the previous chapters love-songs have been examined not as mere literary exercises in a vacuum, but as expressing the varying attitudes to love found in eighteenth-century Scotland. On occasion, love-lyrics serve to render new varieties of love experience when these arise — such as those that appeared among the male writers of the Romantic period, like Shelley or Heine, or among women poets of the twentieth century such as Sylvia Plath. But in the eighteenth century new emotions were not so evident. Then, love-songs were content to transmit tradition; to accommodate present attitudes to those which had come down from the past, such as aristocratic compliment, courtly love, and the feelings congealed in popular tradition. And the general trend of our examination has been to show that those traditions and attitudes were not on the whole specifically or uniquely Scottish, but in the main shared by all the peoples of the British Isles and beyond. They were indeed the record of a 'common pursuit'.

REFERENCES

1.   In *A Collection of 100 Chapbooks* (GUL, BD 20-i.10).
2.   BM, 1346 m.7 *Ballads*. See Chapter I, p. 6 and also Chapter VIII below, where some of these ballads are examined.
3.   BM, 1346 m. 7 (1).
4.   BM, 1346 m. 7 (7).
5.   Robin Hall, Glasgow Street Songs, Vol. 1; *Collector Records* (1959), JES 2.
6.   Kinsley, 406.
7.   *TTM*, I: (1740), p. 76.
8.   St. Clair MS., p. 2.
9.   See A. H. Krappe, *The Science of Folklore* (London, 1930), p. 162.
10.   Burns, 'Sweet Tibbie Dunbar', Kinsley, 285.
11.   *TTM*, II: (1740), p. 150.
12.   'My pretty Turtle-Dove, my Love, and heart's delight', date *c.* 1663, *Roxb. Bds.*, ed. Ebsworth, VI. 213-5.
13.   St. ii, line 2.
14.   Above, p. 58.

15. See e.g. 'Saw ye Jenny Nettles', *LLL* 86, and above, p. 24.
16. *TTM*, IV: (1740), p. 427; Child, 200.
17. *TTM* text, st. i.
18. NLS, MS. 210, fol. 72 (line 1: 'Hae ye heard o' a widow in rich attire?').
19. Motherwell MSS. (GUL).
20. *S.S.S.*, pp. 41-5. 'Have you any pots or pans?' in *TTM*, I: (1740), p. 96; 'The Tinker' in *Merry Drollery* (London, 1661), p. 134; Burns, 'My bonie lass I work in brass', from *Love and Liberty*, discussed below and in my *Burns*, pp. 130-4.
21. In *Three Excellent New Songs*, 1795; printed in Edinburgh by Archibald Martin, Middle of the Old Assembly's-close, pp. 5-7. Nottingham Reference Library Chapbooks, Box 3.
22. Herd (1776), II, 26, st. x, lines 5-8; xii, lines 7-8; xiv. The text in Herd (1769) lacks the chorus 'And we'll gang nae mair a-roving'.
23. Sts. x-xiii.
24. BM, 1346 m. 7.
25. *TTM*, I: (1740), p. 78, st. x (line 1, 'The pawky auld carle came o'er the lee').
26. *Nightingale* (Edinburgh, 1776), p. 68.
27. St. iii: Appendix V to *Rob Roy* (Introduction).
28. By this time the plaid — and plaid-rolling — had acquired considerable sexual symbolism. See W. Donaldson, 'Bonny Highland Laddie: the Making of a Myth', *Scottish Literary Journal*, III (2), Dec. 1976, 30-50.
29. *TTM*, I: (1740), p. 85, sts. iv-v (line 1: 'The lawland lads think they are fine').
30. St. Clair MS., p. 137.
31. *Merry Muses*, pp. 110-11, sts. v-vi.
32. *Merry Muses*, p. 76; H. & H., ii, 304.
33. Thomas Wilkie's MS. Notebooks (1813–1815), NLS, MS. 123, pp. 86-7, st. i.
34. See my *Burns*, pp. 322-3.
35. P. 34.
36. *Wilson's Musical Miscellany* (Edinburgh, 1779), p. 186.
37. St. iv, lines 3-6, in 'The Gallant Sailor', etc., in *A Collection of 100 Chapbooks*, in Euing Collection, University of Glasgow Library, B.D. 20. i. 9.
38. E.g. 'Auld Widow Greylocks', *FSNE*, cxvi.
39. NLS, MS. 123, p. 128.
40. *TTM*, I: (1740), p. 22; line 1, 'While fops in saft Italian verse'.
41. *TTM*, I: (1740), p. 58.
42. C. K. Sharpe, MS. Vol. of old Scottish Ballads, c. 1824, NLS MS. 210, f. 80, sts. 19-20.
43. This song like others discussed in Part II, borders on the work-songs with sexual overtones discussed in the following chapter.
44. *Roxb. Bds.*, ed. Ebsworth, VIII, 245 (n.).
45. *S.S.S.*, pp. 80-1.
46. G. Legman, *The Horn Book* (New York, 1964), henceforth cited as Legman, pp. 136-8.
47. Burns's text, *Merry Muses*, pp. 98-9. The older version in the Herd MS. is even more explicit: 'But she scolds both night and day/Without that Duncan still would play,/ And ay she cries: 'Fy, Duncan Gray,/Come gae me the girdin' o't'. (Hecht-Hd., p. 319.)
48. *S.S.S.*, pp. 73 ff.
49. Text, *Merry Muses*, p. 114.

50. *Scots Nightingale* (Edinburgh, 1779), p. 162.
51. *Chearful Companion* (Perth, 1783), p. 308.
52. E.g. 'Celia's Reflections on herself for slighting Philander's Love', from Durfey's *Massaniello* (1699), which was treated as a genuinely Scottish piece after its appearance in *TTM*.
53. Alexander Whitelaw, *The Book of Scottish Song* (London, Glasgow and Edinburgh, n.d.), henceforth cited as Whitelaw, pp. 253-4, 312.
54. E.g. 'An auld maid in a garret', sung in the Folk Clubs by Lizzie Higgins and others.
55. Above, pp. 28-31.
56. E.g. Burns's second set of 'Duncan Gray' (Kinsley, 394) or his 'Last May a braw wooer' (Kinsley, 503).
57. *Charmer* I (Edinburgh, 1749), p. 243.
58. *TTM*, II: (1740), p. 182.
59. *TTM*, II: (1740), p. 194. 'Lairds in the abbey' — the shopkeepers ruined by their extravagance could take refuge in Holyrood Abbey, a sanctuary for bankrupts.
60. *TTM*, IV: (1740), p. 377 (line 1, 'Ah woe's me, poor Willy cried'); st. i, lines 5-8, sts. ii-iii.

Chapter VII

WORK, SEX AND DRINK

Among the most primitive of all songs are work-songs, arising directly out of the productive process. Their refrains both aid and sweeten labour, and suggest the repetitive choruses of dance-carols and of certain folk-ballads, which may well have been danced.[1] By the twentieth century, and even perhaps by the eighteenth, most work-songs were recreational, sung in *ceilidh*-like gatherings alongside other song-categories after the day's labour was over. A few choruses, however, have survived—some in Burns's contributions to the *Scots Musical Museum*—as indications of the presumably larger number of work-songs that have perished. The chorus of 'The Boatie Row', in Johnson's *Museum*, is sung by fisher women ('And leesome may the boatie row/That wins the bairns breed'), but the lines quoted conceivably reflect an earlier song of the menfolk:

> I cust my line in Largo bay,
>   And fishes catch'd nine,
> There was three to boil, and three to fry,
>   And three to bait the line.[2]

And in 'Here to the Dance of Dysart', that inconsequential tribute to the women of fishing communities, with its chorus derived from the refrain of a work-song, a version of which Burns communicated to the *Scots Musical Museum*,[3] the final stanza carries a stark yet homely undertone of tragic necessity:

> We have sheets to shape
> And we have Beds to make
> And we have corn to shear
> And we have Bairns to bear
> And Hey ca' through ca' through
> For we have muckle to do.[4]

The rhythm of Burns's 'The cardin o't'[5] seems to hark back to a spinning-song:

> I coft a stane o' haslock woo
>   To mak a coat to Johnie o't;
> For Johnie is my only jo,
>   I lo'e him best of onie yet
> The cardin o't the spinnin o't
>   The warpin o't the winnin o't
> When ilka ell cost me a groat,
>   The taylor staw the linin' o't.

The choruses of 'Twine weel the plaiden'[6] ('And twine it weel, my bonny dow,/And twine it weel, the plaiden') and 'Tarry Woo'[7] are pretty certainly the refrains of old labour-songs. The latter begins:

> Tarry Woo, O tarry woo
>   Tarry woo is ill to spin;
> Card it well, oh Card it well,
>   Card it well ere ye begin.
>
> When 'tis carded, row'd and spun,
>   Then the work is haflens done;
> But when woven, drest, and clean,
>   It may be cleading for a Queen.

The most universal labour-songs of all are cradle-songs, such as 'O can ye sew Cushions and can ye sew Sheets/And can ye sing ba-lu-loo when the bairn greets?',[8] a type which can sometimes be given a high level of psychological content, as in the seventeenth-century character-lyric 'Lady Anne Bothwell's Balow',[9] where there may be a folk-basis to an aristocratic composed lyric that itself went through a stage of oral dissemination; or else they may be made to imply a simple dramatic song, like the swaddling song, 'The Reel o' Stumpie':[10]

> Wap and rowe, wap and rowe,
>   Wap and rowe the feetie o't,
> I thought I was a maiden fair,
>   Till I heard the greetie o't.
>
> My daddie was a Fiddler fine,
>   My minnie she made mantie O;
> And I mysel a thumpin' quine,
>   And danc'd the reel o' stumpie O.

The originals of 'The Weary Pund of Tow'[11] and 'Ca' the yowes'[12] may well have been work-songs — the latter sung perhaps when the sheep were driven to the hills.[13] But in many lyrics connected with farming, the work-song has by the eighteenth century become simply the framework for a love-dialogue or courtship lyric, just as in traditional pastoral:

> My brither abuses me daily
>   For being wi' Geordie so free,
> My sister she ca's me hoodwinked,
>   Because he's below my degree.
>
> The mucking of Geordie's Byar,
>   And the schooling the Gruip so clean
> Has aft gart me spend the night sleepless,
>   And brought the salt tears in my een.[14]

There almost certainly existed plough 'Pastimes' in medieval Scotland, in which peasants acted the part of labourers and even of oxen, chanting and miming as the plough was led about the village: this can be deduced from the remarkable 'Pleugh Song' in Forbes' Aberdeen *Cantus* of 1666 (second edition), which may well have originated in the fifteenth century.[15] The 'Pleugh Song' celebrates the productive life of ploughmen in the medieval village community; the bothy ballads comment critically on the productive and social life of ploughmen on nineteenth-century farms. It seems inherently probable that the eighteenth century should have had ploughman-songs that concentrate on work — on horses, hours of labour and working conditions, the personal idiosyncrasies of fellow labourers, the kitchen lassie and the food provided. Those that have come down to us, however, have a strong sexual side to them, just like the more recently collected 'Braes of Broo', printed by Gavin Greig in the early twentieth century, which makes use of popular expressions derived from the eighteenth-century group of songs centred on the Battles of Killiecrankie and Sheriffmuir.[16] And the fact that a plough pulled by oxen is in question ('owsen gaud', 'owsen bow') indicates that the song may go back to the *early* eighteenth century:

> Get up, get up, ye lazy loons,
>   Get up and waur them a', man,
> For the Braes o' Broo are ill to ploo,
>   They're roch and reesky a' man.
>
> *But the plooman laddie's my delight,*
>   *The plooman laddie loes me;*
> *When a' the lave gang to their bed*
>   *The plooman comes and sees me.*

Oh, he's taen up his owsen gaud,
   An't sets him weel to ca', man,
He's laid it owre the owsen bow,
   Says, 'Scurry, come awa', man',
But the plooman laddie's my delight, etc.

It's I will wash the plooman's hose,
   And dry them owre the door, man;
I'll may be be the plooman's wife,
   I've been his lass afore, man.
But the plooman laddie's my delight, etc.[17]

The line 'I will wash my Ploughman's hose' occurs in the text in *The Scots Musical Museum*, Vol. II, 1788.[18] It appears that both this song of Greig's and another collected by him, 'The Ploughman Laddie', are late orally transmitted offshoots of the same piece. One version of this is the *Museum* text, in which Burns had a hand; and that text in its turn belongs to the same complex as Herd's 'The Ploughman' (1769),[19] as well as the *Merry Muses* version where ploughing is an erotic innuendo.[20] Here is Herd's text:

The ploughman he's a bonny lad,
   And a' his wark's at leisure,
And whan that he comes hame at ev'n,
   He kisses me wi' pleasure.

    Up wi't now my ploughman lad,
     Up wi't now, my ploughman;
    Of a' the lads that I do see,
     Commend me to the ploughman.

Now the blooming spring's come on,
   He takes his yoaking early,
And whistling o'er the furrow'd land,
   He goes to fallow clearly;
    Up wi't now, &c.

Whan my ploughman comes hame at ev'n,
   He's often wet and weary;
Cast aff the wet, put on the dry,
   And gae to bed my deary.
    Up wi't now, &c.

I will wash my ploughman's hose,
   And I will wash his o'erlay,
And I will make my ploughman's bed,
   And chear him late and early.

Merry butt, and merry ben,
*   Merry is my ploughman;*
Of a' the trades that I do ken,
*   Commend me to the ploughman.*

Plough you hill, and plough you dale,
    Plough you faugh and fallow,
Who winna drink the ploughman's health,
    Is but a dirty fellow.
        Merry butt, &c.[21]

The Scots Nightingale (1778)[22] prints three stanzas not in Herd that
extend the erotic parallel:

The ploughman he gaes to his bed
    And thinks to get the ease o't,
But he may yoke the stots again
    And brink about the braes o't.
        Up wi't now, &c.

He has three owsen in a plough
    And twa o' them are blind, jo
The seeing ane he goes before,
    The other twa behind, jo.
        Up wi't now, &c.

He plow'd it up upon a brae
    Beneath there was a glen, jo,
Twa of them fell o'er the heugh,
    The third he scrambled in, jo.
        Up wi't now, &c.

With both the Herd and the *Merry Muses* version of this song
'work' is sex, and the actions of ploughing an extended metaphor
for the actions of love.

In a note to his 1911 edition of *The Merry Muses*, Duncan
McNaught quotes 'a licentious ditty current in Ayrshire to this day,
the "owsen" being changed into "pownies".' It, too, is evidently old:

Then he drew out his horses which were in number three,
Three likelier pownies for to draw, their like ye ne'er did see;
There was twa dun pownies on ahin, auld Whitey on afore,
The muzzle-pin for a' the yirth was in the highest bore.

Before he gat the hause-rig turned his horse began to sweat,
And to maintain an open fur, he spurred wi' baith his feet. . . .

A similar equation between ploughing and sex is made in the
English ploughman-songs, and the question has recently been

investigated by James Reeves.[23] The ballad of 'The Painful Plough'
('Come all you jolly ploughmen of courage stout and bold'), noted
by Gavin Greig in N.-E. Scotland,[24] is an English type, like many
others praising particular trades; and both it and the equivocal sort
of ploughman-song can be paralleled in the English broadsides.
Another type of work-song is the trade comparison, found both in
Scotland and England. Gavin Greig, for example, collected 'The
Gairdener and the Plooman', in which the comparison has become
metamorphosed into a compressed lyrical ballad. The singer, who
has long been loved by a gardener lad, keeps her own heart free until
she falls violently in love with a ploughman; that she should do this
so passionately and so irrationally redounds greatly to the credit of
ploughmen as a group. In its concise simplicity, the song rises to the
level of 'pure poetry':

> The firstan time I did you see,
>   You was under a buss o' rue,
> And aye the sweeter 'at ye sang,
>   The nearer the buss I drew — drew,
>   The nearer the buss I drew.[25]

The gardener alone appears in 'The Gardener Lad',[26] and much
earlier in Burns's art-song 'The Gardener wi' his Paidle'. In the
Interleaved Copy Burns wrote: 'The title of the song only is old, the
rest is mine',[27] which means, presumably, that a popular song with
that title existed in the eighteenth century, though I have not come
across any other record of it. The song Greig collected is in the
mode of the traditional ballad. Lady Margaret is courted by many,
but they do not impress the gardener lad in the least. He is sure that
if he makes the effort, she will not say no to him. When he courts
her, he does so with summer flowers; she rejects him, in equally
symbolic terms:

> The driven snaw shall be your shirt
>   Becomes your body neist,
> And the coal-black rain shall be your coat,
>   Wi' a wind-gale in your breast. . . .
>
> The hat that on your head ye wear
>   Shall be the suthron gray;
> And when ye come into my sight
>   I'll wish ye were away.   (sts. xiii, xv)

This ballad, in Greig's text, is extremely interesting, for it begins
as if it were going to develop into a typical wish-fulfilment broadside

type, of the servant who seduces or marries a lady, only to modulate
into a highly poetic and formal confrontation of a summer youth
and a winter maiden. Here the trade-song is fused with the Child
ballad and employs imagery and symbolism considerably removed
from the realism generally found in trade songs.

Many other trade-songs have come down to us — some in fairly
recent oral transmission, such as 'The Gallant Shoemaker';[28] and
then there are weavers' songs, or whalers' songs such as 'The
Diamond was a ship, brave boys' or 'The Whalers' Lamentation',[29]
not to speak of the songs in praise of tinkers or beggars discussed in
our final chapter. The chorus of a traditional shoemaker's song is
preserved in the *Museum* text of 'The Souters o' Selkirk':

> It's up wi the Souters o' Selkirk
> And down wi the Earl of Hume,
> And here is to a' the braw laddies
> That wear the single soal'd shoon:
> It's up wi' the souters o' Selkirk,
> For they are baith trusty and leal;
> And up wi' the lads o' the Forest,
> And down wi' the merse to the deil.[30]

'The Bonny Mason Laddie' may be taken as typical of a large
number of trade-songs in which a girl prefers her lover's occupation
above all others — a special variant of the more ordinary type
where the weaver, souter, blacksmith, collier or cordwainer himself
chants the praises of his occupation:

> I winna ha'e the minister, for a' his many books
> I winna ha'e the dominie, for a' his wylie looks. . . .
>
> I winna ha'e the mautman, for a' his muckle sho'el;
> Nor will I ha'e the miller, for a' his mity meal. . . .
>
> I winna ha'e the ploughman, that gangs at the pleuch;
> Nor yet will I the chaplain, though he has gear eneuch. . . .
>
> I winna ha'e the souter, that rubs upon the shoon;
> Nor yet will I the weaver, that gingles on the loom. . . .
>
> The smith that canna lay an axe is no a man o' craft;
> The wright that canna seam a deal can scarcely lay a laft.
> The lad that canna kiss a lass is no a lad for me;
> But my bonnie mason laddie he can do a' the three.[31]

The miller, too, is apt to be celebrated in similar strains by his lass,
as in 'O merry may the maid be'. Here is the first stanza, which
alone is genuinely traditional:

O Merry may the maid be
  That marries with the miller,
For foul day and fair day
  He's ay bringing till her.
Has ay a penny in his purse
  For dinner and for supper;
And gin he please, a good fat cheese,
  And lumps of yellow butter.

Although there may be a traditional song, or chorus, or just a proverbial expression behind these lines, the other stanzas have all the marks of composed vernacular song — especially the concluding one, with its final pastoral *cliché*:

In winter when the wind and rain
  Blaws o'er the house and byre,
He sits beside a clean hearth stane
  Before a rousing fire;
With nut-brown ale he tells his tale
  Which rows him o'er fou nappy;
Who'd be a king — a petty thing
  When a miller lives so happy?[32]

The author was reputedly Sir John Clerk of Penicuik (? 1680–1755). Much closer to the real folk spirit is 'Hey, the Dusty Miller', exquisitely edited by Burns for the *Scots Musical Museum*:

Hey the dusty Miller,
  And his dusty coat,
He will win a shilling,
  Or he spend a groat.

Dusty was the coat,
  Dusty was the colour,
Dusty was the kiss
  That I got frae the Miller.

Hey the dusty Miller,
  And his dusty sack,
Leeze me on the calling,
  Fills the dusty peck:

Fills the dusty peck,
  Brings the dusty siller;
I wad gie my coatie
  For the dusty Miller.[33]

Many of the miller songs are uncomplimentary, and verge on social satire, because of the miller's traditional rôle as rogue and cheater in the rural community;[34] and many celebrate his sexual un-scrupulousness, as in the *Merry Muses* version of 'The Mill Mill, O'[35], with the traditional onomatopoeic and bawdy chorus:

> As I came down yon water side
>   And by yon Shillin Hill, O,
> There I spied a bonny lass,
>   A lass that I loed right well, O.
>
> *The mill, mill, O, and the kill, kill, O,*
>   *An the coggin' o' Peggy's wheel, O,*
> *The sack an' the sieve, a' She did leave,*
>   *An' danc'd the millars reel, O.*
>
> I spier'd at her, gin she cou'd play,
>   But the lassie had nae skill, O;
> An' yet she was nae a' to blame,
>   She pat it in my will, O.
>
> Then she fell o'er, an' sae did I,
>   And danc'd the millars reel, O,
> Whene'er that bonny lassie comes again,
>   She shall hae her ma't ground weel, O.

'The maid's gane to the mill' combines two aspects, the satirical and the sexual:

> The maid's gane to the mill by night;
>   Hech hey, sae wanton;
> The maid's gane to the mill by night,
>   Hech hey, sae wanton she.
> She's sworn by moon and stars sae bright
> That she wad hae her corn ground,
> That she wad hae her corn ground,
>   Mill and multure free.

When the miller's man came out and swore he would do his best:

> He put his hand about her neck,
>   Hech hey, sae wanton;
> He put his hand about her neck,
>   Hech hey, sae wanton he;
> He dang her doun upon a sack,
> And there she got her corn ground,
> And there she got her corn ground,
>   Mill and multure free.

When other maids went to play 'she sigh'd and sobb'd, and wadnae stay', and had 'a braw lad bairn'.

> Her mither bade her cast it out,
>   Hech hey, sae wanton;
> Her mither bade her cast it out,
>   Hech hey, sae wantonlie;
> It was the miller's dusty clout,
> For getting of her corn ground,
> For getting of her corn ground,
>   Mill and multure free.
>
> Her father bade her keep it in,
>   Hech hey, sae wanton;
> Her father bade her keep it in,
>   Hech hey, sae wantonlie;
> It was the chief of a' her kin,
> Because she'd got her corn ground,
> Because she'd got her corn ground,
>   Mill and multure free.[36]

Altogether lighter and more wistful is 'When I gaed to the mill my lane':

> O I loe the miller laddie!
>   And my laddie loes me,
> He has sic a blyth look,
>   And a bonnie blinking ee.
> What though the laddie kist me,
>   When I was at the mill!
> A kiss is but a touch;
>   And a touch can do nae ill.   (st. ii)[37]

'The Smith's a Gallant Fireman', popular in the late nineteenth century, may well have had an eighteenth-century ancestor. It certainly had seventeenth-century English prototypes like 'The Praise of the Blacksmith' in *An Antidote against Melancholy* (1661),[38] to be sung to the tune of 'Greensleeves'. There are ten stanzas deploying humorous conceits about the Cyclops who made the first Thunderbolts, about Venus, Vulcan, and London place-names like Hammersmith, Seacole Lane, Ironmonger Lane, and Paul's Chain. The ballad next proceeds to enumerate those popular proverbs deriving from the blacksmith's trade—'hit the nail on the head', 'strike while the iron is hot', 'give a man roast and beat him with the spit', 'under lock and key', 'quite off the hooks', 'held hard to it, buckle and thong', 'as plain as a pike-staff' (half a blacksmith's saying!). There is some crude punning:

> There's never a slut, if filth o'er-smutch her,
> But owes to the Blacksmith for her leacher,
> For without *a paire of tongs* there's no man will touch her,
>   *Which no body can deny.*

> Your roaring-boy who every one quails,
> Fights, domineers, swaggers and rayles,
> Could never yet make the Smith *eat his nails,*
>   *Which no body, etc.*

The song ends with 'a good health to Blacksmiths all'. Popular songs in praise of trades, like so many other categories, shade naturally into pastoralism; an early English example is Martin Parker's 'The Milk-Maid's Life . . . to a curious new tune called, The Milke-maid's Dumps'.[39] In spite of winds, cold dews and dark sky, milk-maids are always happy. They never suffer the green-sickness which afflicts 'Those lasses nice and strange,/That keeps shop in the Exchange'. They exist in a conventional landscape; the linnet, thrush and 'dulcid nightingale' sing for them from every bush; garlanded, they dance away sorrow on May-day morning; plough-men are their natural swains. 'God speed the plow, *and blesse the milking paile!*'

In eighteenth-century Scotland, then, there is a wide variety of work-songs ranging from sea- or spinning-songs, through songs in praise of a trade, or dealing more or less lightheartedly with work-mates or conditions of labour, to those involving a love-interest, satirical criticism, and a pastoral colouring. They make constant references to a universe of productive relations whether rural or urban, which are understood by the folk-singers' or ballad-mongers' public, and which constitute an additional dimension of *style*, an inseparable part of the diction of popular literature, as important in its own way as imagery. This framework of known expectations constantly fulfilled, or possible choices postulated at the beginning of the song and brought into the open as the lyric progresses, is something that has to be acquired by the modern singer or reader: but when learnt and appreciated, it is seen as a particularly rich element in the poetic texture of popular song. Once again, it is an element which is by no means exclusively or originally Scottish: it is found in English songs too, and is very much in evidence in the broadside songs and ballads of the seventeenth century.

If it is wrong to restrict our conspectus of work-songs to the comparatively few whose refrains can be traced back to some sort of shared labour, then it is equally limiting to confine our category of 'bacchanalian lyrics' to songs that sing only the praises of wine, 'tippeny' or usquebaugh. After all, Scotland's raciest narrative tells how a tipsy farmer interrupts a dance of witches; her greatest meditative poem centres on a drunk man looking at a thistle. And certainly, in the eighteenth century all classes like their 'dram'. In the first decades, 'gentlemen of figure and fashion . . . enjoyed a bicker of ale as much as a bottle of claret. . . . The *scourging a nine-gallon tree* was then a common feat among lads of mettle. It consisted in drawing the spigot of a barrel of ale, and never quitting it night or day till it was drunk out'.[40] The Scots trade with the West Indies made punch a popular drink; it was at first compounded with brandy, then — after 1745 — with rum; and punch was still drunk by both sexes in good society in the seventeen-seventies, as is clear from Captain Topham's description of a visit to an Edinburgh oyster-cellar in January 1775.[41] Topham approved of moderate drinking because it stimulates good conversation, music, and dancing. But drinking was often excessive, even at funerals and wakes.[42] The Boswell Journals tell us much about the drinking habits of the Edinburgh upper classes towards the end of the century. For example, on 30th June 1774 the Boswells gave a dinner party for nine persons: 'I was in as calm a frame as I ever remember; did not speak much and drank port and water, yet contrived that the company was very social and had five bottles of claret. I rose from table quite cool and several of us drank tea with the ladies. This was an inoffensive day.' On the following day Boswell dined at Lord Monboddo's, where the company were 'sufficiently jovial'; later he supped at the Horse Wynd tavern and drank his customary bottle of old hock, Lord Monboddo again being of the party. On Saturday 9th July he gave a dinner to pay a bet to several of his cronies:

> Dr [Alexander] Webster was with us as chaplain; and we had . . . abundance of drinking. While Webster sat, we had several good stories and songs. He left us between seven and eight, and then we grew very noisy and drunk, but very cordial as old friends. In short we had a complete riot, which lasted until near twelve at night. We had eleven Scotch pints of claret, two bottles of old hock, and two of port, and drams of brandy and gin. . . . I sat after the rest were gone and took a large bowl of admirable soup, which did me much good, for I was not sick; though after I was in

bed my dear wife was apprehensive that I might die, I
breathed so ill.

It is clear from the Journals that such drinking was general amongst
the legal aristocracy. On the morning of Saturday, 30th July,
Boswell met the Solicitor-General, Henry Dundas, later (1782)
Keeper of the Signet and the 'uncrowned King of Scotland', who
became Viscount Melville in 1802:

> I found the Solicitor, who had been with us last night and
> drank heartily, standing in the outer hall looking very ill.
> He told me he was not able to stay, so he went home.
> He had struggled to attend his business, but it would not do.
> Peter Murray told me he had seen him this morning come
> out of a dram-shop in the Back Stairs, in all his formalities
> of large wig and cravat. He had been trying to settle his
> stomach. In some countries such an officer of the Crown as
> Solicitor-General being seen in such a state would be
> thought shocking. Such are our manners in Scotland that it
> is nothing at all.[43]

In the Highlands, and among the farming and working classes,
whisky was drunk; as Robert Forsyth put it, writing in 1805, 'a
woman of low rank is scarcely to be found, whatever her character in
other respects may be, who does not at forty-five years of age become
less or more addicted to the use of spiritous liquors'.[44] Fifty years
before, we are assured by a traveller that claret was on sale 'in every
public-house of any note except in the heart of the Highlands, and
sometimes even there'; and a decade or two earlier, in 1726–30,
Captain Burt noted that the people, when drinking plentifully of
their staple twopenny ale, 'interlace it with brandy or whisky'.[45]

The most popular bacchanalian song amongst all classes was
'Todlen Hame'. Burns called it 'perhaps the first bottle-song that
ever was composed'.[46] As in so many other songs, 'Todlen Hame'
unites the theme of drink with the theme of love; the inn was, indeed,
sometimes a favourite resort for courting couples, with the hostess
as confidante. The minister of the Ayrshire parish of Galston
reports:

> When a young man wishes to pay his addresses to his
> sweet-heart, instead of going to her father's, and professing his
> passion he goes to a public house; and, having let the
> land-lady into the secret of his attachment, the object of his
> wishes is immediately sent for, who never almost refuses to

come. She is entertained with ale and whisky, or brandy, and
the marriage is concluded on.[47]

The several sets of another extremely popular drinking song,
'There's cauld Kale in Aberdeen', unite drink and sexual double-
entendre in various ways, because 'cogie' generally has two meanings,
a literal and a bawdy. The set in Johnson's *Museum*, attributed to
Alexander, 4th Duke of Gordon (1743–1827), is a fine piece of sly
social commentary: 'the Reel o' Bogie' is sometimes a synonym for
the act of love, sometimes the dance which is its prelude; while the
'cogie' is drunk only in the intervals of 'dancing promisky' and the
couple kiss before they dance:

> In foursome Reels the Scots delight,
> The Threesome maist dance wondrous light;
> But Twasome ding a' out o sight,
>   Danc'd to the Reel of Bogie. . . .
>
> Now, Piper lad, bang up the Spring;
> The Countra fashion is the thing,
> To prie their mou's e'er we begin
>   To dance the Reel of Bogie.
>
> Now ilka lad has got a lass,
> Save yon auld doited Fogie,
> And ta'en a fling upo' the grass,
>   As they do in Strabogie.
>
> But a' the lasses look sae fain,
> We canna think oursel's to hain;
> For they mae hae their come-again
>   To dance the Reel of Bogie.
>
> Now a' the lads hae done their best,
> Like true men of Strabogie;
> We'll stop a while and tak a rest,
>   And tipple out a Cogie:
>
> Come now, my lads, & tak your glass,
> And try ilk other to surpass,
> In wishing health to every lass
>   To dance the Reel of Bogie.[48]

It is interesting that the composer of this set was an aristocrat
working in a popular tradition, and that he almost achieves the
abandon of the rustic orgy whose best known examplar in Scotland
is 'The Ball of Kirriemuir'. By the end of the century, however,

drink began to take precedence over love in songs of the 'Cauld
Kail' group, as in the version which Burns refers to as an 'old song':

> *My Coggie, Sirs, my coggie, Sirs,*
> *I canna want my coggie;*
> *I wadna gie my three-girr'd cap*
> *For e'er a quine on Bogie.*

> There's Johnie Smith has got a wife
> That scrimps him o' his coggie,
> If she were mine, upon my life
> I wad douk her in a bogie.
> *My coggie, Sirs, etc.*   (chorus, st. ii)

This set continues, in *Dale's Collection of Sixty Favourite Scotch Songs*
(probably printed in 1794) with four stanzas depicting the drunk-
ard's starving 'twa-three toddlin weans'.[49] Originally a January and
May piece about the octogenarian first Earl of Aberdeen (d. 1720)
who fell in love with a young girl, 'Cauld Kail' has turned into a
mal-marié(e) song where the alehouse is at once a refuge from a shrewish
wife, and the cause of her discontent. By the early nineteenth
century William Reid, the Glasgow bookseller (of the famous firm
of Brash and Reid) had produced a purely bacchanalian version.
A subsequent transformation was into what can only be termed
'teetotal propaganda' — a sorry tale of how young Will neglected
his wife for the drink but learnt his lesson when he 'miss'd the brig'
and found 'Bogie o'er him foamin':

> And aye the sang through Bogie rang,
> O! haud ye frae the cogie!
> The weary gill's the sairest ill
> On braes o' fair Strathbogie.[50]

Many drinking songs, then, involve women. They can also be
highly pathetic, like 'The Barren Wife', with its ballad-like treatment of youth and age:

> There was a wife and she had nae bairns,
> Sing hey! ba', lillie-loo;
> And she took the pint-stoup in her arms,
> Sing hey! ba', lillie-loo:
> And aye she liltit, and aye she sang,
> Sing hey! ba', lillie-loo;
> Sweet's yer breath, but cauld's your mow,
> Hey! ba', lillie-loo.

> Gin Robin had been like other men,
> O hey! ba', lillie-loo;
> The weans had been toddlin' but & ben;
> Hey! ba', lillie-loo:
> But now nae other joy hae I,
> Sing hey! ba', lillie-loo:
> But sit & drink when I am not dry,
> Hey! ba', lillie-loo.[51]

In general, however, the treatment of tippling women in Scottish Literature is comic. There is, for example, a broadside of 1719 that recaptures the Edinburgh town life of that period: 'An excellent new Ballad, intituled, The Four drunken Wives that live at Belsie hil. To the tune of Four Drunken Maidens at the Nether-bow. . . . Newly corrected and amended by Thomas Rutherfoord . . . in Colingtoun Paper-Mill, Edinburgh.' The main part of the broadside describes, in hack doggerel, a spree that the four women engaged in at a time when some person or persons unspecified were expelled from their tenements, possibly at the instigation of 'Noble Hags', a knight, who sends them off to paint the town red. The third stanza is typical:

> They went to Margaret Hunter's
>   they drank her Bots all dry;
> And they came to Jean Marwood,
>   her Brandy for to try:
> If that your Brandy it be good,
>   we'll have another Gill:
> And there four drunken Wives,
>   that live at *Belsiehil*.[52]

'The Four Drunken Wives', though utterly lamentable as poetry, is one of the earliest dated writings by a Scottish plebeian poet that we have — the shadowy papermaker, Rutherfoord, and the song which gives its name to the tune, 'Four Drunken Maidens', must obviously be earlier than 1710, the date of the parody.[53]

Most of the popular drinking-songs involving women overlap the categories of love and comedy, and some have already been discussed. The heroine of that vigorous example of the folk-mode, 'My wife's a wanton wee thing',

> . . . sell'd her coat, and she drank it,
> She sell'd her coat and she drank it,
> She row'd hersell in a blanket,
>   And winna be guided for me.

In the fourth stanza of the *Museum* text, probably added by Burns, the husband 'took a ring and clawed her' till she became a good 'bairn'.[54] In 'Hooly and Fairly' the wife drank all her own clothes — her hose and shoon, gown and sark, then pawned her husband's Sunday coat and best blue bonnet:

> At kirk and at mercat I'm covered but barely —
> Oh, gin my wife wad drink hooly and fairly.

The *Tea-Table Miscellany* set of 'Andro and his cutty gun' has as protagonist a young woman who drinks till her cash is done, but is unwilling to emulate the wife of 'Hooly and fairly' and pawn her 'shoon'. The gallant Andro providentially pays for the rest of the liquor, whereupon the cunning ale wife brings through her cheese and well-toasted girdle cakes, thus increasing the demand for drink. They all keep up the binge till morning, and Andro is the best drinker of them all:

> He did like ony mavis sing,
>   And as I in his oxter sat,
> He ca'd me aye his bonnie thing,
>   And mony a sappy kiss I gat.
>
> I hae been east, I hae been west,
>   I hae been far ayont the sun;
> But the blythest lad that e'er I saw,
>   Was Andro' with his cutty gun.[55]

Burns himself is our witness for the song's popularity; in his day it was 'an intimate favourite at bridal trysts and house-heatings' (i.e., it was a song for mixed company), and he was so enamoured of its quality that, anonymous though it is, he described it as 'the work of a master'.[56]

The male aristocracy in their clubs, and mixed company in oyster-cellars such as Lucky Middlemass', sang these 'realistic' songs in Scots; but they also trolled catches, and knew polite lyrics in the anacreontic tradition. Catches, most of them originally English, were printed in the song-books of eighteenth-century Scotland, often in special appendices. The most popular could hardly have been *more* English: 'Hark! the bonny Christ-church bells', where the three voices imitated their ding-donging, 'But the ne'er a man will leave his cann,/Till he hear the mighty Tom'.[57] In the catches, however brief, the humours of Bacchus were linked to the humours of Venus, exactly as in the more classic-sounding anacreontic songs. One begins 'Let us love, and drink our liquor',[58] while another

expresses, joyfully and succinctly, the opposition between the all-
male *Kameradschaft* of the tavern or the club, and the restricted
atmosphere of the home, 'whaur sits our sulky, sullen dame . . .
nursing her wrath to keep it warm':

> None but a cuckold, a cuckold, a cuckold, a cuckold,
> Bully'd by his wife for coming, coming,
> Coming, coming, coming late, fears a domestic strife,
> I'm free, I'm free, and so are you, so are you, so are you too,
> Call and knock, knock boldly, knock boldly,
>   Knock boldly, knock boldly,
> Tho' watchmen cry Past two o'clock.[59]

Volume III of *The Tea-Table Miscellany* popularised such well-
known southern songs as 'Since we die by the help of good wine',[60]
'Bacchus is a flower divine',[61] 'Jolly mortals fill your glasses',[62]
'Here's a health to the king and a lasting peace',[63] more familiar
under the title of 'Down among the Dead Men', and 'He that will
not merry, merry be',[64] with its characteristic final stanzas:

> He that will not merry merry be,
>   With a comp'ny of jolly boys,
> May be plagu'd with a scolding wife,
>   To confound him with her noise:
>   *Let him be merry merry there*
>   *And we'll be merry here;*
>   *For who can know where we shall go,*
>   *To be merry another year?*
>
> He that will not merry merry be,
>   With his mistress in his bed,
> Let him be buried in the church-yard,
>   And we put in his stead:
>   *Let him be merry, etc.*

In anacreontic verse, the preferred deities are Cupid and
Bacchus; the favourite emblems — roses, garlands and the Bowl.
Alexander Robertson of Struan is the most interesting Scottish
writer of 'straight' anacreontics, just as he is the most notable
aristocratic purveyor of *erotica*.[65] The 'cogie' of the 'Cauld Kail in
Aberdeen' group is parallel to the anacreontic bowl, and the
pastoral nymphs of Struan's songs danced the 'reel of Bogie' after
their own aristocratic fashion. In his highly formal and non-
singable lyric, the *Ode against Sobriety*, Robertson wittily adopts the
Shaftesburian position that the heart is superior to the head in order
to state that drunkenness is well worth a hangover:

Since Wisdom bids indulge the nobler Part,
I'll sacrifice my Head to cheer my Heart.

Paradoxically, the pleasures of drink are those of a quiet life, and
it is Sobriety that is attended by the emotions traditionally associated
with drunkenness — Envy, Hatred and Despair.[66] Robertson's
Jacobitism gives an original touch to a song entitled 'To a Humdrum
Company on the First Day of the new Year', and directed to the tune
'Ne parlez plus de politique':

> Since Wine alone wants Pow'r to move ye
>   To be more gay:
> Let's rouze our Joy, by drinking to the
>   Health of the Day.
>
> Then here's to him, crown all the Glasses
>   Till they run o'er,
> Whose growing Worth our Care defaces
>   Still more and more.
>
> Let some repine, still we will quaff it
>   Against their Wills,
> This happy Moment makes us laugh at
>   [An] Age of Ills.[67]

In the following song of Struan's, which is even closer to the spirit
of 'ne parlez plus de politique', partisanship disappears in an
anacreontic miasma:

> Ambitious Wights run mad and fight
>   And Life, and Love, and Wine despise,
> Tho' VENUS ever gives Delight,
>   And healthy BACCHUS never cloys;
> Let JAMES and GEORGE each other teaze for me,
> I'll arm me with Indiff'rence Cap-a-pee.
>
> Draw near me, then, my lovely lass!
>   Kind CUPID bids us closely join;
> The jolly God fills up our Glass
>   To make our pleasures all divine;
> Endless Delights must be the Boon of Love,
> When thus they're prompted by the Pow'rs above.[68]

The sentiment of Robertson's first stanza is precisely that of one of
the most popular vernacular songs of the second half of the century,
the Rev. John Skinner's *Tullochgorum*:

> Let Whig and Tory all agree,
> Whig and Tory, Whig and Tory,
> Let Whig and Tory all agree,
>   To drop their Whig-mig-morum. . . .[69]
>   (st. i, lines 5-8)

In 'Solomon Corrected', Robertson has written a bacchanalian song of considerable sophistication, where the anacreontic strand is cunningly dovetailed with pastoral simple-lifeism, the comic anachronism of the 'Coach and eight', and the identification of Solomon with Diogenes in:

> With vast Expence and princely Care
>   He [Solomon] rais'd a sumptuous Pile,
> On downy Bed and Velvet Chair
>   His sorrows to beguile;
> But he had fetch'd a Nap as sound
> On a straw-Bed upon the Ground
>   *With a fa,la, la, la, la, la, la.*
>
> He then endeav'ring to be gay,
>   Roll'd in a Coach and eight,
> By which he hop'd to drive away
>   From his uneasy Thought;
> He might as well, without his Wheels,
> Tripp'd it like us upon his Heels
>   *With a fa, la, &c.* . . .
>
> At last, since nought away could rub
>   The Causes of his Pain,
> He rais'd him in his royal Tub,
>   And preach'd that all was vain:
> Since there's no Help for Vanity,
> We'll drink, and be as vain as he,
>   *With a fa, la, &c.*   (sts. v, vi, ix)[70]

When the anacreontic poet felt tired of sex, he destroyed the customary unity of Bacchus and Venus and turned drink into the sovereign cure for Love. It is again Struan Robertson who gives us one of the most lively variations on this theme, when in a song entitled 'Liberty preserved, or Love destroyed' he promises, if Cupid should ever again desert him, to 'drown the little Bastard in my bowl'.[71] There are dozens of songs and catches in the collections which celebrate the unity of love, wine and friendship; or of love and wine only; or which present love and wine as irreconcilable opposites. And 'popular' drinking songs do not differ in principle from upper-class anacreontics which go back at least as far as the seventeenth century. What else does Burns's protagonist do in 'My love she's but a lassie yet' but 'drown the little bastard' in 'a drap o' the best o't'?[72] In late eighteenth-century England the true descendant of the Restoration 'Good Fellow' was the 'Choice Spirit', a member of the society of that name founded by George Alexander Stevens the singer and ballad writer. In the preface to his *Songs, Comic and Satyrical*,[73] Stevens gives the following satirical history of the Choice Spirits:

> After *Circe*'s elopement with *Ulysses*, they became wanderers upon the Face of the Earth, and like *Jews*, and *Strolling-players*, continue *Itinerants* even unto this day; they have nevertheless multiplied exceedingly, propagating their Convivialities into the different *Orders of Grigs, Gregs,* and *Gregorians; — Anti-Gallicans, Free Masons,* and *Macaroni; Sons of Sound Sense* and *Satisfaction; Sons* of *Kit,* and *Old Souls; True Blues, Purples,* and *Albions; The Beef Steak, Jockey* and *Catch Clubs;* the *Magdlens,* and *Lumber Troop,* with many Others; all which acknowledge the Affinity they bear to their paternal Society, by celebrating their Evening Mysteries with a *Song* and a *Sentiment.*
>
> The *Choice Spirits* have ever been famous for their Talents as Musical Artists. They usually met at the harvest-homes of Grape-gathering; There exhilarated by the pressing of the Vintage, they were wont to sing Songs, tell Stories, and show Tricks, from their first emerging, until their Perihelion under the Presidentship of Mr. *George Alexander Stevens, Ballad-Laureat* to the Society of Choice-Spirits, and who appeared at Ranelagh in the Character of *Comus,* supported by the Droles of merry Memory.

These clubs were of course London clubs and they were exclusively male societies; the Edinburgh clubs have been examined in detail by Dr McElroy.[74] The most bacchanalian of all Edinburgh's Choice Spirits was Robert Fergusson, whose 'Hollo! keep it up boys' is a vigorous but undistinguished piece in the English tradition, moving towards what might almost be termed a note of 'anti-poetry':

How all things dance round me! — 'tis life, tho' my boys:
Of drinking and spewing how great are the joys![75]

Fergusson's other songs for the Cape Club are interesting as commemorating specific club occasions as well as for their vivid portrayal of personalities and scenes. 'How happy a State does the

Cape knight possess' elicits yet another picture of vomiting club-
men roistering against the background of Edinburgh low life;
'The Progress of Knighthood, by the Knight of Precentor' calls up
the 'brisk laughter' of a score of Vocal Knights who later sing in
chorus, together with a visual impression of their surroundings:

> On all around bright Candles shine
>   And Broun Stouts Coal burns clear
> A coal whose influence divine
>   The dullest Knight can chear.

'Brown Stout' was the Club title of one of the members, Thomas
Law. Another song, put in the mouth of 'the Knight of Complaints'
(a certain Alexander Clapperton) begins with a firmly etched
vignette of an Edinburgh burgess cutler:

> How blyth was I ilk day to see
>   Auchleck come tripping doun
> His ain forestairs at Netherbow
>   To drink his dram at Noon.

Clapperton has moved house to the Canongate; his motto is 'What
should I do up town my business lies all in the Canongate'; his
greatest regret is that he can no longer partake of 'the Warmest
dram That Eer in Mouth did burn' in 'Tam Dicks House', but must
stay in his new locality, 'a dismal place and dry'. Fergusson's Cape
Club songs exhibit on a miniature scale the comical realism and
mastery of urban detail that give distinction to his major poetry.[76]

To sum up — there is very little point in dividing bacchanalian
songs into 'popular' and 'non-popular'; all were popular, though
sometimes in different circles (e.g., almost all, apart from 'Todlen
Hame' and, later on, 'Auld Lang Syne', are men's songs originally,
and some were confined to specific male clubs). The nature of
the subject ensures that the various changes which can be rung
upon it will occur equally to rich and poor, educated and un-
educated. Favourite beverages are praised; friends, clubs, localities
and the singer's nation are celebrated; women — either as a sex or
as individuals — are toasted with geniality or abandon. Sometimes
fellow-drinkers are presented in character-portraits; sometimes
friendship and the good old times are nostalgically hymned.
Outside the warm interior, be it alehouse or rose-strewn bower,
lurks old Care, Lord of the Kill-joys, surrounded by cankered
puritans and shrewish wives. The best of the drinking songs in
vernacular Scots have an insouciance and an inconsequence that
sometimes suggest the comedy of free association, as in the traditional

'Rattlin, Roarin Willie', to which Burns added a stanza in compliment to William Dunbar, W.S., a member of the convivial club of the Crochallan Fencibles. Drink is the other side of the medal to work, for it is as much 'sore labour's bath' as sleep ever was; it is closely associated with sex either as supplement or antagonist; and the literary sources of the bacchanalian songs are often anacreontic. Not surprisingly it is to Burns that we have to turn for the most original bacchanalian works of the century — his transcript of the utterly traditional 'John Barleycorn', where the creativity comes entirely from folk-symbolism, even myth, and his masterpiece, *Love and Liberty*, the subject of our final chapter.

REFERENCES

1, G. H. Gerould, *The Ballad of Tradition* (1932: N. York, 1959), pp. 198 ff; A. L. Lloyd, *Folk Song in England* (London, 1967), pp. 54, 57, 89; 267-315.
2. *Museum*, 427; *LLL*, 35.
3. Kinsley, 381.
4. St. Clair MS., p. 106; *LLL*, 34.
5. *Museum*, 437; Kinsley, 567.
6. *Museum*, 31.
7. *Museum*, 45.
8. *Museum*, 444.
9. *Watson's Choice Collection of Comic and Serious Scots Poems*. The Three Parts, 1706, 1709, 1711 in one volume (Repr. Glasgow, 1869), henceforth cited as *Watson's Collection*. Part III, pp. 79-82.
10. *Museum*, 457.
11. *Museum*, 350.
12. Kinsley, 185 and 456.
13. See the pre-Burns text, *LLL*, 36.
14. *Museum*, 96, st. iv. For Herd's text, see *LLL*, 42.
15. 'Pleugh-Song' in Forbes, *Cantus: Songs and Fancies* (Aberdeen, 1666), pp. [105-10]. See also H. Shire and K. Elliott, 'Pleugh Song and Plough Play', in *Saltire Review*, II (1955), No. 6, 39-44.
16. For some treatment of these songs see my article 'Political and Protest Songs in Eighteenth-Century Scotland, I: Jacobite and Anti-Jacobite' in *Scottish Studies*, XIV (1970), 1-33.
17. *FSNE*, lxv, sts. i-ii, vii. On ploughing technique, W. Alexander observes: 'The extinction as an operative agency of the old plough, with its team of ten or twelve oxen, was quite gradual. In 1770, it was still in all but universal use in the North-East; twenty years thereafter it had to a certain extent given place to a better-fashioned implement and a lighter team. . . . In Cromer, the Garioch, and other districts of Aberdeenshire, the 'tual owsen' plough was pretty common as late as 1792; and in exceptional cases it was in use a few years after the commencement of the present (i.e. nineteenth) century.' (W. Alexander, *Notes and Sketches*, Edinburgh 1877, pp. 33-6.) In the Lothians and Burns's Ayrshire, ploughing by oxen became obsolete by the mid-eighteenth century.

18.   No. 165.

19.   P. 317.

20.   *Merry Muses*, pp. 117-18; *LLL*, 40.

21.   Also in the 1776 edn., II, 144, and *Nightingale* (Edinburgh, 1776), an indication of their popularity at this date.

22.   Pp. 314 ff.

23.   In *The Everlasting Circle* (London, 1960), pp. 25 ff.

24.   *FSNE*, lxvi. For the English predecessors and analogues, see Robert Bell, *Ancient Poems, Ballads and Songs of the Peasantry of England* (London, 1857), pp. 46-9, and *Roxb. Bds.*, ed. Ebsworth, VI, 523-5, VII, 273-7, 278, 818; IV, 384, 526-8, VII, 171-2, VII, 682.

25.   *FSNE*, cxxvi, st. vii.

26.   *FSNE*, xlii. Child 219.

27.   *Museum*, 220; Kinsley, 291.

28.   *FSNE*, xlii.

29.   *FSNE*, lxxxv-lxxxvi.

30.   *Museum*, 438. Not too much should be made of the tradition, expounded by Stenhouse, *Illustrations*, pp. 383 ff., that this song refers to the brave service of 80 burgesses of Selkirk at the battle of Flodden, or the other tradition that it celebrates a football match between the burgesses and the family of Hume. But the appeal to intensely local loyalties is obvious.

31.   Whitelaw, p. 119, st. ii, lines 1-2; iii, lines 1-2; iv, lines 1-2; v, lines 1-2; st. vi.

32.   *Museum*, 123; *LLL*, 38.

33.   *Museum*, 144; Kinsley, 201. The original fragment in the Herd MS. is *LLL*, 39.

34.   Feudal arrangements for grinding corn prevailed in many parts of Scotland in the eighteenth century, and certainly in the North-East. Alexander (pp. 148-9) quotes James Anderson, *General View of the Agriculture and Rural Economy of the County of Aberdeen, with Observations on the means of its Improvement* (1794), as saying that 'in Aberdeenshire the tenants in some cases paid the seventeenth peck in thirlage, plus multure, or the price of grinding, which is often the thirty-second peck. They pay also to the miller a *lick of good will*, or a bannock, which tenants have sometimes allowed to be measured; and there are instances where another unmeasured lick has crept in. Even the seeds sifted from the bannock are sometimes paid. When all these items are added together, they amount at some mills to a twelfth or eleventh part of the whole corn carried to the mill.' Since the miller's customers had no option but to come to him, under the system where tenants were 'thirled' to a particular mill, he had no need to take much trouble over his duties.

35.   *Merry Muses*, p. 101. For Allan Ramsay's polite version, see *LLL*, 110.

36.   *Museum*, 481.

37.   Herd (1776), II, 228; *LLL*, 75. Cp. the tea-table and popular songs on kissing cited in Chapter IV, above.

38.   *Roxb. Bds.*, ed. Chappell, II, 127-30.

39.   *Ibid.*, 116-20.

40.   Ramsay of Ochtertyre, II, 78 ff.

41.   Topham, pp. 128-31.

42.   Ramsay of Ochtertyre, II, 74-5 (for upper classes); *Stat. Account*, Campsie, XV, 372 (for lower classes).

43.   *Boswell for Defence 1769–1774*, ed. W. K. Wimsatt Jr. and F. A. Pottle

(London, 1960), pp. 229, 234-5, 246. The Scotch pint referred to in the second extract equals three Imperial pints.

44. Forsyth, 'The Beauties of Scotland', I, 35, quoted in Rogers, II, 96.
45. Alexander, pp. 131-4.
46. Burns, *Notes*, p. 49. For the text of 'Todlen Hame', see *LLL*, 24.
47. *Stat. Account*, Galston, II, 80.
48. *Museum*, 162, st. ii, lines 5-8; st. iii, lines 5-8; sts. iv-v.
49. Burns, *Notes*, p. 31; Stenhouse, *Illustrations*, pp. 151-2; *LLL*, 26.
50. Whitelaw, p. 256.
51. NLS, MS. 123, p. 26.
52. NLS, Ry III a 10 (82).
53. I have not located the original of 'Four Drunken Maidens'. Charles Kirkpatrick Sharpe, the early nineteenth-century antiquarian, seems to have known it, for he printed a version for private circulation, three stanzas of which are printed as *LLL*, 25.
54. *P. & S.*, p. 1330.
55. 'Blyth, blyth, blyth was she' in *TTM*, IV: (1740), p. 423.
56. To Thomson, 19th Nov. 1794, in *Letters*, II, 276.
57. *Charmer* II (Edinburgh, 1751), 339 and in nine other song-books published in Scotland before 1786.
58. *Scots Nightingale* (Edinburgh, 1778), p. 341.
59. *Ibid.*, p. 350.
60. *TTM*, III: (1740), p. 293.
61. P. 294.
62. P. 293.
63. P. 291.
64. P. 292.
65. Above, pp. 46-8.
66. A. Robertson, *Poems*, p. 261; sts. ii-iii.
67. *Ibid.*, p. 240.
68. *Ibid.*, p. 142.
69. *Nightingale* (Edinburgh, 1776), p. 13.
70. The whole song is printed in *LLL*, 23.
71. The whole song is printed in *LLL*, 153.
72. Kinsley, 293, *LLL*, 154.
73. London, 1801, pp. x ff.
74. D. D. McElroy, *The literary Clubs and Societies of eighteenth-century Scotland and their influence on the literary publications from 1700 to 1800*. Ph.D. Thesis (Edinburgh, 1952).
75. St. iii, lines 7-8. The whole song is in *LLL*, 27.
76. *The Poems of Robert Fergusson*, ed. M. P. McDiarmid (S.T.S. edition, 2 vols., Edinburgh, 1956), II, 168-72, 296-8.

Chapter VIII

THE BROADSIDE MODE

Throughout most of this book I have treated eighteenth-century Scottish song as a single conglomerate – as a total culture with subcultures within it. Yet each of the three or four thousand songs that have come down to us, however conventional it may seem to the sophisticated, is in its own way unique. Even the 'purest' of folksongs are not made by some mysterious supra-rational communal entity, but are brought into being by a sequence of individual composer-performers and traditional singers;[1] the singing and composing are done in a group where the singer is in a two-way relation with his audience on *particular* occasions, no two of which are ever exactly the same; the songs *respond* to situations, they are 'actions' and 'reactions'. When some of the people become literate and broadsides and chapbooks circulate among them, a medial term – print – is introduced into the equation; the transaction is more impersonal, for poet, vendor and singer need not be the same person, though they sometimes are. Writing at a distance is writing for money. Broadsides like 'The Four Drunken Wives' discussed in the previous chapter[2] often report an unusual incident in a city or smaller town; they are full of human-interest stories, which were as avidly read two hundred years ago as the crime and scandal pages of the modern popular press.

By far the most sensational of the journalistic broadsides were the execution-ballads – printed sheets or small chapbooks hurriedly composed by hacks to be sold at public hangings and sung thereafter. Very often they took the form of the supposed last words of the criminal concerned, and an allied type purported to give the testaments of other villains of the popular imagination, such as misers. In the early nineteenth century these themes were expressed in prose rather than verse, like the following in the National Library of Scotland: 'A Full, True, and Particular Account of the wretched death on Wednesday last of a Notorious Miser who resided in the Cowgate, and was in the constant practice of gathering up rags and bones off the streets and begging about the country, – and of the enormous sums which were found hidden in various curious places in his miserable dwelling, amounting to nearly L2000'.[3]

A hundred years before, Allan Ramsay had written in the vernacular 'Habbie' stanza[4] his 'Last Speech of a Wretched Miser':

O DOOL! and am I forc'd to die,
And nae mair my dear siller see,
That glanc'd sae sweetly in my e'e!
It breaks my heart!
My goud! my bands! alackanie!
That we should part.[5]

'The Wretched Miser' is the title of one of the Pepys Ballads, which dates from c. 1690,[6] with a similar content. It would seem, then, that a connection can be established between this English broadside and one of the earliest masterpieces of the Scots vernacular revival; they are in a broad popular tradition which cuts right across national differences.

In so far as it is possible to compare English 'Last Words' ballads with Scottish, the former seem to be even more moralistic in tone.[7] There are, in fact, a number of Scottish pieces, such as 'Gilderoy' and 'Macpherson's Rant', which positively glorify the criminal, and it was these which entered the 'folk' repertoire. Among the earliest English songs in praise of robbers are of course the Robin Hood ballads, which, since they were also popular in Scotland, no doubt made their contribution to the native variety. In the seventeenth-century English examples, however, any defiant note of protest is generally buried under pious sentiments.[8] One of these, a song called 'Captain Johnston's Last Farewell', seems to have circulated widely in Scotland, where it is found on a broadsheet as late as 1776, even although Johnston 'was arraigned for being assisting in stealing a young Heiress, for which he was executed at Tyburn' as early as the 23rd of December, 1696.[9] No doubt the ballad's appeal in the north was due to Johnston's Scottish origin, his motive of pure friendship for the main abductor, and his excuse that, being a Scotsman, he did not understand that abduction was a crime! He was betrayed by his landlord for fifty pounds' reward, and his lady refused to hear his 'moan' while 'dying words he sent'. He ends on the traditional note:

My landlord and his subtile wife
I do forgive them here;
Farewell this transitory life
The laws are most severe.

An early 'last words' ballad featuring a Scotsman was 'A Confession and Lamentation, recommended to Mr Madder to subscribe before his Death that thereby he may Appease his Countrey Mens wrath thats hot against him for his unaccountable Hardness, SAY, To the Tune of Captain JOHNSTONS lament'.[10] Madder, involved in the murder of a certain Drummond during an act of piracy on the Malabar Coast in 1703, is much more defiant of orthodox morality than the rogues in the English broadsides we have mentioned: thus st. vi begins 'I did GOD's Deputes here revile: Thinking them to Outbrav'. What is most interesting, however, is the pronounced nationalism of the piece, expressed in the same measure as 'Macpherson's Rant':

> I from my Yeuth upward did hate
> my Countrys Povertie.
> Although I know Its only Spring
> Is Her pure Honestie.
> To *England* therefor I did go
> To won money to spend,
> I won, and spent much, GOD knows how
> For which I make this end. . . .
>
> To ev'ry SCOT that this doth come
> I this advice commend.
> That He his Countrey don't deny
> For any Selfish end.
> Or Sure and Just GOD shall pursue
> With such reward as Mine.
> And then be sure he shall Repent,
> When it is Out of Time.   (sts. iv, vi)

Commonplace pietism is here subsumed under the more significant emotion of Scots patriotism. Other examples are 'Captain Thomas Green's Last Farewell',[11] and 'The last Speech and Confession of Janet Riddle, who was Execute for Murthering her own Child, in the Grass Market of Edinburgh, 21st January 1702'.[12] The farewell of Green, Madder's captain, was addressed 'to the Ocean and all the World', and he 'was Execute with two more of his Crew at Leith within the Flood-Mark, 11 April 1705, for Piracie and Murder'. Green protests his innocence: he never saw the man he is supposed to have murdered, and he — like Johnston — has been betrayed, by one who had eaten his bread and served him. And there is a strongly puritanical strain, too. Even though he is innocent of the crime for which he has been tried, nevertheless the punishment is merited by his 'youthful sins' in general. He forgives everybody, and hopes his soul will find mercy.

Another ballad, put into the mouth of an Englishman, assumes that Green is guilty: 'A seasonable Advice, TO ALL who encline to go in Pirrating; drawn from what has happ'ned to Captain Green, As it were from his own mouth, One of that Rank, To the Tune of, *To the Weaver if ye go, etc.*'[13] In this ballad, Green is made to bow to the Scots, whom his crew thought would never dare to sentence an Englishman, and national feeling finds its appropriate symbol in the heroes of the War of Independence:

> And tho' it's true WALLACE is dead,
>   Yet take no hope from that,
> For sure there are some in his stead,
>   Who some way fill his Hat.

Green is even made to say that God is at the right hand of those who are his executioners — God is on Scotland's side:

> Therefore my Country Men I pray
>   by War ye wrong the SCOTS,
> For GOD 'mongst them doth open Lay,
>   what's done 'gainst them in Plots.

Janet Riddle, too, is convinced that she deserves the severest punishment for the murder of her child, and the Kirk's voice can be heard in her last words:

> The Div'l helpt me to go on,
>   and paved out the way.

Witnesses claimed they heard the child crying, but Janet denied them,

> Saying it was by me dead Born,
>   and I had laid it there,
> Least any Person should me Scorn,
>   and Church be too severe.

She dies, fearing eternal misery and woe, but hoping for God's mercy or at least 'the blessing . . . of thy word'.

The complex interaction between the Scots and English popular traditions is well illustrated by the ballad of 'Gilderoy'. It seems to have had the following history. Composed in or near 1638 in Scotland, the date of the bandit's execution, it spread to England by oral or MS. transmission or both, and came into the popular heritage during the Civil War. At about 1660 two quite separate English broadside treatments appeared, one of which was later printed in the *Westminster Drollery* of 1671, entitled 'A Scotch Song called Gilderoy', the other, *c.* 1685, under the heading 'The Scotch Lovers Lamentation; Or, Gilderoy's Last Farewell': both in the course of time influenced the texts orally current in England and Scotland. Lady Wardlaw (1677–1727) combined the two (English) versions, and in the eighteenth century the ballad became increasingly Scottified, though it continued to be sung in southern as well as Irish versions.[14] The subject of 'Gilderoy', the idealisation of the Highland freebooter, is a theme which made its contribution a hundred and fifty years later, *via* the Waverley Novels, to the paraphernalia of English romanticism and, in particular, to continental opera plots. After quoting a correspondent who pointed out 'how in native ballad and song the Highlander is almost always a hero, and as a lover usually prevails against Lowland rivals', Gavin Greig[15] comments that 'this may be due to the fact that much of our minstrelsy has had a Celtic origin'. Another reason might well be that by the eighteenth and nineteenth centuries, the Erschemen whom Dunbar felt to be alien[16] were now regarded by ballad-singers and some young women as sufficiently naturalised, sufficiently part of the common weal, to become not ogres but romantic heroes. This is recognised quite explicitly by Scott in the introduction to *Rob Roy* when he quotes from Jamieson's version of 'Bonny Babby Livingstone', spirited away by the Highlander Glenlyon, and from a ballad about Robin Oig, or Rob Roy the younger, on the subject of his abduction of Jean Key or Wright. The wish-fulfilment rôle of the Highlander has already been noted in our discussion of amorous *motifs*, and he even plays his part in Burns's *Love and Liberty*, as we shall see in Chapter X.

The Scottish execution-ballad which has lasted longest in oral transmission is 'Macpherson's Rant'. The account of its hero given in a letter in the *New Monthly Magazine* (1821)[17] illustrates many features of popular myth. Macpherson was the child of a gipsy woman and a Highland gentleman, who acknowledged him and brought him up in his own house, until his death in a fight over cattle with neighbouring clansmen. Next summer the gipsy took away her son, though she kept in touch with the clan, who often gave her money and clothes for the boy. When he grew up he robbed like a gentleman, and saw that his 'tribe' committed no atrocities. 'He often gave the spoils of the rich to relieve the poor; and all his tribe were restrained from many atrocities of rapine by their awe of his mighty arm.' But it is unlikely that his victims, the settled farmers and merchants, saw him as anything other than a petty bandit who stole horses and cattle and broke into houses and henroosts. His tribe was a body of 'gipsies' or outlaw 'sorners', and the theme of 'Macpherson's Rant' is an especially heroic variant of the general wish-fulfilment myth of beggar-pastoral. Chambers' imaginative description of the 'Egyptian Band' is quite in the spirit of the ballad:

> There seems to have been thirty of them in all, men and women; but it was seldom that more than eight or ten made their appearance in any one place. It was quite a familiar sight, at a fair or market in Banff, Elgin, Forres or any other town of the district, to see nearly a dozen sturdy Egyptians march in with a piper playing at their head, their match-locks slung behind them, and their broadswords or dirks by their sides, to mingle with the crowd, inspect the cattle shown for sale, and watch for bargains passing among individuals, in order to learn who was in the way of receiving money.

Yet there is some foundation for this picture in the records of the 'Process against the Egyptians'. One witness 'deponed' that he saw twenty-seven of them, armed and with a piper, in Keith on 2nd September 1698; another, 'that he seed about twelve men, with a piper, come in to Keith, at St. Ruffus' Fair was two year, where of the pannals were a pairt'; and several, that 'the women who uses to follow the pannals has a particular language peculiar to themselves' (i.e., neither Gaelic nor Scots).[18]

Duff, Laird of Braco, was then the leading administrator in Banffshire. To bring to book Macpherson's band he had to counter the opposition of the Laird of Grant, whose tenants some of the 'gipsies' nominally were, and who wished to try them under his own heritable jurisdiction. Two of the gang in particular, Peter and Donald Broun, had lived for six months very close to Castle Grant. According to an account in Baird's *Genealogical Memoirs of the Duffs* (*c.* 1773), which the antiquarian and publisher Robert Chambers held to be authentic, Braco decided to attack Macpherson, the Brouns and their gang when he found them at the Summer's Eve fair at Keith:

> As soon as he observed them in the fair [the account goes on], he desired his brother-in-law, Lesmurdie, to bring him a dozen stout men, which he did. They attacked the villains, who, as they had several of their accomplices with them, made a desperate resistance. One of them made a pass at Braco with his hanger, intending to run him through the heart; but it slanted along the outside of the ribs, and

one of his men immediately stabbed the fellow dead. They
then carried Macpherson and [Peter] Broun to a house in
Keith, and set three or four stout men to guard them, not
expecting any more opposition, as all the rest of the gang
were fled. Braco and Lesmurdie were sitting in an upper
room concerting the commitment of their prisoners, when
the Laird of Grant and thirty men came calling for them,
swearing no Duff in Scotland should keep them from him.
Braco, hearing the noise of the Grants, came down-stairs,
and said, with seeming unconcern and humour: 'That he
designed to have them sent to prison; but he saw they were
too strong a party for him to contend with, and so he must
leave them'; but, without losing a moment, he took a turn
through the market, found other two justices of peace, kept
a court, and assembled sixty stout fellows, with whom he
retook the two criminals, and sent them to prison.

On 7th November 1700 Macpherson, the two Brouns and James
Gordon were charged before the sheriff at Banff 'of being knowne
habit and reput to be Egiptians and wagabonds, and keeping the
mercats in their ordinarie manner of theiving and purse-cutting, or
guilty of the rest of the crimes of thift, masterfull bangstrie and
oppressione'. The Laird of Grant's agent demanded that the two
Brouns be surrendered for trial in 'the court of his regality', and
offered a pledge for them; but the demand was not granted. The
depositions of the witnesses stated that the prisoners had stolen
sheep, oxen and horses; forcibly entered houses and stolen the
occupants' property; filched purses; and oppressed farmers by
taking possession of their kiln barns and refusing to move for a
fortnight or even a month. One witness alleged that Macpherson
'came into his house and spilt his ale, and stobbed the bed seeking
the deponent'; another, that he had drunk and danced with the
company all night long at the witness's house. After his arrest
Macpherson is supposed to have composed the tune 'Macpherson's
Rant' and marched to the place of execution, a mile from the town,
playing it on his violin. 'He even danced it under the fatal tree. Then
he asked if any one in the crowd would accept his fiddle, and keep it
as a memorial of Macpherson; and finding no one disposed to do so,
he broke the instrument over his knee, and threw himself indignantly
from the ladder'.[19]
    Macpherson broadsides seem to have been printed very soon
after the bandit's execution, but the text most generally known in
the late eighteenth century was David Herd's:

I've spent my time in rioting,
   Deabuch'd my health and strength;
I've pillag'd, plunder'd, murdered,
   But now, alas! at length,
I'm brought to punishment direct,
   Pale death draws near to me;
This end I never did project,
   To hang upon a tree.

To hang upon a tree! a tree!
   That curs'd unhappy death!
Like to a wolf to worried be,
   And choaked in the breath.
My very heart would surely break,
   When this I think upon.
Did not my courage singular,
   Bid pensive thoughts begone.

No man on earth that draweth breath,
   More courage had than I;
I dar'd my foes unto their face,
   And would not from them fly;
This grandeur stout, I did keep out,
   Like HECTOR, manfullie:
Then wonder one like me, so stout,
   Should hang upon a tree.

Th'Egyptian band I did command,
   With courage more by far,
Than ever did a general
   His soldiers in the war.
Being fear'd by all, both great and small,
   I liv'd most joyfullie:
O! curse upon this fate of mine,
   To hang upon a tree.

As for my life, I do not care,
   If justice would take place,
And bring my fellow plunderers
   Unto this same disgrace.
For PETER BROWN, that notour loon,
   Escap'd, and was made free;
O! curse upon this fate of mine,
   To hang upon a tree.

Both law and justice buried are,
    And fraud and guile succeed,
The guilty pass unpunished,
    If money interceed.
The Laird of Grant, that Highland saint,
    His mighty majestie,
He pleads the cause of PETER BROWN,
    And lets MACPHERSON die.

The dest'ny of my life contriv'd
    By those whom I oblig'd,
Rewarded me much ill for good,
    And left me no refuge.
For BRACO DUFF, in rage enough,
    He first laid hands on me;
And if that death would not prevent,
    Avenged would I be.

As for my life, it is but short,
    When I shall be no more;
To part with life I am content,
    As any heretofore.
Therefore, good people all, take heed,
    This warning take by me,
According to the lives you lead,
    Rewarded you shall be.[20]

In this text there is no mention of the freebooter's attempt to
dispose of his fiddle (symbolising the wild abandon of his life) to
the bystanders at the Cross of Banff: here, the cateran's complaint
is the possibly unhistorical one that his 'fellow-plunderers' — in
particular, Peter Broun — were set free by the Laird of Grant,
contemptuously dismissed as 'that Highland saint'. The trial of
Peter Broun, and his brother Donald, seems to have been completed
later than that of Macpherson and Gordon, for sentence of death
was not passed upon them till 21st February 1701, to be carried out
on the Gallow Hill on 2nd April. The Brouns were, in fact, reprieved
— until the second Wednesday in June 1701; and it is to be presumed
that they were then hanged.[21]

Macpherson, in Herd's version, is the victim not so much of the
law as of fate, 'the destiny of my life' — in the original broadside,
simply 'the Destinie'; and yet fate is seen as the product of his
chosen actions throughout life. In some of the early texts there is
an even greater degree of moralising, coupled with the suggestion

that sheer will-power, or lust for revenge, is capable of triumphing over Hell itself:

> For neither Death nor Divels power
>   this rage of mine shall break,
> For in the place to which I go
>   some Office I expect.

This same broadside ends with lines which, although they do not refer to it in so many words, are thoroughly consonant with the legend of Macpherson playing his fiddle up to the very foot of the scaffold itself:

> Than wantonly and rantingly
>   I am resolv'd to die
> And with undaunted courage I
>   shall mount this fatall Tree.[22]

Burns's 'McPherson's Farewell', which transmutes his broadside sources into a superbly economical lyric, should perhaps be mentioned here rather than in the final chapter.[23] Not only does his last stanza build with assurance on the lines just quoted from this early broadside,

> Now farewell, light, thou sunshine bright,
>   And all beneath the sky!
> May coward shame distain his name,
>   The wretch that dares not die!—

but they resemble a Jacobite imitation of the hundred and thirty-seventh psalm:

> If thee, *O Scotland*, I forget,
>   Even with my latest Breath;
> May foul Dishonour stain my Name,
>   And bring a Coward's Death.[24]

This example sums up perfectly and in miniature Burns's creative relationship to the whole popular culture.

The line of development seems to have been as follows. First, the English 'Last Words' ballads of the sixteenth and seventeenth centuries; then, the Scottish derivatives, which may be just as lachrymose and moralistic as their English originals, though they may on occasion breathe a Robin Hood spirit of defiance; next, the transformation of the type from the last words of an executed criminal to the last words of any interesting or low-life character. Ramsay attached the 'Habbie' measure to the genre ('Last Speech

of a Wretched Miser', already quoted, or 'Lucky Spence's Last
Advice' on a famous Edinburgh bawd), and naturally enough with
this form, as with the couplet, there was no question of a piece being
actually sung. Standard Habbie's association with the comic was
strengthened by Allan Ramsay, and maintained in broadsides like
'The Highland Man's Lament for the Death of *Donald Bayn* alias
Mcevan Vanifranck who was Execute in the Grass Market of
Edinburgh on Wednesday the 9th day of January 1723',[25] which
is noteworthy for its attempt to make humorous use of Highland
English. The broadside begins with a reference to those archetypal
freebooters Rob Roy and Gilderoy, assumes familiarity with the
Macpherson story and such characters as the 'Laird of Grant', and
manages to get in a considerable amount of political satire:

> *Tonald Bayn* her nane dear Shoy
> Maks a' folk sad save *Robin* Roy
> Who kend him sin he was a Boy,
>   hernane sell Swons,
> To think he'd hangs like *Gilderoy*,
>   by *Loulan* Louns.

> Ohon, ohon, for Land of Refe
> Sin *Tonald's* hang'd for common Theif,
> Not on kind Gallows at the *Crief*,
>   indeed no fair,
> Pra Shentlemen her nane sels Cheif,
>   did a hing there. . . .

> *Donald* and her [i.e. Rob Roy], for mony a Day,
> Eat Kebbecks, and drank Huskiebae;
> And syne took up te Trumps to play,
>   *McPherson's* Rant
> We liv'd as Blyth as the Lord *Gray*
>   or Laird of *Grant*.

> Throu *Murray*-Land and *Huntly* Heth
> We chas'd the *Gypsies* out of *Breth*,
> Put them, and *Tinklers* a' to Death
>   and spoil'd their Carcks:
> The Chapmen fand out Highland Wrath,
>   We toom'd their Packs.[26]   (sts. i-ii, vii-ix)

The broadside depicts conditions in the N.-E. highlands and
neighbouring farmlands that are very like those ascribed to all
Scotland by Fletcher of Saltoun in 1698.[27] Interestingly enough,
Donald Bayn's band massacre other rivals in pillage – gipsies like

Macpherson himself, less heroic beggar-folk such as tinkers, and common chapmen. There are four stanzas describing guerrilla fighting against Mar's Swiss and Dutch mercenaries, and quarrels with Rob Roy and the McGregors. The character of a Highland swashbuckler is wickedly caricatured, together with the laments of his victims:

> Pe sure, her nane sell never saw,
> Te man tat valued less te Law,
> For he gae Folk cald Coals to blaw,
>   which gard them groan,
> And when he carried all away,
>   cry'd Pockmahon.

Now that 'her heart will plead/For his pare Arse to grace the Gallows', Macleods, Macdonalds or Macbanes, and all the Macs 'tat kend him anes/Hing toun te Head, and mak great Mains, we Cronons fair',

> Te Clans will make te firy fery,
> Frae *Fokoburrs* to *Inverary*,
> And frae *Glensheils* down to *Glengary*,
>   for *Tonald Bayn*,
> I fear te Plots will a' miscarry,
>   Sin *Tonald's* gane.

In 'The Highland Mans Lament', a form that was originally a song set to a popular tune has, under the influence of a traditional lowland Scottish stanza that lends itself peculiarly to colloquial expression, become a satirical poem expressing the lowlander's judgement of Highland freebooting, and at the same time a vehicle for creative stylistic experiment in rendering a new level of usage.[28]

At about mid-century, the balance in verse-journalism changes. The broadsides and chapbooks, while still continuing to print 'Last Words' songs (including pieces dating from as far back as eighty years before) contain more and more items of the sentimental and romantic kind. The latter are very often English — and old favourites at that. In the Aberdeen ballads,[29] for example, there were atrocity stories such as 'The Babes in the Wood', or 'The Yarmouth Tragedy, shewing how by the Cruelty of their Parents, two lovers were distroyed'. In 'The Gosford Tragedy: or the Perjured Carpenter', a ship's carpenter kills the girl he has seduced and made pregnant before he goes to sea; when her ghost appears on board the ship he is forced to confess, after which he dies, 'raving distracted'. Another broadside of this class, 'The Blackamoor in the Wood', is an early instance of the literature of colour prejudice; it tells how a Moor, in revenge for being corrected by his master, rapes his lord's wife and massacres their children in view of their father. When the master begs 'O save her life and now demand of me the thing thou wilt', the reply is 'Cut off thy nose, and not one drop of her blood shall be spilt'. When the lord obeys, the Moor lets her fall from the tower on which these deeds take place. The husband dies, and the Moor hurls himself to his destruction. This English and indeed international type was imitated by Scottish ballad-mongers, as in 'Young Grigor's Ghost', where Kitty's cruel father arranges for Grigor to be pressed into the army. He is murdered by Indians near Fort Niagara on 30th July 1750, one of whom cuts off his finger with Kitty's ring on it. Grigor's ghost appears to her in distant Scotland and tells her of his fate; she wastes away, and her mother dies — a truly lamentable tale, told in bathetic verse of incredible ineptitude. Some ballads hover on the brink of real atrocity, but the villain repents and all ends happily, as in 'The Bonny Lass of Bennachie', where the girl's cruel father causes the hero to become a soldier in Germany. When the father spreads the false rumour that he is slain, she seeks and finds him in High Germany, whereupon the father relents, procures his free discharge — 'and now we hear he's a wealthy squire/And lives near Aberdeen'. It is interesting that English social terms such as 'squire' and 'parson' are included in these ballads printed for a Scottish public; even if the borrowing was done quite mechanically, the implication is that a Scottish audience would have understood them. And crudely plebeian satire continues to find a place in the broadside 'poetry of action' of the last quarter of the century, warning its audience about the common rogueries of everyday life. Thus 'The Humours of the Age' adjures 'gentlemen farmers' to keep their hands in their pockets for fear they are picked, and lists the evils to which farmers are subject — death of cattle, high wages to pay, landlords' rent, taxation, hard labour while gentlemen hunt and hawk, lawyers who must be bribed, cunning millers, deceitful weavers and tailors, not to speak of barbers, shoemakers, tanners, skinners, glovers, hatters, bakers, butchers, go-slow day labourers, doctors and surgeons living by extortion, shopkeepers, the blacksmith ('He's always choked up with a damnable thirst'), the painter, the exciseman, the brewer, diversity of religions, overdressed servant girls, tea-drinkers of every degree, and

> Your ladies of pleasure that walk in the night
> With their watches and tweezer[s], and laces so bright
> If they meet with a stranger that loves the old game
> They will pick his pocket it's twenty to one.

This doggerel is evidently a Scottified version of an English broadside because specifically English words such as 'tithes' appear, together with 'the old Church of Scotland I'll ever adore', where one feels 'Scotland' has been substituted for an original 'England'. It is as much a Complaint as a satire, for its burden is that farmers have every other social class on their backs.

The simple-lifeism of an older generation disapproving of the softness and luxuriousness of the young often forms the basis of popular satire. 'The Roving Maids of Aberdeen'[30] illustrates this perfectly, at the same time as it provides a vigorous glimpse of feminine life in a mid-eighteenth-century Scottish city:

> Now to behold the pretty maids;
>   as they walk on the causey,
> With ruffle cuffs and capuchins,
>   and wow but they be saucey.
>   Fal de ral lal de ral. . . .
>
> The roving maids of Aberdeen,
>   when they go to the dancing,
> The young men all admires the sport,
>   they are so neat and handsome.
>   Fal, etc.
>
> They curse and swear and domenier,
>   and scold like any randy;
> Their morning drink I really think,
>   is whisky gin or brandy.
>   Fal, etc.
>
> And if they chance to prove with child,
>   or lose their reputation,
> O they set up a baudy house,
>   and that's their occupation.
>   Fal, etc.
>
> Such bauds and bullies then turn thieves,
>   observe the dismal story,
> By hangies hand, their lives they end,
>   and that's call'd gallows glory.
>   Fal de ral lal de ral.   (sts. ii, xi, xv-xvii)

The moralism of the piece converts a satire upon dress into an exemplum, a northern *Harlot's Progress*; as with 'The Humours of the Age', its broad comic moralism is almost Hogarthian in spirit.

Like the execution-ballads and broadside satires, the political and patriotic songs were action songs. Each was a response to a specific occasion or to a group need.[31] The earliest Jacobite songs were meant to encourage and confirm commitment; to enhance the Jacobites' public and private image by belittling their opponents'; and to give expression to universal emotions – patriotism, devotion to a hero, self-sacrifice – as these appeared in peculiarly Jacobite contexts. The satire and partisanship of Whig songs was similar, but they did not show any of the nostalgic melancholy and sentimental eroticism which were the curse of Jacobite song and prose fiction in the nineteenth century. Whig songs were either polemical, or broadly patriotic, like the following stanzas:[32]

> (1)   O Brother Sandie, hear ye the news?
>   Lillibulero, bullen a la,
>   An army's just coming without any shoes,
>   Lillibulero, bullen a la. `. . .`

> (2)   O'er the hills and far away
>   O'er the hills and far away,
>   The Rebel Clans in search of prey,
>   Come o'er the hills and far away. . . .

> (3)   As lang as *Scottish* bards draw breath,
>   The British HERO they shall sing;
>   As lang as fame her trump can bla'
>   His praise through distant lands shall ring.

(This last is from a song in praise of the Duke of Cumberland)

Masonic songs, of course, helped to keep *their* group together. In so far as they were Scottish they appear to have taken over into the Enlightenment some of the worst aspects of Calvinism, as, for example, the notion of an elite of Freemasons, harsh scorn for the lesser breeds without the craft and an element of persecution mania.[33] The vehicles of an anti-Calvinist and libertarian creed, they yet expressed attitudes in many respects akin to those of a religion to which Masonic theory was opposed. The revolutionary slogan of Fraternity is the Masonic virtue *par excellence*: as one song put it, 'Our Maxims are justice, morality, friendship, and brotherly love'. Another, 'Though bigots storm and fools declaim', by Brother Blacklock of the lodge at Dumfries,[34] combines exclusive elitism with the spirit of a rather vague *Internationale*. It is worth quoting as a historical document, in spite of its bathos:

> O'er all the earth let masons join,
> To execute one grand design,
> And strike amazement into fools,
> Who laugh at masons and their tools.

Brother Blacklock's third stanza, though still concentrating on individual self-improvement, adds an ominous new virtue to the traditional fraternity:

> Let ev'ry mason then prepare
> By virtue's mould his work to square;
> And ev'ry task adjusted be
> By the level of equality.

Equality and the other virtues are nevertheless exclusive: they are not to pass over into society at large but are to be practised within the lodge, behind an impenetrable barrier of secrecy.

For industrial protest songs, trade union verse, and songs and poems expressing a typically proletarian outlook, one has to go to the nineteenth and early twentieth centuries; yet these more recent working-class songs are no doubt descended from, or at the very least analogous to songs of earlier centuries. Very few such proto-types have survived in Scotland and it is the great English collections of broadsides that contain the ancestors of Burns's 'Man was made to mourn',[35] such as 'The Poor Folks Complaint' of *c.* 1675:[36]

> Whilst you so surfeit with Excess,
>   and with great plenty are rewarded,
> The Poor do languish in distress,
>   and still their Cryes are not regarded. . . .   (st. ii)

Broadsides of general plebeian social protest, of English origin, were widely known in Scotland and widely sung. It is hard to draw any other conclusion from Burns's mention of his grand-uncle whose 'most voluptuous enjoyment was to sit down & cry, while my Mother would sing the simple old song of *The Life & Age of Man*'[37] —a song similar in tone and treatment to 'The Poor Folks Complaint'. And the matter is almost clinched, so far as this one piece is concerned, by the inclusion of two related pieces in the Aberdeen broadsides of the late 1770s.[38]

But the social criticism of 'The Poor Folks' Complaint' and 'The Life and Age of Man' is stoical and passive. Before the French Revolution, militant class feeling and the emotions of plebeian democracy come to the surface only indirectly, and often in songs about wars and soldiers, as in the various version of 'Deil tak the wars hurried Billy from me', which go back to the late seventeenth century.[39] In a nineteenth-century piece preserved by oral trans-mission, which formed part of the repertoire of the late Jeannie Robertson, 'Twa recruitin sergeants',[40] the sergeants paint condi-tions in the army as much less dangerous than those experienced by a ploughman on the average farm, and they pointedly criticise the ploughman's employer, 'the greedy auld farmer', and the mouldy fare he provides for his workmen. The theme that life in the army guarantees freedom from the oppression of civilian life is exactly that of a song of the mid-eighteenth century, here reproduced in full:

My yellow-mou'd mistress, I bid you adieu,
For I've been too long in slavery with you,
With washing and scouring I'm seldom in bedy
And now I will go with my sodger laddie.
    My sodger laddie, my sodger laddie,
    The kisses are sweet of a sodger laddie.

With the crust of your loaf, and the dregs of your tea,
You fed your lap doggie far better than me,
With rinning and spinning, my head was unsteady,
But now I will go with my sodger laddie.
    My sodger laddie, etc.

For yarn, for yarn, you always did cry,
And look'd to my pirn, ay as ye went by;
Now the drums they do beat, and my bundle is ready,
And I'll go along with my sodger laddie.
    My sodger laddie, etc.

As women with men are always for use,
For washing and dressing, or plucking a goose;
Or drawing a chicken to make his diet ready,
O happy I'll be with my sodger laddie.
    My sodger laddie, etc.

A soldier that's married, I always do see,
Has always most money, if so they agree,
He calls her his honey, his dear and his lady,
Then I will go with my sodger laddie.
    My sodger laddie, etc.

If my fortune be bad, the truth I will tell,
It was through a bad mistress that so it befell;
If she sent me an errand, she cry'd, ay, where stay'd ye,
For which I will go with my sodger laddie.
    My sodger laddie, etc.

I went to the well, and lost a burn stoup,
And when I came home, she kicked my doup;
O was not this hard, by such a fine lady,
For which I will go with my sodger laddie.
    My sodger laddie, etc.

I'll always be ready, with needle and soap,
For possing and patching to serve the whole troop,
I'll be loving and kind, and live like a lady,
When I go abroad with my sodger laddie.
  My sodger laddie, etc.

In heat of battles, I'll keep on the flank,
With a stone in a stocking, and give them a clank.
If he be knock'd down, though he be my daddy,
I'll bring all his clink to my sodger laddie.
  My sodger laddie, etc.

For robbing the dead is no thievish trick,
I'll rifle his breeches, and then his knapsack,
But yet on a friend I'll not be so ready,
If he's been acquaint with my sodger laddie.
  My sodger laddie, etc.

Then as rich as a Jew, I'll return yet I hope,
And ask my old lady if she's found her burn stoup,
And all my days after, I'll live like a lady,
On the gold I've got, with my sodger laddie.
  My sodger laddie, my sodger laddie,
  The kisses are sweet of a sodger laddie.[41]

This song can well be taken as a test piece for the appreciation
of the popular lyric in broadside style. To many it will seem the
merest doggerel, but to those attuned to popular conventions,
more especially the Scottish ones, it will seem excellent of its kind —
first, because of its perfect adaptation of words to tune (it is a parody
of 'My sodger laddie is over the sea' in *The Tea-Table Miscellany*);
second, because of the frequently adroit management of assonance
and half rhyme in the second couplet of many stanzas; third,
because of the repeated fulfilment of the expectations aroused by
the contrast between the initial masculine and final feminine rhyme
patterns within each stanza; and fourth, because its social criticism
is so perfectly fused with the character of protagonist. In several
ways the piece looks forward to Burns; for example, the servant's
'You fed your lap doggie far better than me' foreshadows the
criticism of luxury in *The Twa Dogs*. The conflict of classes is manifest
at the individual level in a clash of *wills* between mistress and slavey,
and the latter's dearest wish is for revenge — to vanquish her ex-
employer through the use of sarcastic humour, and then to have
riches and luxury herself. One of the finest oppositions in the song
appears in st. iii between the mistress's nagging economic exploitation and the drumbeats that ironically symbolise freedom; and

another is the contrast within the girl's own character between her self-will and her generosity — once away from her immediate cramping environment, she will be 'loving and kind' to her own man and, in addition, serve the whole troop. Altogether delightful is this strong personality's unhesitating acceptance of her femininity — the principal way to freedom open to her is through her rôle as woman, to love and to serve. Even in the grim context of a battle-field where the camp followers loot the corpses, she will still serve, though in a superficially unfeminine way, by attacking some perhaps wounded man with a stone wrapped in a stocking. The grim realism of this piece demonstrates what could be achieved, even before Burns, by the popular tradition itself. Like so many broadsides, and so many of the action and national songs discussed in the next two chapters, its technique is one of formal parody. Its values are those of the more radical English and Scottish beggar songs, and its social attitude is a forerunner of *Love and Liberty*.

REFERENCES

1. See David Buchan, *The Ballad and the Folk* (London, 1972), *passim* and esp. pp. 166-73.
2. Pp. 134. For a definition of broadside, see Chapter I, pp. 5-6.
3. In *A Collection of broadsides and newspaper cuttings printed mainly in Edinburgh*, supposed to have been made by James Maidment. NLS, L.C. 1268.
4. The stanza made popular by Robert Sempill of Beltrees (?1595–1668) in *The Life and Death of Habbie Simson* and later known as the 'Burns Stanza'.
5. 1728; st. i.
6. In *The Pepys Ballads*, ed. H. E. Rollins, 8 vols. (Harvard, 1929–32), henceforth cited as *Pepys Bds.*, V, 300. See also Rollins, *The Pack of Autolycus* (Harvard, 1927), pp. 31-5.
7. E.g. 'Disny's Last Farewell' (*Pepys Bds.*, III, 127-30) where the protagonist is a traitor who had printed Monmouth's treasonable declaration in 1685, and the moral is 'be loyal to the powers that be'; 'The High-way Man's Advice to his brethren. Or, Nevison's Last Legacy to the Knights of the High-Padd; By way of Caution, to deter them from following their Un-lawful Enterprizes' (*Pepys Bds.*, III, 173), where the advice is 'lead an honest life'; and 'The Sorrowful Lamentation and last Farewel of John Price, alias Jack Ketch', in which Ketch is suitably overcome by remorse for his 'cruel and most barbarous murder of Mrs White'.
8. E.g. 'The Penitent Highwayman: or, The Last Farewel of Mr Biss, who was . . . Executed at Salisbury, on the 12th of March, 1695' (*Pepys Bds.*, VIII, 202), and a group of pieces on a certain Whitney, who was betrayed by his mistress (*Pepys Bds.*, VI, 310 ff.).
9. BM, 1346 m. 7 (32)
10. In *Old Scotch Ballads*, 1679–1830, NLS, Ry III a 10 (91). Line 1: 'My Countrey Men come here I'le tell . . .' For Madder and Thomas Green,

see Hugo Arnot, *A Collection and Abridgement of Celebrated Criminal Trials in Scotland from A.D. 1536 to 1784* (Glasgow, 1812), pp. 279-94.

11. NLS, Ry III a 10 (104).

12. *Ibid.* (103).

13. *Ibid.* (105).

14. See *Bagford Bds.*, ed. Ebsworth (Hertford, 1878), I, 101 ff.

15. *FSNE*, xliii, 2.

16. E.g. 'Dance of the Sevin deidly Synnis', lines 109 ff.

17. B.G., 'Anecdotes of J. Macpherson, the Ancient Freebooter and Musician' in *The New Monthly Magazine and Literary Journal* (Original Papers) I (1821), 1423. See also *The Scottish Songs*, ed. R. Chambers, 2 vols. (Edinburgh, 1829), I, 84-5 (n).

18. See 'Process Against the Egyptians at Banff' in *Miscellany of the Spalding Club*, III (Aberdeen, 1846), 175-91.

19. R. Chambers, *Domestic Annals of Scotland*, 2 vols. (Edinburgh and London, 1858): quoted from R. Chambers, *Domestic Annals of Scotland*, 1 vol. abridged edition (Edinburgh, 1885), pp. 374-8; Alexander, pp. 164-6.

20. *Scottish Songs*, 1776, I, 99-101.

21. W. Cramond, 'Macpherson the Freebooter' in *Annals of Banff*, 2 vols., New Spalding Club (Aberdeen, 1891), I, 112.

22. NLS, Ry III a 10 (29).

23. Kinsley, 196; *LLL*, 22.

24. NLS, Ry III a 1 (39), st. iv.

25. NLS, Ry III a 10 (36).

26. For another comment on this ballad, see W. Donaldson, '*Bonny Highland Laddie*: The Making of a Myth', *Scottish Literary Journal*, III (2), Dec. 1976, 30-50.

27. See below, pp. 188-9; Fletcher, *Political Works* (Glasgow, 1749,) pp 86, 100-1.

28. This ballad displays considerable artistry. Another, 'The Life and tragical End of Alastair Mackalaster, who was hanged at Aberdeen the 31st of May 1723' (NLS, Ry III a 10 (37)) is more representative of the bathos endemic in the type. Mackalaster, a native of Campbeltown, went around Scotland extorting 'Charity' by force. When apprehended in Aberdeen, he dug up the flags from his own prison floor and slew the keeper's servant when he came up with his food. When put in irons, he proceeded to 'sharpen the ends of them/Some others for to kill'. The poor wretch, tongue-tied before the judge, was deemed to have condemned himself by his silence, and was hanged by the neck 'betwixt the Cross and Trone/a Death too good for Bloody Men/Who of GOD have no fear'. The ballad, of course, is designed to be sung to the standard tune for this type, 'Captain Johnston's Lament'. For another example, see 'An Elegy On the never to be lamented Death of Mrs McLeod, who was Execute on *Wednesday* the 8th of *March*, 1727', which employs the Standard Habbie stanza in a poem that applies the comedy of the Mock Elegy to the hanging of a forger, thief and bawd (*LLL*, 18).

29. BM, 1346 m. 7. See above, p. 6.

30. BM, 1346 m. 7 (18), *LLL*, 20.

31. See my articles, 'Political and Protest Songs in eighteenth-century Scotland': Part I, 'Jacobite and anti-Jacobite' and Part II, 'Songs of the Left', in *Scottish Studies*, XIV (1970), 1-33, 105-31.

32. From three separate songs, quoted in *Scottish Studies*, XIV, 22-4.

33.   For scorn at the uninitiated, see the contempt for cowans (masons 'without the word') in st. iii of 'Let worthy brethren all combine' in *The Freemason's Pocket Companion. . . . The Second Edition* (Edinburgh, 1763), p. 215:

> Ye fools and Cowans, all who plot,
> For to obtain our mystery;
> Ye strive in vain, attempt it not,
> Such creatures never shall be free.

The persecution mania is reflected in st. i of 'In praise of Masonry' in *Wilson's Musical Miscellany* (Edinburgh, 1779), p. 307:

> In spite of the prejudic'd hate
> The vulgar against us retain,
> Let us new attachments create,
> And strengthen each link to our chain:
> Without ceasing, they slander us still,
> And fling at us many a joke;
> But those, who of Masons speak ill,
> Are not worthy their wrath to provoke.

34.   *The Freemason's Pocket Companion*, Edinburgh, 1761, pp. 81-2.

35.   Kinsley, 64, *LLL*, 44.

36.   *Pepys Bds*, III, 12-15.

37.   Burns, *Letters*, I, 246.

38.   BM, 1346 m. 7. One is called 'The Six Stages of Man's Life Displayed'; the other, entitled 'The Mourning Soul for Christ', has four stanzas with the refrain 'And why should I not mourn?', and one (the last) ending 'I'll never cease to mourn'.

39.   T. Durfey, *Wit and Mirth: or Pills to Purge Melancholy* (London, 1719-20: repr. New York, 1959), I, 294.

40.   Jeannie Robertson, *The Songs and Ballads of Scotland: Lord Donald, etc.*, Collector Records, London, 1960, JFS 4001.

41.   *The Universal Scots Songster* (Edinburgh, 1781); *LLL*, 37.

Chapter IX

THE ACTION LYRIC

Freemason, Whig and Jacobite writers were merely doing what came naturally to hundreds of people, ordinary and not so ordinary, who wrote in the popular medium. It was a medium which could be *used* by men and women in every walk of life to render their experiences, however slightly these might differ from their fellows'. Burns's first song, 'O, once I lov'd a bonnie lass',[1] is of this kind. It was written when he was about fifteen for Nelly Kirkpatrick, 'a bonnie, sweet, sonsie lass' of fourteen who was his neighbour in the harvest field, and as such it was both an outpouring of personal feeling and an incident in a conventional rural courtship where the young lover was expected to sing to his girl if he had any voice at all. The whole action began with Nelly herself singing to Robert a song composed in the locality by 'a small country laird's son, on one of his father's maids, with whom he was in love; and I saw no reason why I might not rhyme as well as he, for excepting shearing sheep and casting peats, his father living on the moors, he had no more Scholar-craft than I had'.[2] Burns's career provides a more telling example still. On Fasten-e'en (the evening before Lent) in 1785 he attended a traditional 'rockin' or small social gathering where women spun on the distaff or wove stockings while each member of the company sang a song in turn. One song pleased him above the rest, a rather Anglified piece called 'When I upon thy Bosom Lean', which he was told had been written by John Lapraik, an eccentric fellow who lived near Muirkirk;[3] and it is especially significant that Lapraik, a countryman, should have been attracted to the tea-table style. It looks as if by 1785 urban modes had become familiar enough to be made the vehicles of rural experience.

Nor were matters so different in the upper classes. The men and women of the very families whom we regard as typical of the Enlightenment were familiar with popular song, and moved from the tea-table to the plebeian with equal facility as subject and occasion demanded. We know that the upper classes performed both English and Scots songs from the beginning of the century – Ramsay of Ochtertyre, for instance, tell us that in the 1720s 'persons of wit and fashion . . . attempted to write Scottish poetry' and he makes an obvious comparison when he says that 'a song in the dialect of Cumberland or Somersetshire could never have been generally acceptable in England, because it was never spoken by people of fashion'.[4] The songs set down by Elizabeth St. Clair between 1771 and 1786 form perhaps the most remarkable record of the inter-action between popular tradition and upper-class individual talent.[5] Take, for example, this family song about the Hamiltons of Binning, dating from the early part of the century:[6]

> Some cry up little Hendy for this thing & for that
> And others James Dalrymple[7] tho' he be somewhat fat
> But of all the pretty Gentlemen of whom the town do tell
> Emelius Emelius he bears away the Bell. . . .
>
> Some cry up Binning's father for fighting at Dunblane,[8]
> But Binning says he shit his breeks for fear of being ta'en. . . .
>
> I have nae skill in politicks, therefore I'll had my tongue
> But you'll think I hae gab enough tho' I be somewhat young.
> But I'll tell you a secret my fairy Binning Elf
> Emelius Emelius I swear it is yourself.

It is a strangely intimate political-satirical song whose traditions are entirely popular, and despite the contemptuous 'shit his breeks' it is difficult not to feel that the author was a woman.

In the same manuscript there is a delightful parody on 'Willie's gane to Melville Castle' where the protagonist throws all the lassies into confusion when he is forced to leave for a watering place.[9] The women are all mentioned by name in succeeding stanzas – the Duchess of Ross, Miss Ross, Jeany Hamilton, Betty Ross, Betty Dalrymple, Betty Graham and Lady Betty Montgomerie. They all 'greet' when Billy leaves, then 'dry up their e'en' and give him a loud Huzza. The last two stanzas read:

> O Lady Ross sat knotting by
> And wondered at them a'
> Dear lasses trust in providence
> And ye's get Husbands a'.
>
> But what care we if he come back
> Or he return at a'
> For a' our Lasses shall be wives
> Or Billy comes frae spaw.

Another song, definitely by Alison Cockburn, applies the street-singer's style to an aristocratic occasion – a Ridotto at Holyrood

House.[10] Certain persons present are mentioned, and a peculiarity of each is detailed, just as in the crude popular style of the nineteenth-century bothy ballads. Take, for example, st. xii, on the writer of the manuscript herself:

> Bess St. Clair was there so charming & gay
> As red as the morning & bright as the day

Or st. xiv, most maliciously:

> Seven virgins laid hold of one man woes me
> Alas for the Ladies Monboddo was he.

The songs in the St. Clair MS. give us fascinating glimpses of Dukes and Duchesses, lawyers, politicians, upstarts enriched by the plunder of the Indies, virtuosi, improving landlords, philosophers and tart-tongued cultured hostesses—a society aware of the latest ideas in science and history, yet able without affectation or embarrassment to make use of popular traditions for satire or for expressing their personal feelings. They are the occasional poems of a small in-group who knew all about folk-ballads, who indeed collect them, and to whom it is the most natural thing in the world to write their own 'lyrics of action'. Not that occasional poems of the more formal and orthodox sort were lacking in Scotland. Sir William Bennet filled two notebooks with such compositions between 1702 and 1729, including the poems on his father's birthday that he turned out in eight successive years after 1702.[11] But he copied out at least one dramatic lyric written for what in effect was a school play, a translation of Terence's *Eunuchus*, 'as it was acted by the scholars of Kelso' on 18th August 1727. The lyric was inserted into the Prologue, 'spoken by a young Lady, fam'd for a fine voice, followed by a sett of others, all habited like Amazons, with gully knives in sheaths, hanging at their Girdles'. After the first stanza of the Prologue 'and betwixt all the stanzas following the Lady's did draw their gullys and flourished the same, round their heads, singing the Chorus to the Tune, of geld them, Lasses, geld them'. Like many great landed families the Clerks of Penicuik were deeply imbued with literary culture; there are a number of letters on poetical subjects in the Clerk correspondence, as well as such occasional poems as an anonymous Epithalamium on the marriage of John Clerk the younger to Lady Margaret Stewart[12] and Sir John's almost archetypal descriptive poem, *The Country Seat*.[13] But it is not so generally realised that the Clerks were probably as familiar with folk and popular song as the Elliots and Dalrymples of a later date.

As has been noted above in Chapter VII, all but the first stanza of
the text of 'O merry may the maid be that marries the miller'[14]
were apparently written by this same Sir John.

The Clerk papers even include an example of group (if not
communal) composition, dating from c. 1708. It is 'The Pennicuick
Song . . . about Nanse Weston . . . composed by John Clerk,
younger, of Pennicuick, Dr John Clerk, and Dr Arthure. . . . To its
proper tune composed by the same hands. First part for a grave tune
in common time'.[15] The manuscript is set out just like a printed
broadside and the piece is written in the broadside style, colloquial
and sometimes even Scottish in idiom, though not in dialect. The
rather English-sounding chorus almost sings itself:

> Come sit thou down my Nanse
>   thou art my only fancy
> The Lily & Rose they cheeks compose
>   and thy breath's sweat like a Tansy.

That the habit of singing occasional songs survived in the Clerk
family is evident from a manuscript volume of verses written
between 1755 and 1762, mainly in heroic couplets; it does contain,
however, one eight-lined stanza, in the folk-style, beginning 'Johnny
was the Lad of a' the men I saw'.[16]

James Boswell, in so many ways the embodiment of the contradictions in Scottish thought and behaviour during the second half
of the century, produced verses from his earliest years and was
familiar with both the English and Scottish popular traditions.
The Beggar's Opera was a favourite of his, and his imagination was
at one time haunted by the figure of Macheath. What could be
more natural than that he should himself attempt a ballad opera in
the manner of Gay? It was written in 1760 when he was trying to
gain his father's consent to a military career in the Guards and
significantly entitled *Give your son his Will*. The verses are competent
words for music, for they fit their tunes very well, as do most of
Boswell's later songs. He wrote on his own legal cases, as well as on
others that engaged his imagination like the famous Douglas Cause,
which he celebrated in Scots in a song beginning 'Gif ye a dainty
mailing want/And idleseat prefer to working'. He also wrote on his
amours ('A Crambo song on losing my mistress') and on that most
glorious of beings, himself (B——, a Song: To the Tune of 'Old Sir
Simon the King'), used in *The Beggar's Opera* and by Burns for the
Merry-Andrew's song in *Love and Liberty*. This last piece dates
from 1760, and was in all probability meant for the Soaping Club,

founded in Edinburgh after Boswell's return from his first visit to London, with the motto of 'Let every man soap his own beard' — i.e., do what he likes. It uses the popular lyric to deploy quite extra-ordinary powers of self-analysis; as Frederick Pottle has said, it is 'the best description extant of the mask which Boswell wore to make himself easy . . . no less a mask because it reproduced to some extent his natural features':[17]

> B[oswell], of Soapers the King,
>   On Tuesday's at Thom's does appear,
> And when he does talk or does sing,
>   To him ne'er a one can come near.
> For he talks with such ease and such grace,
>   That all charm'd to attention we sit,
> And he sings with so comic a face
>   That our sides are just ready to split.
>
> B[oswell] is modest enough,
>   Himself not quite Phoebus he thinks;
> He never does flourish with snuff,
>   And hock is the liquor he drinks. . . .
>
> B[oswell] is pleasant and gay,
>   For frolic by nature design'd,
> And heedlessly rattles away
>   When the company is to his mind.
> This maxim he says you may see,
>   We can never have corn without chaff;
> So not a bent sixpence cares he,
>   Whether *with* him or *at* him you laugh.
>
> B[oswell] does women adore
>   And never once means to deceive
> He's in love with at least half a score;
>   If they're serious he smiles in his sleeve.
> He has all the bright fancy of youth
>   With the judgment of forty-and-five;
> In short, to declare the plain truth,
>   There is no better fellow alive.[18]
>   (sts. i, ii lines 1-4, iii, iv)

In other songs Boswell uses the popular lyric for a diametrically opposite purpose, objective not subjective, to hit off — crudely no doubt, but with the same cast and powers of mind that make him the finest of all biographers — the character of others:

(1)   Of all the judges in the land
I surely must be held the chief,
For, none so cleverly can hang
A bloody murderer or thief. . . .

Tweedle, tweedle, tweedle didum,
Up with the Justiciary Court!
('Song on the Character of Lord Kames', dated 1766, st. i)[19]

(2)   My name is J[oc]k M[ille]r, I care not who knows it,
For I am the laird of the lands of Glenlee,
And I am the man that can parritch and brose it,
And drink strong liquors, if you'll keep me free.
I, J[ock]y [Mille]r, was there e'er such another,
I'm laird of Glenlee, Lord Justice Clerk's Brother,
And twenty fat wethers like rabbits I'll smother,
And eat them myself at the mill of Glenlee.
('The Laird of Glenlee', Tune *Langolee*, st. i)[20]

It was in 1776 that Boswell was involved in a broadside-type concoction called 'The Justiciary Garland', featuring the luminaries of the Scottish law-courts in exactly the same way as Alison Cockburn treated aristocratic women, mentioning each by name and briefly indicating their peculiarities: Auchinleck (Boswell's own father), Macqueen (later Lord Braxfield), Kames, Hailes, Dundas, and Monboddo are only a few of the names that crop up.[21] Among the Boswell papers at Yale are plans for a ballad opera on a Scottish law theme, with songs assigned to many of the same characters; it is clear that the Garland records a considerable part of this *Justiciary Opera*. The Prisoners' Chorus, quoted here as a sample, asks for banishment in these terms:

O send us owr the wide seas
Our ain kind Lordies
To the Plantations where you please
Our ain kind Lordies;
For gang this trial as it will
Our ain kind Lordies
In Scotland we can fare but ill
Our ain kind Lordies.[22]

The tunes to which the songs in *The Justiciary Opera* are directed to be sung are in the main Scottish — 'Mary Scott the Flower of Yarrow', 'Tarry Woo', 'Coming through the Broom', 'Saw ye my Father', 'Fie let us a' to the Wedding', 'Here awa' there awa' ',

'Fie on the Wars', 'Dusty Miller', 'Maggie Lauder', 'John Anderson, my Jo' and 'Aiken Drum'. This proves both Boswell's extensive knowledge of his country's popular song, and the legal profession's familiarity with these same tunes and their original words.

Among the Yale MSS. two songs in Boswell's handwriting that do not appear to be connected with the later ballad-opera are worth reproducing for the light they cast on this Anglo-Scot's creative familiarity with the folk mode. The first, a dialogue between a man and a woman, is obviously meant to go to the tune 'Haud awa frae me Donald':

He

There's mony a man that taks his Wife
And licks her wi' a rung, Jo
But I'se tak a contrairy gate
And lick you wi' my tongue, Jo.

She

O lick awa lick awa
Lick awa my Dearie
Ye winna hurt my winsom mou
Tho ye lick till ye be weary.[23]

The second is entitled 'Cut him down Susie':

Cut him down Susie,
Haste ye wi your gully knife
Ye'se get him for your ain Gudeman
Gin ye contrive to save his life.

Cut him down and tak him hame
And send for folk to dance and sing
And pit your arms about the neck
That on the gallows tree did hing.[24]

When Boswell settled down as a man of law in Scotland he founded a family that shared his enthusiasm for Scottish song. He proudly noted in his journal that his daughter could chant half a dozen tunes before she could speak; significantly, none of those he names are English. A final piece of evidence: Boswell's son, James the Younger, was as musical as Veronica and at the age of twelve (in 1790–1) composed his own ballad-opera with twenty-two songs, for performance by the family circle. Like his father's in *Give your Son his Will* and *The Justiciary Opera*, young Jamie's lyrics are to specific tunes, most of them Scottish (e.g. 'Dumbarton Drums', 'Over the water to Charlie', 'Birks of Endermay'). Thus the records of the Boswell family, just like the deductions that can be made from the St. Clair MS., bear out what can be gleaned from Captain Topham, Ramsay of Ochtertyre, and other memoir-writers about the rôle of sung lyric in upper class households.

We have seen that the Clerk family's 'Pennicuick Song about Nanse Weston' seems to have been produced in an extraordinary outburst of group spontaneity. Some at least of *The Justiciary Opera* was written in the same way, for Boswell notes on 17th March 1778: 'Crosbie and I amused ourselves at times during this journey with making more of *The Justiciary Opera*, adapting the proceedings of the Criminal Court to tunes and putting them in rhyme, with much merriment produced by parody and ludicrous contrasts of various kinds'. The opera had been begun two years before by Andrew Crosbie, John Maclaurin (later Lord Dreghorn), and Boswell, the occasion being the acquittal of certain clients of theirs. Boswell writes on 4th March 1776 that they 'went to eat a beefsteak at Princes Street Coffee-house. We grew exceedingly merry; and who begun it I cannot say. But we three advocates made a number of sketches of songs, by way of a Criminal Opera. . . . Such ludicrous extravagance diverted us extremely. We laughed and sung and drank claret till past eleven at night. Though I drank above two bottles I was not at all intoxicated, which was strange.'[25]

Boswell, the Clerks of Penicuik, Elizabeth St. Clair, Alison Rutherford, the Dalrymples and their circle — all these, we have suggested, did not differ in their song writing from many humbler amateurs who used the lyric to help in the business of daily living. How, then, did their action songs contrast with what have been termed national songs — the deliberate, creative and systematic attempt by the professionals, Ramsay and Burns and a number of lesser men and women, to produce a new corpus of song for the whole people of Scotland by a combination of purposive editing and the fitting of new words to old tunes? The answer is that there is no absolute contrast; although action songs were private and familial whereas national songs were intended for a wider public, yet many of the finest national songs were, to begin with, personal or occasional. If there is a difference of kind rather than degree, it is that Ramsay and Burns were truly dedicated, having an essentially dramatic attitude to their material; and that they saw themselves as (in a modern metaphor) cultural engineers, consciously preserving and recreating the nation's songs. In his study of music and society in eighteenth-century Scotland, David Johnson draws attention to the curious fact that Ramsay wrote a Scots Cantata, 'The Tune after the Italian Manner, compos'd by Signior Lorenzo Bocchi', the words published in Vol. I of the *Tea-Table Miscellany* in 1723 and — almost simultaneously — the 'Elegy on Patie Birnie' attacking classical music and poking fun at *castrati* singers. He comments: 'Allan Ramsay's position was undecided, to say the least'.[26] But it is not necessarily a question of the poet's own consciously held attitude as man and citizen. Ramsay himself had surely no position; in each of these pieces he, or his *persona*, was adopting a rôle; as Burns so often did, he wrote from behind a mask. Some have seen in Ramsay's songs a missionary purpose: to improve and modernise the taste of Edinburgh and the Scottish provinces as Addison and Steele's essays had aimed to refine the English middle-classes a couple of decades earlier. But even the lyrics which most clearly fulfil a propagandist purpose are dramatic. 'Love inviting Reason' is written from the point of view of a 'true' country laird scorned by a girl who has fallen for urban fashions and fripperies — lap-dogs, monkeys, new manteaus and Flanders lace, and who is about to jilt him for a Frenchified popinjay. Its real interest is in contrasts of character and of attitudes *behind* character, in a conflict between reason and affectation:

> Rouze up thy reason, my beautifu' *Annie*,
>   And dinna prefer a paroquet to me;
> O! as thou art bonny, be prudent and cany,
>   And think on thy *Jamie* wha doats upon thee
> (st. ii, lines 5-8)[27]

It is no doubt proper to sneer at such songs. Ramsay was quite lacking in self-criticism, and was sometimes more uncertain in setting English words to Scots tunes than his collaborators Hamilton of Bangour or Robert Crawford. But, like Burns after him, he experimented on occasion with quite other traditions than those of the Tea-Table or the pseudo-Scots songs of Durfey; he was as much a laureate of the streets as of the drawing-room, and in any full assessment the consciously literary *Gentle Shepherd* and the anti-quarian *Ever-Green* should be balanced against the songs hawked for a penny among market throngs. He could write in a derivative of the folk-style, best seen in 'Fair Widow are ye Waking', the source of Burns's 'Wha is that at my bower-door?':

> O wha's that at my chamber door?
>   'Fair widow, are ye wawkin?'
> Auld carle, your suit give o'er,
>   Your love lyes a' in tawking.

Gi'e me a lad that's young and tight,
   Sweet like an *April* meadow;
'Tis sic as he can bless the sight,
   And bosom of a widow.

'O widow, wilt thou let me in,
   I'm pawky, wise, and thrifty,
And come of a right gentle kin;
   I'm little mair than fifty.'
Daft carle, dit your mouth,
   What signifies how pawky,
Or gentle born ye be, – bot youth?
   In love you're but a gawky.

'Then, widow, let these guineas speak,
   That powerfully plead clinkan,
And if they fail, my mouth I'll steek,
   And nae mair love will think on.'
These court indeed, I maun confess,
   I think they make you young, Sir,
And ten times better can express
   Affection, than your tongue, Sir.[28]

English expressions like 'sight and bosom of a widow', 'ten times better can express affection than your tongue, sir' are integrated into the surrounding vernacular Scots in a natural and acceptable way: only the formula 'young and tight' grates on a modern ear, perhaps because the sense of 'tight' as 'well-proportioned' is quite obsolete. 'Bessie Bell and Mary Gray',[29] on the theme of 'How happy could I be with either', is less successful. Classical allusions are not fully integrated with the Scots ('When Phoebus starts frae Thetis' lap', 'O Jove, she's like thy Pallas'), and there is an even more unfortunate use of the word 'tight' in one line – 'She blooming, tight and tall is'. But the assured last stanza points forward to Burns's later successes in the dramatic lyric, though some may jib at its rather complacent air of male superiority:

Dear *Bessy Bell* and *Mary Gray*,
   Ye unco sair oppress us;
Our fancies jee between you twa,
   Ye are sic bonny lasses:
Wae's me! for baith I canna get,
   To ane by law we're stented;
Then I'll draw cuts, and take my fate,
   And be with one contented.

But there are no flaws in 'Up in the Air':

> Now the sun's gane out o' sight,
>   Beet the ingle, and snuff the light;
> In glens the fairies skip and dance,
>   And witches wallop o'er to *France*.
>   Up in the air
>   On my bonny grey mare,
>   And I see her yet, and I see her yet.
>   Up in, etc.
>
> The wind's drifting hail and sna',
>   O'er frozen hags, like a foot-ba';
> Nae starns keek thro' th'azure slit,
>   'Tis cauld, and mirk as ony pit.
>   The man i' the moon
>   Is carousing aboon;
>   D'ye see, d'ye see, d'yee see him yet?
>   The man, etc.
>
> Take your glass to clear your een,
>   'Tis the elixir heals the spleen,
> Baith wit and mirth it will inspire,
>   And gently puffs the lover's fire.
>   Up in the air,
>   It drives away care;
>   Ha'e wi' ye, ha'e wi' ye, and ha'e wi' ye, lads, yet.
>   Up in, etc.
>
> Steek the doors, keep out the frost;
>   Come, Willie, gi's about your toast;
> Til't, lads, and lilt it out,
>   And let us ha'e a blythsome bout.
>   Up wi't there, there,
>   Dinna cheat, but drink fair:
>   Huzza, huzza, and huzza, lads, yet.
>   Up wi't, etc.[30]

The song has real development and several delightful touches of surprise. It begins just after sunset, with a background of vigorous rural folk-lore that anticipates Hogg's comic use of the super-natural a hundred years later. The second stanza makes its un-obtrusive transition to drink *via* another folklore motif, the man in the moon; only with the third stanza do we fully realise that it is a

drinking-song we are hearing, that 'up witches' has been transformed into 'up glasses'. By the final stanza, all dangers, whether
from witches or winter weather, are forgotten in the warm fellowship
of the drinkers. For once Ramsay has proved himself a gifted artist in
popular song, uniting antiquarian folk-lore with other traditions,
including the anacreontic strain treated in Chapter VII ('And
gently puffs the lover's fire'). If any piece deserves to be called a truly
'national' song, it is 'Up in the Air'.

National songs, once they appear, become part of the general
medium, to be used and transformed, in whole or in part, by later
writers for occasional purposes. For an instance we need go no
further than Allan Ramsay himself, who transformed the almost
classical 'Fy, let us a' to the bridal'[31] into a satire on extreme
presbyterianism that anticipates Burns's religious satires, in 'The
Marrow Ballad: On seeing a strolling congregation going to a
field meeting, May 9th, 1738'.[32] Here a writer of national song is
making a parody on a 'classic' that fits in perfectly with the objects
and moods of *broadside* satire, as examined in the previous chapter.
A more central illustration of the links between 'national' and
'action' song is provided by 'The Flowers of the Forest'. The tune
came first. The old air was locked away in the Skene MS. (*c*.1630)
and not printed until 1838, but it survived in oral transmission and
became transformed into an eighteenth-century tune, published by
Oswald in the seventeen-fifties and in McGibbon's Scots Tunes
(1768).[33] There are three sets of words to it, all written at about the
same time by ladies who knew each other. Although it is by no
means certain that the best known set, 'I've heard of a lilting at our
ewes' milking', composed *c*. 1755 by Jean Elliot (1727–1805), sister
of Hume's friend Sir Gilbert Elliot of Minto, is the earliest, it is
convenient to take it first because it probably uses *two* lines of the
lost traditional song:

> I've heard of a lilting at our ewes' milking . . .
> The flowers of the forest that are wede away.

Miss Elliot wrote it as a literary exercise when her father, the Lord
Justice-Clerk of Scotland, bet her that she could not write a ballad
on the Battle of Flodden; it was published in 1769 in Herd's *Scots
Songs* (p. 338), and thought by many to be an old song, more or less
contemporary with the battle. Its inspiration is patriotic and
antiquarian; its language is Scots; and it is shot through with that
nostalgia which has coloured Scottish attitudes to lost causes from
that day to this:

O dool for the order sent our lads to the border!
    The English for ance by guile gat the day;
The Flower of the forest that ay shone the foremost,
    The prime of our land lyes cauld in the clay.

We'll hear nae mair lilting at our ewes milking,
    The women and bairns are dowie and wae,
Sighing and moaning on ilka green loaning,
    Since our braw foresters are a' wede away.

                                             (sts. v, vi)

The second set, by Alison Cockburn (Elizabeth St. Clair's friend),
beginning 'I've seen the smiling of fortune beguiling', was first
published in *A Choice Collection of Scots and English Songs* (Edinburgh,
1764), p. 279. Scott thought its subject was the depopulation of
Ettrick Forest, but Chambers tells us that the song referred to a
commercial disaster, 'a crisis of a monetary nature, when seven
good lairds of the Forest were reduced to insolvency, in consequence
of imprudent speculations':

        I've seen the forest
        Adorn'd the foremost
    With flowers of the fairest, most pleasant and gay;
        Sae bonny was their blooming,
        Their scent the air perfuming;
    But now they are wither'd and weeded away.

If Chambers is right, Mrs Cockburn's inspiration was local, but she
successfully generalised it to make it fit any disaster involving the
death or exile of a community's leaders. It, too, became a national
song, for it seems for a time to have been more popular than
'I've heard of a lilting'.[34]
    A third set (l. 1 'Adieu! ye streams that smoothly glide'), by
Anne Home (1742–1821), who later married Dr John Hunter the
celebrated anatomist, was printed in *The Charmer* Vol. I (Edinburgh,
1765, p. 361) and *The Lark* (Edinburgh, 1765, p. 10). Its subject
is entirely personal; it is a lament, not for a local community or a
nation's chivalry, but for one young man who has been drowned,
expressed not unpleasantly in conventional pastoral English. Anne
Home's song, too, became a national one in its own day. It was
printed in ten Scottish miscellanies between 1765 and 1786 (more
frequently, in fact, than 'I've heard of a lilting') and all three sets
achieved the distinction of being included in *The Scots Musical
Museum*.
    Oral composition (re-creation in performance), the essence of

folk-song, is replaced by parody — which may be serious as well as comic — in broadside song; and parody, as we have just seen, is also one feature of a live tradition of *national* song. 'The Broadswords of Old Scotland'[35] is a case in point. It ironically parodies Fielding's 'The Roast Beef of Old England', and may also be in attitude a direct ancestor of Burns's *Scots Wha Hae*:

> The Romans, the Picts, and the Old Britons too,
> Us by friend and by guile, did attempt to subdue;
> But their schemes proved abortive, while we did prove true.
> O the broad swords of Old Scotland,
> And O the Old Scottish broad-swords. . . .
>
> Our Scottish ancestors were valiant and bold,
> In learning ne'er beat, nor in battle controul'd;
> But now — shall I name it? — alas, — we're all sold
> O the broad-swords, etc.
>
> (sts. ii, vi)

Like many Jacobite art lyrics, 'The Broadswords of Old Scotland' conveys the message that, at the union of 1707 and after, Scotland was 'sold' by the Whigs. But its first appearance in a song book was over thirty years after the Forty-five and nearly seventy years after the Union. Almost immediately, a second parody, deriving from the first, was printed in Aberdeen, and entitled *The Scottish Kail Brose*:

> When our ancient forefathers agreed wi 'the laird,
> For a wee piece grund to be a kail-yard,
> It was to the brose that they paid their regard;
> O! the kail brose of auld Scotland;
> And O! for the Scottish kail brose. . . .
>
> Our sodgers were drest in their kilts and short hose,
> With bonnet and belt which their dress did compose,
> With a bag of oatmeal on their back to be brose.
> O! the kail brose, etc. . . .
>
> But when we remember the English, our foes,
> Our ancestors beat them wi' very few blows;
> John Bull oft cried, O! let us rin — they've got brose;
> O! the kail brose, etc.
>
> But, now that the thistle is joined to the rose,
> And the English nae longer are counted our foes,
> We've lost a good deal of our relish for brose;
> O! the kail brose, etc.

Yet each true-hearted Scotchman by nature jocose,
Likes always to feast on a cog o' guid brose,
And thanks be to Heaven we've plenty of those.
   O! the kail brose, etc.

(sts. i, iii, v-vii)[36]

What a falling off is here! The writer is closer in spirit to the real nature of the Scottish compromise — reluctantly accepted Union with England and regret for vanished independence, and there is also a nineteenth-century, 'kailyard' quality about the sentiment. But the main point remains valid: previous national songs are being used in a continuing process, each building on its predecessors.

In the thirty years or so before Burns, minor versifiers continued the practice; and one major poet, Robert Fergusson, who gave us his two masterly stanzas of 'The Lee Rigg',[37] while the genre-piece 'Hallow Fair', beginning 'There's fouth of braw Jockies and Jennys' and published by David Herd in 1776,[38] has also been ascribed to him. Like Ramsay's 'Marrow-Ballad', considered earlier in this chapter, it was written for that ever-popular tune 'Fy, let us a' to the bridal'. Both these pieces are in vernacular Scots. Fergusson's drinking songs for the Cape Club[39] (occasional-action rather than national songs) employed either a much thinner conversational Scots or else Scots-English, while the lyrics which he added to the Edinburgh performance of Arne's *Artaxerxes* on 31st July and 5th August 1769 were in the most unexceptionable Augustan English. Exactly the same linguistic and cultural variations are shown by the lesser writers of these decades.

English pastoral modes were naturalised and developed by a number of cultivated men, such as Sir Gilbert Elliot of Minto[40] ('My sheep I neglected, I lost my sheep-hook', *The Charmer*, I, 1749); Dr Austin ('For lack of gold she's left me, O'), a song at once conventional and occasional, about Jean Drummond who threw him over for the Duke of Atholl (*The Charmer*, II, 1751); William Falconer ('The Smiling plains, profusely gay'), an elegantly wrought song about separation, in Ruddiman's *Edinburgh Weekly Magazine* December 1773 and *The Charmer*, II, 1782; the Rev. John Logan (1749–1788), who sang the praises of the Esk in terms reminiscent of Gray's 'Elegy' ('A Helen has pined in the grove;/ A Homer has wanted his name'), John Lowe (1750–98), whose 'Mary's Dream', an effectively dramatic lyric about a drowned lover's ghost, was published in the 1791 edition of Herd's *Scottish Songs*; and Dr Thomas Blacklock (1721–91), notorious for his advice to Burns that he should concentrate on English. Of the authors just listed, only Blacklock can be counted professional; and even he (despite the opprobrium which Burnsians cast upon his polite English) was able to use the neo-classic parts of the song-culture to some effect in his marry-in-haste-and-repent-at-leisure song 'The Wedding Day' (*The Nightingale*, 1776, p. 200):

> What would I give for a wedding day!
> Who would not wish for a wedding day!
> Wealth and ambition, I'd toss ye away,
> With all ye can boast, for a wedding day. . . .
>
> Horns are the gift of a wedding day;
> Want and a scold crown a wedding day;
> Happy the gallant who, wise when he may,
> Prefers a stout rope to a wedding day
>
> (lines 5-8, 29-32)

The Scots part of the song-culture, as well as the neo-classical, was in continuous use for pastoral during the half-century which followed *The Gentle Shepherd*—for example by the author of the comic broadside-type 'Nae dominies for me, laddie' (ascribed by Robert Chambers to the Rev. Nathaniel Mackay of Crossmichael, Kirkcudbright—d. 1781, and by David Laing to the Rev. John Forbes of Deer, Aberdeenshire—d. 1769); by the Rev. James Muirhead (1742–1808), minister of Urr in Galloway, whose 'Bess the Gawkie' is a rather painfully kailyardish comedy of rural courtship; by the ballad editor John Pinkerton in his pseudo-antique lament of a girl for her dead lover, 'Bothwell Bank'; by the author of the couthily domestic 'There's nae luck about the house' sometimes ascribed to the professional writer William Julius Mickle, and sometimes to the amateur Mrs Jean Adams, schoolmistress of Crawford's Dyke, near Greenock (*c.* 1772); by Alexander Ross, schoolmaster of Lochlee, Forfarshire (d. 1783), particularly in 'The Spinnin o't', a dialect character-song with satirical undertones, and in 'The Bridal', another dialect piece celebrating marriage as a joy for the whole rural community; and, finally, by the Rev. John Skinner (1721–1807), episcopal minister of Longside near Peterhead in Buchan, whose 'Tullochgorum', termed by Burns 'the best Scotch song Scotland ever saw' was a favourite all over the lowlands. More than most of Burns's predecessors, Skinner wrote for instrumental tunes, rather than the tunes of older songs, and his inspiration was often satirical; a favourite theme was '*O tempora, O mores*', the decline from ancient virtues. 'A Song on the times' treats this stock subject in vigorous English; 'Old Age' sings of the virtues of a couple who are happy though poor, from a point

of view very like Burns's in 'The Twa Dogs', though Skinner also
stresses the continuity of the generations; the 'Marquis's Reel' —
characteristically, to a dance tune — is an occasional 'action' piece
for a family celebration at Castle Gordon; the 'Ewie wi' the Crookit
Horn' is at one level a lyrical mock elegy on an animal, at another
a humorous poem about a whisky still. Finally, 'Lizy Liberty'
— a late piece — shows the tradition used to the full for political
purposes, exactly as Ramsay used it for religious satire in the
'Marrow Ballad'.[41] Not only does Skinner write for the tune of
'There's ower many wooing at her', but he expects his audience to
be aware of the words of the older song that he is parodying:

> Now Lawrie French has ta'en the whim,
>   To toss his airs, and frisk about her,
> And Malcolm Fleming puffs and swears
>   He disna value life without her
>   Wooing at her, fain wad ha'e her,
>   Courting at, but canna get her;
>   Bonnie Lizy Liberty,
>   There's o'er mony wooing at her. . . .
>
> Ah! Lawrie, ye've debauch'd the lass,
>   Wi' vile new-fangled tricks ye've played her;
> Deprav'd her morals; — like an ass,
>   Ye've courted her, and syne betray'd her.
>   Wi' hanging of her, burning of her,
>   Cutting, hacking, slashing at her;
>   Bonnie Lizy Liberty,
>   May ban the day ye ettled at her.

By 1785-6, when Burns came upon the scene, all the various
strands of the common medium, folk and 'national', broadside and
'art', Scots and English, were being used in Scotland for the
composition of private, occasional, action and 'national' lyrics.
Skinner's songs, indeed, sum up in themselves the unity that had
been achieved. The words are always perfectly accommodated to
the tunes; judged as a poetic craftsman purely, he is a master of
verse technique; when he writes entirely in Scots-English, he is as
assured as when he is employing mainly the vernacular; and he can
modulate with ease from the one language to the other:

> (1)   But for the dirty, fawning fool,
>   Who wants to be oppression's tool,
>   May envy gnaw his rotten soul,
>   And discontent devour him!

> May dool and sorrow be his chance,
> Dool and sorrow, dool and sorrow,
> May dool and sorrow be his chance,
>   And nane say, Wae's me for 'im!
>
> ('Tullochgorum', st. vi, lines 1-8)

(2)   Lay aside your sour grimaces
>   Clouded brows and drumlie faces,
>   Look about and see their Graces,
>   How they smile delighted:
>   Now's the season to be merry
>   Hang the thoughts of Charon's ferry,
>   Time enough to come camsterry,
>   When we're auld and doited.
>
> ('The Marquis's Reel', st. ii)

It is tempting to draw a parallel with the present day. In Scotland now, thanks to the achievements of Hugh MacDiarmid and those who wrote in Scots from the nineteen-twenties to the nineteen-fifties, and of Edwin Muir and his followers in English, it is now possible for a poet unselfconsciously to choose either Scots or English for a work of any length or complexity, depending on the natural bent of his mind. By the last quarter of the eighteenth century in Scotland a similarly wide choice was open to the writer of sung lyrics or of comic and satirical verse, but not (if there were any such 'benorth the Tweed') to the philosophical, tragic or epic poet. And the song-writer had yet another choice open to him. Not only could he move from one language to another within the same song, he could also move from one stratum of the common lyrical heritage, from folk to broadside to tea-table to the imitation of aristocratic and classical models. This follows from the comprehensive nature of the song-culture in Scotland.

REFERENCES

1. Kinsley, 1.
2. To Dr Moore, *Letters*, I, 108.
3. My *Burns*, pp. 1-2, 88-9. Lapraik had once been a small laird.
4. Ramsay of Ochtertyre, I, 19.
5. For Elizabeth St. Clair, see above, p. 5.
6. St. Clair MS., p. 119. If it is by Alison Cockburn (*née* Rutherford), it must have been written in her girlhood when the memory of the fifteen was fairly fresh. She was born in 1712.
7. Presumably the second son of Lord Stair (fl.1714), and not Elizabeth St. Clair's husband.

8. *I.e.*, Sheriffmuir (1715).
9. P. 122.
10. Pp. 198-201.
11. Scottish Record Office, GD 205/Box 38, portfolio 8.
12. SRO, GD 18/4396.
13. SRO, GD/18/4404/1/2/3.
14. Above, p. 126.
15. SRO, GD 18/4396.
16. SRO, GD 18/4423, p. 43.
17. F. A. Pottle, *Boswell: The Earlier Years*, p. 70.
18. *A Collection of Original Poems by Scotch Gentlemen*, II (Edinburgh, 1762), 90.
19. Printed in F. A. Pottle, 'Three new legal ballads by James Boswell', *Juridical Review*, XXXVII (1925), 201-11, and in J. Werner, *Boswell's Book of Bad Verse* (London, 1974), p. 92.
20. In *A Collection of Songs and Poems on Several Occasions by Isabel Pagan* (Glasgow, 1803), pp. 24-6: this stanza quoted in F. A. Pottle, *The Literary Career of James Boswell* (Oxford, 1929), p. 269. 'The Laird of Glenlee was John Miller, elder brother of Thomas Miller, Lord Justice Clerk, later Lord President and a baronet, a person whom Boswell disliked because of his Hamiltonian bias in the Douglas Cause, and whom he found occasion to attack anonymously in the newspapers because of his refusal to recommend a pardon for a certain John Reid, sentenced to be hanged for sheep-stealing' (*Ibid.*, p. 268).
21. A later text, 'The Court of Session Garland, By James Boswell, Esq. Tune —Logan Water', was published in Robert Chambers' *Traditions of Edinburgh* (1825). See F. A. Pottle, *op. cit.*, pp. 273-4.
22. Boswell MSS., Yale University Library.
23. *Ibid.*
24. *Ibid.*, LLL, 19.
25. *Boswell: The Ominous Years, 1774–1776*, ed. C. Ryskamp and F. A. Pottle, p. 244. The skit was published in part by Sir Alexander Boswell in *Songs in the Justiciary Opera* (1816), but with additions. Until the practice died out in the mid-nineteenth century the opera was regularly performed, with each legal generation making its own topical alterations.
26. D. Johnson, *Music and Society in Lowland Scotland in the Eighteenth Century*, p. 192.
27. *TTM*, I: (1740), 32.
28. *TTM*, II: (1740), 154; *LLL*, 84. For the Burns song, see Kinsley, 356.
29. *TTM*, I: (1740), 53.
30. *TTM*, II: (1740), 73.
31. *TTM*, I: (1740), 82.
32. See *Poems by Allan Ramsay and Robert Fergusson*, ed. A. M. Kinghorn and A. Law (Edinburgh, 1974), henceforth cited as Ramsay-Fergusson, p. 116.
33. Burns, *Notes*, p. 113.
34. It seems to have been published in seventeen song-books printed in Scotland between 1764 and 1786, compared with only six appearances of Jane Elliot's text in these miscellanies.
35. *The Nightingale* (Edinburgh, 1776), p. 199; Hogg, *Jacobite Relics* (1819: repr. 1874), I, 78. Hogg claims it is 'said to have been written by an English gentleman who was sojourning here after the time of the Union, and witnesses the feelings of the country-people on that occasion. The nationality of the song has made it a favourite, although the air be originally an English one' (I, 260).

36. *The Songs of Scotland* (3rd edn., Glasgow, 1893), pp. 188-9.
37. Ramsay-Fergusson, p. 141, *LLL*, 124.
38. Herd (1776), II, 169-71. This must not be confused with the better-known poem of the same title, beginning 'At Hallowmas, whan nights grow lang' (Ramsay-Fergusson, pp. 132-7), which is definitely by Fergusson.
39. Above, p. 139.
40. The brother of Jane Elliot whose set of 'The Flowers of the Forest' has been considered above. That 'My sheep I neglected' achieved national status by the early nineteenth century is indicated by an allusion in Scott, *Lay of the Last Minstrel*, Canto i, lines 295-8. See my note in Scott, *Selected Poems* (Oxford, 1972), p. 283.
41. Texts of these songs may be found in *A Miscellaneous Collection of Fugitive Pieces of Poetry, by the late Reverend John Skinner . . . Volume III of his Posthumous Works* (Edinburgh, 1809), pp. 135-67. The texts cited here are from *The Songs of Scotland* (Paisley and London, 1893), pp. 177-87.

Chapter X

BURNS, LOVE AND LIBERTY

Skinner's achievements in one or two songs were equalled or surpassed by Burns in some three hundred and thirty which he either
wrote outright or refurbished, however slightly, in the editing.
Burns was the Allan Ramsay of the end of the century, but a Ramsay
able to take advantage of all the developments in popular song
during the previous seventy years. He was much more successful
than Ramsay at fitting new words to old tunes, vocal or instrumental, and he was also the most assiduous collector of his day – a
practising folk-lorist deeply influenced by enlightenment antiquar-
ianism.[1] And he was also the masterly exponent in practice of an
aesthetic of music and words which had been developing in Britain
from Dryden onwards, and which fitted in with current European
trends, particularly with some of Rousseau's speculations about
music.[2] He both summed up the past and, through the content of
his songs, their simplicity and intense personal emotion, deeply influenced the romantic poets of the three or four decades after his death.

In the Preface to the Kilmarnock edition Burns described a kind
of composition that did not differ in kind, though it did in quality,
from that practised by other Scots of his century – 'he sings the
sentiments and manners he felt and saw in himself and his rustic
compeers around him'. This is what John Lapraik and David Sillar
had done, and the author of Nelly Kirkpatrick's harvest song.
With the substitution of aristocratic or urban for rustic, it is what
Alison Cockburn, Boswell and the Clerks of Penicuik had achieved
for their own circles, and equally it is how the in-group Jacobites,
anti-Jacobites and Freemasons had reacted. Yet Burns's lyric range
was far wider than theirs, and he excelled in all types of lyric current
during the century. 'A Highland Lad my love was born'[3] and
'McPherson's Farewell'[4] are the apotheosis of the broadside or stall-
type; 'Comin thro' the rye'[5] of the pure folk-song; 'O Willie brew'd
a peck o' maut',[6] of the composed bacchanalian; 'To the weaver's
gin ye go'[7] and 'My Collier laddie'[8] of the love-song which is also a
craft-song; 'There's news, lasses, news'[9] and 'O can ye labor lea'[10]
of the song uniting love, labour and sex; 'Clarinda, mistress of my

soul'[11] of the artificial love-lyric; 'The Lass that made the Bed'[12] of an intensely sensual love; 'Yestreen I had a pint of wine'[13] of physical passion flaunting all social convention and 'The rantin Dog the Daddie o't'[14] of the deep devotion that can grow out of such a flaunting; 'On a bank of flowers in a summer's day'[15] of the artificial pastoral rencontre; 'My Lord a hunting he is gane'[16] of the Lady Chatterley situation; 'O let me in this ae night'[17] of the love-dialogue and the night-visit; 'Corn Rigs'[18] of passionate rustic courtship; 'Duncan Gray'[19] and 'Last May a braw wooer'[20] of love's comedy; 'Sic a wife as Willie's wife'[21] of *mal-marié(e)* comedy; 'O poortith cauld, and restless love'[22] of the song based on the opposition between love and money; 'The Fornicator'[23] of the opposition between sex and the Kirk; 'My love she's but a lassie yet'[24] of alcohol as the solace for a jilted lover; 'I hae been at Crookieden'[25] of Jacobite political pastiche; 'Strathallan's Lament'[26] of the dramatic Jacobite art-lyric; 'O'er the water to Charlie'[27] of the simple, compressed song of loyalty for the Stewart cause; 'Ye sons of old Killie'[28] of masonic minstrelsy; the Heron election-ballads of ephemeral propagandist parodies;[29] 'Scots wha hae'[30] of the antiquarian patriotic song with revolutionary overtones; 'Is there, for honest poverty'[31] of the songs inspired by the French revolution and Tom Paine's *Rights of Man*; 'Does haughty Gaul invasion threat?'[32] of the progressive patriotic song; and 'As I stood by yon roofless tower'[33] of the lyric of a political movement on the ebb. Each of the songs cited here can be fitted into one or more categories within the popular traditions we have been examining, and many have another aspect too: they are *personal* responses to experience, action-songs and national songs at one and the same time.

When Burns moved beyond simple collecting and editing to composition in the folk mode, his technique was generally dramatic, involving the use of a *persona*. For example, both James Kinsley[34] and Iona and Peter Opie[35] are of the opinion that the nursery rhyme 'Wee Willie Gray' is not a collected piece but by Burns himself. If they are right (and there is as yet no means of proving it, one can only rely on one's own subjective response), then the piece shows Burns's absolute mastery of the form. It is as if, in the writing of it, he has *become* Jean Armour, or any other Ayrshire mother singing to her children:

> Wee Willie Gray, an' his leather wallet;
> Peel a willie wand, to be him boots and jacket,
> The rose upon the breer will be him trouse and doublet,
> The rose upon the breer will be him trouse and doublet.

Wee Willie Gray, and his leather wallet;
Twice a lily-flower will be him sark and cravat;
Feathers of a flee wad feather up his bonnet,
Feathers of a flee wad feather up his bonnet.[36]

There is a similar fusion of folk sources and techniques with
dramatic imagination in 'My love she's but a lassie yet' (1790),
where Burns again identifies with the jilted young man in the alehouse,[37] and there is an even more miraculous empathy in the songs
where the *persona* is a young girl, like 'Thou hast left me ever,
Jamie' (Sept. 1793),[38] 'Last May a braw wooer' (July 1795)[39] and
'Tam Glen' (Nov. 1788).[40] In these last four songs, dating from
the Dumfriesshire years, Burns's final period, the poet reacts to
experience like a novelist or short-story writer building on chance
events in his locality or on characters casually met.

But in *Love and Liberty*, the masterpiece of Burns's early Ayrshire
period, the stimulus was simple, direct, overwhelming — and
dramatic. In reacting to the original experience Burns seized on two
traditional *media*, one specifically Scottish (the series of 'brawl
poems' on orgiastic festivities which descend from 'Christis Kirk on
the Green' and other pieces of the fifteenth century), the other more
generally British — popular beggar pastoral, with all the expectations aroused by the mode; and the resulting work of art arises from
the creative interplay between these two and the experience itself,
their conflict and final synthesis. But first, the stimulus — an autumn
evening in 1785 spent with a group of uproarious vagabonds in
Poosie-Nansie's, a disreputable tavern and lodging house in
Mauchline. Writing in his Commonplace Book some eighteen
months before (March 1784), Burns noted: 'I have often coveted
the acquaintance of that part of mankind commonly known by the
ordinary phrase of Blackguards, sometimes farther than was consistent with the safety of my character; those who by thoughtless
Prodigality, or headstrong Passions have been driven to ruin';[41] and
his delight, ten years later, in similar company was one of the
complaints which the Dumfries 'unco guid' had against him.[42]
'Prodigality' and 'headstrong passions' of course echo the establishment view of the mendicant poor in all ages; but Burns in the same
passage goes on to claim that these fascinating outcasts sometimes
exhibited the very qualities which official society found heroic:
'though disgraced by follies, nay sometimes "Stain'd with guilt, and
crimson'd o'er with crimes"; I have yet found among them, in not
a few instances, some of the noblest Virtues, Magnanimity, Generosity, disinterested friendship and even modesty, with the highest

perfection'.[43] There is thus an additional tension at work within the cantata to the contradiction between immediate stimulus and inherited *literary* tradition — an opposition within Burns's experience itself, between the values of Prudence, Regularity and Order and the beggars' guiding ethical principles, embracing both 'Do what you Will', for which Burns had an instinctive sympathy, and qualities which the moral philosophers of the Enlightenment would have placed high on the list of virtues.

For one of the most significant expressions of the upper-class view of beggars, one has to go back nearly a hundred years, to Andrew Fletcher of Saltoun's *Second Discourse concerning the affairs of Scotland*, written in 1698: since they are idle, dissolute and ill-disciplined, beggars should either be forced to work under masters in a kind of servitude, or else sold to the galleys or the West Indian planters. Fletcher was no doubt correct when he said 'there have always been in Scotland such numbers of poor, as by no regulations could ever be orderly provided for; and this country has always swarmed with such number of idle vagabonds, as no laws could ever restrain'. But he cannot possibly have had any evidence, other than wild surmise, for the statement that there were then in Scotland 'two hundred thousand people begging from door to door'. The rest of his account also suffers from exaggeration, though it probably had a certain basis in fact:

> These are not only no way advantageous, but a very grievous burden to so poor a country. And though the number of them be perhaps double to what it was formerly, by reason of this present great distress, yet, in all times, there have been about one hundred thousand of those vagabonds, who have lived without any regard or subjection either to the laws of the land, or even those of God and nature; fathers incestuously accompanying with their own daughters, the son with the mother, and the brother with the sister. No magistrate could ever discover, or be informed, which way one in a hundred of these wretches died, or that ever they were baptized. Many murders have been discovered among them; and they are not only a most unspeakable oppression to poor tenants (who, if they give not bread, or some kind of provision to perhaps forty such villains in one day, are sure to be insulted by them), but they rob many poor people who live in houses distant from any neighbourhood. In years of plenty many thousands of them meet together in the mountains, where they feast and riot for many days; and

at country weddings, markets, burials, and other the like
public occasions, they are to be seen, both men and women,
perpetually drunk, cursing, blaspheming, and fighting
together.[44]

Although in the passage just quoted Fletcher is referring mainly
to those wretches hurled into abject poverty during the near-
famine of the last ten years of the seventeenth century, he nevertheless attributes to them the ways of life which gipsies and highland
caterans were thought to follow. A similar disapproval is found in
Baron Hume's attempt to define a Gipsy:

Touching the proof of such a charge, it is not sufficient to
prove, in general, that the pannel [i.e., the accused] is
habite and repute a sorner, or a vagabond, or a thief, or that
he is addicted to those pilfering and vitious courses, which
are common to Egyptians with other wandering and
dissolute societies. The special opinion of him as an Egyptian,
or one of a different breed from the other inhabitants of
this land, must be established; and this proceeding on those
noted and peculiar circumstances of manner and appearance
by which, in all countries that they have visited, this loose
and lazy race have so remarkably been distinguished.[45]

'Loose', 'lazy', 'a thief', 'pilfering', 'vitious courses' — such are the
characteristics of the uprooted *lumpenproletariat* of all periods,
who by their very existence seem a threat to the smug stability of
the 'unco guid'. And they are characteristics which are certainly
to be found in Burns's beggars.

There was, however, a further circumstance which complicated
the rural community's view of the beggar — namely, that there were
two distinct sorts: the blue-gowns and the outcast *déracinés*. The
former (or 'gaberlunzies'), were licensed by the Kirk Session to beg
in their own parishes, and they carried little lead badges stamped
with the name of the parish. As late as 1845 such badges were issued
to paupers in Brechin, while according to the Poor Law Commis-
sioners report of 1842, 'in most of the burghs and smaller towns the
paupers are allowed to beg on one or more days of the week'.[46]
Henry Grey Graham sums up as follows:

If the parish or town was large they were divided into
different bands, so that they in turn might traverse each
division in one day, and the whole parish in the course of a
fortnight. In this way there was one continuous stream of
mendicancy passing through the neighbourhood; knocking

at the door, not only of the laird, but also of the farmer and labourer, presenting their 'meal-pokes', which beggars never took away empty, for none refused to put into the wallet a handful of oat or barley meal. . . . The restriction was made that only persons who had resided three years in the bounds were to have this qualification; and all others, as well as beggars from other districts, were without fail brought before the Kirk Session and duly 'advised' (that is, commanded) to betake themselves to their own place — the constable, in the rare case of there being such an official, being rewarded with 2s. 6d. Scots (or 2½d. sterling) for every one whom he lodged in jail. . . . A 'communion season' in a parish attracted crowds from all quarters, for it was well known that on the Monday after the sacrament the elders would distribute to the poor the collections from the huge gatherings of worshippers made during the preceding days of preaching. There accordingly assembled a motley and unruly ragged lot, who sat on gravestones, or stood amongst the long grass and nettles of the kirkyard till the service was over, to share in the division of bodles or turners.[47]

When Burns thought he might well end his life as a beggar, he imagined himself sleeping in kilns and deserted barns, enjoying an equality of perfect comradeship with other victims of society as 'commoners of air', taking pleasure in landscapes of 'sweeping vales' and foaming floods, complete with daisies and blackbirds.[48] The Jolly Beggars themselves are less sentimental than the idealised projections of the 'Epistle to Davie', each with an 'honest heart that's free frae a'/Intended fraud or guile' — not blue-gowns but sorners, the most independent of whom were the 'cairds', thus characterised by William Alexander: 'The pronounced caird hardly deemed it necessary to approach you with a whine; an unshrinking and, it might be, an insolent demand suited his temper better; and the remark applies not to the male caird alone'.[49] There seems, indeed, to have been a considerable number of vagrants — cairds and others — towards the end of the century, despite the improvement in economic conditions since Fletcher's time.[50] The writer of the account of Kinettles (Forfarshire) in the Old Statistical Account has this to say:

We have bands of sturdy beggars, male and female, or, as they are usually called, tinkers; whose insolence, idleness, and dishonesty, are an affront to the police of our country. These persons are ready for prey of all kinds. Every thing

that can supply them with provisions, or bring them money,
is their spoil, if it can be obtained with any appearance of
safety. They file off in small parties, and have their place of
rendezvous, where they choose to billet themselves at least
for one day; nor do they fail generally to make good their
quarters, as the farmer is afraid to refuse to answer their
demands, or to complain of the oppression under which he
labours.[51]

The minister of Peterculter has the same story to tell:

This country is often infested with vagrants of various
descriptions, who, by threats or otherwise, compel people to
give them money, and the best *vivres* their houses afford.
They likewise pick up poultry, apparel, and what they can
lay hold of. Their exactions are oppressive, their numbers
often formidable, and it hurts the feelings of the humane to
see so many young people trained up to the same pernicious
courses.[52]

But the most vivid description of vagrancy comes from Ayrshire
itself, in William Aiton's report:

Begging from door to door is still practised all over the
county of Ayr. The streets of the towns and villages, and
public and private roads, in all parts of Ayrshire, are
occasionally infested with vagrant beggars, and sometimes
with tinkers and gypsies, who sorn and thieve, and pilfer
and extort alms from the weak and timid, to the disgrace of
the police, the terror of the inhabitants, and discredit of
humanity. In several of the towns and villages, houses are
open at all times, for the reception of these vagrant beggars,
where these depraved and wretched creatures spend 'their
sinister gettings in the grossest riot and debauch'. In the day
time, they prowl through the towns, or roam in the country,
begging, stealing, or swindling, as opportunity may offer. At
night, they return to their miserable haunts to consume
their spoils, in feasting, drinking, swearing, and carousing
at the expense of the simple, whom they have duped, or the
timid whom they have terrified; and insulting and
disturbing the virtuous inhabitants. It is no way uncommon
to see from ten to twenty lodgers, in one of these *hotels de
vagrants*, with half a dozen teapots, three or four dram
bottles and several gill or half-mutchkin stoups, in rapid
circulation, in their *common-hall*. . . .

Feuds and quarrels are not unfrequent, in these heterogeneous companies. In passing the streets of a market town, to the inn, I found, near midnight, a crowd of people collected before the door of one of these lodging houses, amused or terrified with a mutiny among the lodgers. The threats and curses were loud and reiterated, and the blows at times severe. The diversity of dialects of the combatants, their grounds of complaint, manner of stating them, novelty of their oaths and curses, diversity of aspect and of dress, and degree of intoxication, &c, exhibited a picture truly hogarthian.[53]

Love and Liberty, then, grew out of drinking with a group of sorners, sharing their company. To this stimulus from personal experience was added a second, purely literary stimulus — the Cantata form. It is not always realised just how original Burns was being here. He cannot possibly have heard any sort of Cantata before the autumn of 1785, when *Love and Liberty* was written, and it is hardly probable that he envisaged a performance of the piece by a narrator and singers, whether costumed as beggars or not. The piece must have existed purely within the theatre of his own mind, or rather within his mental picture of Poosie Nansie's, as the setting of an imagined action. He first met the Cantata form in print — in *The Tea-Table Miscellany*, Vol. I (1723), which included 'A Scots Cantata. . . . Composed by Signor Lorenzo Bocchi', with a tune described as being 'after the Italian manner' and its words (Ramsay's own) in Scots. Its sentiments were of the simplest, and the versification of its two recitatives supremely unimaginative: two iambic quatrains, 5a5b5a5b. In Vol. IV of Ramsay's collection, however, there were two pieces without recitatives where the subject is a beggar's life — 'The Happy Beggars', where the Queen of the Beggars and six other women each sing a stanza;[54] and 'The Merry Beggars', where six men do likewise.[55] Professor Kinsley sees these last two pieces, which will be discussed in more detail below, as examples of a 'rudimentary cantata form';[56] their main significance is that they were a bridge between Burns, reacting imaginatively to real Ayrshire beggars in Poosie Nansie's, and a whole series of popular treatments of the vagabond in English and Scottish literature, some of which he must have known from oral tradition and some from his reading.

The first of the English pieces in the beggar tradition which I wish to examine, Ben Jonson's masque *The Gypsies Metamorphos'd* (1621), does not ascribe any sort of superiority to the declassed.

As is only to be expected, since the masque was written for Court performance, Jonson's gipsies flatter the King, and the only approach to social criticism is in the fantastic humour of a song in the broadside style, 'Cock Lorell would needes have the Divell his guest', which tells how the Devil's Arse in the Peak District got its name, as the result of a mighty discharge of wind from Satan's rear after he had been regaled on such dishes as pickled tailors, sempsters, tirewomen, feathermen, perfumers, a stewed usurer, a lawyer's head in green sauce, a cloven sergeant's face, roasted sheriffs, a mayor, a London cuckold, a lecher's chine, a plump harlot and a pandar's 'pettitoes', 'a large fat pastie of a midwife hot', 'a reuerend painted lady', a justice of the Peace and two Clerks, a jailor's jowl, a constable, and 'two aldermen lobsters asleepe in a dishe, a deputie Tart, a Churchwarden Pye'. Its main quality is a destructive energy with Rabelaisian overtones, and there is considerable stylistic novelty in Jonson's experiment with cant, as we can see from the following passages, addressed to a child:

> Therefore (till with his painefull Progenitors he be able to beate it on the hard hoofe to the *ben bowse* or the *stauling Ken*, to nip a *Ian* and *cly the iarke*) 'tis thought fitt he march in the Infante equipage,

> > With the *convoy*, *cheates* and *peckage*,
> > Out of clutch of *Harman-beckage*,
> > To theire *Libkens* at the *Crackmans*
> > Or some *skipper* of the *Blackmans*.[57]

In Fletcher's *Beggar's Bush* (?1622) there is a King of Beggars (really the disguised father of the rightful heir to the Earldom of Flanders) who imposes on his subjects not anarchy but a parody of individualism — a beggardom where each enjoys his own:

> He will not force away your hens, your bacon,
> When you have ventur'd hard for't, nor take from you
> The fattest of your puddings: under him
> Each man shall eate his own stolne eggs, and butter,
> In his owne shade, or sun-shine, and enjoy
> His own deare Dell, Doxy or Mort, at night
> In his own straw, with his owne shirt, or sheet,
> That he both filch'd that day, I [aye], and possesse
> What he can purchase, backe, or belly-cheats
> To his own prop. . . .[58]

Beggar's Bush contains one song that looks forward to the anarchic wish-fulfilment of the later beggar literature:

> Where the Nation live so free,
> And so merry as do we?
> Be it peace, or be it war,
> Here at liberty we are,
> And enjoy our ease and rest;
> To the field we are not prest;
> Nor are call'd into the Towne,
> To be troubled with the Gowne.
>
> Hang all Officers we cry,
> And the Magistrate too, by;
> When the Subsidie's encreast,
> We are not a penny ceast.
> Nor will any goe to law,
> With the Beggar for a straw.
> All which happinesse, he brags,
> He doth owe unto his rags.[59]

Here in 1622 with Fletcher we already have an almost Burnsian emphasis upon Liberty: some of the values of the pastoral tradition have become attached to the figure of the Beggar, and are beginning to move forward towards the praise of anarchy. Yet that anarchy, that mood of rebellion are merely peripheral to *Beggar's Bush*; the real interest is a romantic plot involving disguises and changes of identity. The beggars are there mostly for their picturesque colouring; they are not the vehicle for a truly radical assault on society's values; the principal figures are all members of the upper class; and the play's happy ending celebrates the marriage of the rightful heir of Flanders with the formerly abducted heiress of Brabant—a finale paralleled in the union of Florizel and Perdita in *The Winter's Tale*, of Patie and Peggy in *The Gentle Shepherd*, and of the heroes and heroines of many other pastoral dramas concerning shepherds, not beggars.

Richard Brome's *A Jovial Crew, or the Merry Beggars* (1641) injects a more pointed satire and looks forward in some respects to Gay's *Beggar's Opera*. For instance, in the opinion of one character, courtiers are merely 'court Beggars', and a woman remarks: 'Does he think us Whores too because sometimes we talk as lightly as great ladies?' Brome also carries on Ben Jonson's practice of writing in thieves' cant as in the following song where the beggars' argot achieves all the vigour of which colloquial Scots is also capable. The singer is an ancient female, Autumn Mort:

This is bene bowse, this is bene bowse;
  Too little is my skew.
I bowse no lage, but a whole gage
  Of this I'll bowse to you.
This bowse is better than rom-bowse;
  It sets the gan a giggling.
The autem-mort finds better sport
  In bowsing than in niggling.[60]

The stage direction indicates that she then 'tosses off her Bowle, falls back and is carryed out'. There are at least seven other songs in the later editions of Brome's play, including 'A-begging we will go', which circulated as a broadside ballad and entered the oral tradition of England, Scotland and Ireland, to become later (in altered versions), almost the trade song of the beggars themselves. But just as in Fletcher's *Beggar's Bush*, Brome's protagonists are all, with one exception, members of a higher social group who join the beggars for a frolic. That exception is Springlove, now steward to a country squire, but formerly a declassed vagabond; every spring he has an impulse to take to the roads again. The plot is picaresque, involving disguises and a chase of the beggars. The Beggar's Chorus, 'A begging we will go', already mentioned, was not in the earliest edition of *A Jovial Crew* printed in 1652, but, despite that, the song seems to have been popular before 1660. The following quotations indicate its contributions to the tradition:

With ev'ry Man a Can in's Hand,
  and a Wench upon his knee . . .
And when that we're disposed,
  we ramble on the Grass,
With long patch'd Coats
  for to hide a pretty Lass
And a begging we will go, we'll go, we'll go,
  And a begging we will go. . . .
Within a hollow Tree,
  I live, and pay no Rent;
Providence provides for me,
  and I am well content,
And a begging, &c.
I fear no Plots against me,
  but live in open Cell,
Why who would be a King,
  when a Beggar lives so well?
And a begging, &c.

A broadside, 'A beggar, a beggar, a beggar I'll be', given by Henley and Henderson as a prime source for Burns, was printed as a black-letter, probably before 1672, with a title uniting those of Fletcher's and Brome's plays, viz., 'The Jovial Crew, or Beggar's-Bush, In which a mad Maunder doth vapour and swagger, with praiseing the Trade of a bonney bold Beggar'. A reference in the early editions to the regicide Hugh Peters, executed in October 1660, perhaps indicates that the broadside was originally composed very shortly after the Restoration. Texts appear in *Windsor Drollery* (1671) and Durfey, *Pills to Purge Melancholy* (1719–20). 'Still later', says Ebsworth, 'it was sung by Hemskirk, at Sadlers' Wells, and published as a single sheet of music.'[61] It also appeared in *The Muses Delight (Apollo's Cabinet)*, Liverpool, 1754–7; the words alone in an eighteenth-century *Collection of Diverting Songs* and *The Choice Spirits Chaplet* (1771).[62] Thus on the bibliographical evidence alone, this broadside ballad was available throughout the eighteenth century in England, and could perfectly well have been known to Burns either in printed form or in some orally transmitted derivative.

Brome's play influenced the later eighteenth century in yet another way — through the refurbished text of 1731, *The Jovial Crew*, transformed by Edward Roome, Sir William Yonge and Matthew Concanen, and made into a comic opera in 1760 with musical arrangements by William Bates. There, the beggars are true Choice Spirits, the bowl goes round, and the theme of *carpe diem* is crossed with anacreontic and pastoral strands:

> Our Wants we can't help, nor our Poverty cure:
> Tomorrow mayn't come, of To-night we'll make sure,
> We'll laugh, and lie down, although we are poor,
> And our love shall remain, tho' the Wolf's at the Door.
>
> Then brisk, and smart, shall our Mirth go round,
> With antick Measures we'll beat the Ground,
> To pleasure our Master in Duty bound
> We'll dance, till we're lame, and drink till we're Sound.[63]

It is a virtue that 'we can fall no lower', and

> The dame of rich Attire that brags,
> Wou'd willingly unrig her:
> Did she but know the Joys of Rags,
> And the Life of a Jovial Beggar.[64]

Again,

> Beggars alone are free;
> Free from Employment,
> Their life is Enjoyment
> Beyond Expression. . . .[65]

There is one song in the opera, however, which almost certainly made a direct contribution to *Love and Liberty* — the piece already referred to as 'The Merry Beggars', in Vol. IV of *The Tea-Table Miscellany* (1737) and reprinted throughout the century. It is Air xix:

1. Beg. Man: I once was a Poet at London,
              I keep my heart still full of Glee;
              There's no man can say that I'm undone,
              For Begging's no new trade to me.
                                Tol derol, &c.

2. Beg. Man: I was once an Attorney at Law,
              And after, a Knight of the Post;
              Give me a brisk Wench in clean straw,
              And I value not who rules the Roast,
                                Tol derol, &c.

3. Beg. Man: Make room for a Soldier in Buff,
              Who valiantly strutted about;
              Till he fancy'd the Peace breaking off,
              And then he most wisely — sold out.
                                Tol derol, &c.

4. Beg. Man: Here comes a Courtier polite, Sir,
              Who flatter'd my Lord to his Face;
              Now Railing is all his Delight, Sir,
              Because he miss'd getting a Place.
                                Tol derol, &c.

5. Beg. Man: I still am a merry Gut-Scraper,
              My Heart never yet set a Qualm:
              Tho' poor, I can frolick a vapour,
              And sing any Tune, but a Psalm.
                                Tol derol, &c.

6. Beg. Man: I was a Fanatical Preacher,
              I turn'd up my Eyes when I pray'd;
              But my Hearers had half-starv'd their Teacher,
              For they believ'd not one Word that I said.
                                Tol derol, &c.

1. Beg. Man: Who'er would be merry and free,
                Let him list, and from it he may learn;
            In Palaces who shall you see,
            Half so happy as we in a Barn!
                        Tol derol, &c.

A Dance of Beggars.[66]

Burns creatively transforms the suggestions in this song. At the social level, he makes the satire into something far more radical than the original. And at the formal level, the soldier, fiddler and poet are retained, while the fanatical preacher moves off stage to become the martial chuck's 'sanctify'd sot'. The last stanza of Air xix in *The Jovial Crew*, expressing the ideology of beggar-pastoralism, is given to the ex-poet, who is therefore the only beggar allowed two stanzas; similarly, the final song of *The Jolly Beggars*, expressing the ideology of beggar-anarchism, is sung by the 'bard of no regard', who is – once again – the only beggar to sing twice. The difference in content is seen in their treatment of Peace. In 'Air xix' the soldier is a *miles gloriosus* who leaves the army as soon as there is any chance of peace ending; the satire is routine fun at the expense of a stock literary type. In *The Jolly Beggars*, ten paradoxical words reveal the ultimate obscenity of both poverty and war: 'But the Peace is reduc'd me to beg in despair'. If the text of *The Jolly Beggars* as printed by John C. Weston,[67] without the incident of the Merry Andrew or his song, really reproduces Burns's intention, then we can be certain that Burns based his formal structure on Air xix of *The Jovial Crew*, for there would then be exactly seven airs in *The Jolly Beggars*, shared between six characters, as there are seven stanzas in Air xix, also shared between six characters. But we cannot be sure that Burns's intention was of this kind, since we know from reported oral testimony that the cantata at one time included other airs – for a sweep, a sailor and possibly Racer Jess, the innkeeper's whorish daughter.[68] It would seem likely, then, that Burns's original plan was to have more than seven songs, and that the formal parallel with Air xix is either accident or afterthought.

As we have seen, *The Tea-Table Miscellany* also contains 'The Happy Beggars'[69] where there are again seven stanzas – one given to the Queen of the Beggars, the others to separate beggar women. There certainly *is* a connection with Burns's cantata, and it has been claimed that Burns 'took from it his main theme of natural freedom and perhaps some hints for his woman pickpocket'.[70] One may feel, rather, that Burns took his main theme in the first instance from life, from the real beggars in Poosie Nansie's, and in the second instance from countless literary sources, not just from 'The Happy Beggars'. The importance of 'The Happy Beggars' is probably not so much direct as indirect — that is, in its contribution to one of the several traditions of popular lyric in which Burns was working. Moreover, it unites beggar-pastoral with bacchanalian abandon in a way that Air xix does not. The Queen of the Beggars sings in st. i:

> How blest are beggar-lasses,
>   Who never toil for treasure!
> Who know no care, but how to share
>   Each day successive pleasure.
>
> Drink away, let's be gay,
>   Beggars still with bliss abound,
> Mirth and joy ne'er can cloy
>   Whilst the sparkling glass goes round.

The last four lines of this stanza link the beggar-pastorals with the Restoration good-fellow ballads and the European anacreontic tradition referred to in Chapter VII.

Nor must the contribution of specifically Scottish songs to this whole complex be forgotten, although their effect on *The Jolly Beggars* is not immediately obvious. One such piece is 'In Scotland there liv'd a humble beggar', first printed by David Herd[71] — a fine vernacular song about a beggar who dies, is mourned by 'lads and lasses of a high degree', suddenly starts up from his coffin at the 'late-wake', and escapes from it a second time as he is about to be laid in earth. The only features it shares with Burns are the beggar's irrepressible and irreverent vigour: when he first gets up, it is to call a woman 'limmer' and rumple her cockernonie, and the joyful conclusion is that 'he was first hame at his ain ingle side,/ And he helped to drink his ain dirgie'. The beggar, symbol of unrestrained pleasure, is comically victorious over Death. A second song is 'The Gaberlunzie Man' ('The pawky auld carle cam ower the lee')[72] with an elopement plot, which may have contributed to Burns's vernacular recitative rather than to his songs — particularly the last stanza:

> Wi' cauk and keel I'll win your bread,
> And spindles and whorles for them wha need,
> Whilk is a gentle trade indeed,
>   To carry the gaberlunzie on.

> I'll bow my leg, and crook my knee,
> And draw a black clout o'er my e'e,
> A cripple or blind they will ca' me,
>   While we shall be merry and sing.

A third song, 'The Jolly Beggar' ('There was a jolly beggar, and a begging he was bound'),[73] influenced Thomas Stewart's choice of adjective in the title given to the first printing of the cantata in 1799 but had little effect on the *matter* of Burns's work, unless we count as influences such individual words as 'meal-pocks' and 'duddies'. It would seem, then, that even when due weight is given to the native sources, the general content of *The Jolly Beggars* is affected by traditions of which our principal records are English, not Scottish.

The last contribution we must consider is *The Beggar's Opera*. Gay's burlesque affected *The Jolly Beggars* in two ways—the first indirect and even tortuous, the second direct and obvious. Its indirect influence came through the opera version of *A Jovial Crew*, which owed much to Gay, as well as through later satirical songs stemming from Gay. And it had a direct influence because Burns probably knew its entire text as well as the songs reprinted in *The Tea-Table Miscellany*. The 'Newgate pastoral' almost certainly helped to organise the social comment in Burns's cantata. Gay's intention is ironically brought out in Act III, sc. xvi, when his anonymous choric Beggar addresses the Player:

> Through the whole Piece you may observe such a similitude
> of Manners in high and low Life, that it is difficult to
> determine whether (in the fashionable Vices) the fine
> Gentlemen imitate the Gentlemen of the Road, or the
> Gentlemen of the Road the fine Gentlemen. Had the play
> remain'd, as I at first intended, it would have carried a
> most excellent Moral. 'Twould have shown that the lower
> Sort of People have their vices in a degree as well as the
> Rich: And that they are punish'd for them.

The irony of course consists in this—that the rich are not always punished for *their* vices. In the very first air Peachum, receiver of stolen goods and two-faced informer, makes a precise parallel between the criminal and the respectable:

> Through all the Employments of Life
>   Each Neighbour abuses his Brother;
> Whore and Rogue they call Husband and Wife:
>   All Professions be-rogue one another.

> The Priest calls the Lawyer a Cheat,
>   The Lawyer be-knaves the Divine;
> And the Statesman, because he's so great,
>   Thinks his Trade as honest as mine.

And Jenny Diver the pickpocket sees gamesters, lawyers and — significantly — gypsies as the same at bottom:

> The gamesters and lawyers are jugglers alike,
>   If they meddle, your all is in danger;
> Like gypsies, if once they can finger a souse,
> Your pocket they pick, and they pilfer your house,
>   And give your estate to a stranger.[74]

There are two positives in *The Beggar's Opera* — Polly's simple love for Macheath, and the highwayman's irrepressible amorality. Against these are placed the paradox of man's animal ferocity which exists alongside his social nature. In Act III, sc. ii, Lockit the Keeper of Newgate says: 'Lions, Wolves and Vulturs don't live together in Herds, Droves or Flocks. Of all Animals of Prey, Man is the only sociable one. Every one of us preys upon his Neighbour and yet we herd together.' Lockit's prose sentiment is made much more vivid by the image at the end of Air xliii:

> Thus Gamesters united in Friendship are found,
> Though they know that their Industry all is a Cheat:
> They flock to their Prey at the Dice-Box's Sound,
> And join to promote one another's Deceit.
>   But if by mishap
>   They fail of a Chap,
> To keep in their Hands, they each other entrap.
> Like Pikes, lank with Hunger, who miss of their Ends,
> They bite their Companions, and prey on their Friends.

The underlying idea of *The Beggar's Opera*, then, is no wishfulfilment dream, but the animality of all self-seekers, rich or poor, with ultimate value residing only in a few simple, uncorrupted characters.[75] It is essentially the standpoint of Pope's *Moral Essays* or of *Gulliver's Travels*.

What, then, is the underlying idea of *Love and Liberty*, and what, if anything, is its message? Recent judgements have often been about how the cantata reflects or comments on the world beyond its action. Thus when John C. Weston sees in the poem the triumph of the 'natural' man against notions of the 'social' man,[76] he is claiming that the poem extols extreme individualism whose inevitable

extension is towards various forms of anarchy. And when Hermann
Nibblelink argues that *Love and Liberty* works through from an
individualistic hedonism to a transient social communion in the last
almost ritual chorus, where the beggars are not a collection of
mutually hostile individuals but a group who have, literally,
abandoned themselves to become 'a community not dependent on
impersonal, institutional forms',[77] the implication is that the poem
moves from 'bad' anarchy to 'good', from a Hobbesian all-against-
all to the temporary analogue of a commune. In his 1974 Warton
lecture, however, James Kinsley reacts very firmly against all
attempts to make the work into a radical critique of eighteenth-
century society, or a celebration of values that inhere in the beggars
themselves.[78] To Kinsley, Burns is an orthodox moralist; there is no
love in the poem, only lust; its liberty is a fake, since none of the
singers is free 'of his or her past'; all their lives are senseless, violent
and disordered. Positive value inheres (1) in the 'stable, relatively
innocent society outside' the poem, and (2) in Burns's own attitude,
a Chaucerian 'indulgent humorous affection' for the beggars, a
comic vision which, paradoxically, at one and the same time gives
an ironic sanction to their lives and forms a *cordon sanitaire* which
preserves the poet from ultimate self-identification with his outcasts.

I shall take Professor Kinsley's second point first. It is only in
some very short lyrics that self-identification is the norm for Burns;
in longer flights like 'The Twa Dogs', 'Halloween', 'The Holy Fair',
or 'Tam o' Shanter' he is always in some degree distanced from his
characters. And 'indulgent, humorous affection' for the predatory,
the lecherous and the violent is not incompatible with finding
positives within them; it merely proclaims 'a man's a man for a'
that' at a level far more compassionate than 'an honest man's the
noblest work of God', since the beggars are neither honest nor noble.
The poem's theme, for me, combines two Blakeian aphorisms, —
'Everything that lives is holy' (here, everything human) and
'Energy is eternal Delight' — the holiness of the thieves on the cross,
the energy of Barabbas.

Professor Kinsley says '*Love and Liberty* is not mythopoeic; its
character is energetic and satiric realism'.[79] But there is nothing
to prevent it, like Joyce's *Ulysses* on a much larger scale, from
being both things at once. And in fact it does manage to straddle
both worlds; though its techniques are realistic and comic, it is
mythopoeic in the way it sets the human world over and against
the natural world. Man's fragile group-life, in which co-operation
emerges so painfully from competition and strife, is represented by
the songs and action within the howff; the hostile environment, as in

'Tam o' Shanter', by the wind and rain outside. The first couple, a soldier and his 'tozie drab', may embrace mechanically, as Professor Kinsley claims; the woman may hold up her mouth for kisses as greedily as she presents her begging-bowl to the passers-by during the daytime, but we know, and Burns knows, that receiving is always the counterpart of giving. The soldier bestows kiss after 'skelpan' kiss in a comic emblem of his ruling virtue, generosity. The two are grotesque, no doubt, but at the mythopoeic level they are still Mars and Venus, a comic Antony and Cleopatra: age withers neither of them. In the soldier's song to 'stand the winter's shocks,/Beneath the woods and rocks often-times for a home' elaborates the tension between Man and Nature of the first recitativo and glances, ever so lightly, at another mythical pattern, that of the hero who 'loses favour with the gods and/or his subjects, and is driven from throne and city'.[80] In *The Gentle Shepherd*, as we have seen, the rôle of fate is taken over by the historic process; here, it is rather the way contemporary society is organised, the class-structure that treats common soldiers as expendable, which is to blame. The point of view is almost exactly that of Dr Johnson in his essay on the bravery of the English common soldiers:

> It is not to any great esteem of the officers that the *English* soldier is indebted for his spirit in the hour of battle; for perhaps it does not often happen that he thinks much better of his leader than of himself. . . . There are some, perhaps, who would imagine that every *Englishman* fights better than the subjects of absolute governments, because he has more to defend. But what has the *English* more than the *French* soldier? Property they are both commonly without. Liberty is, to the lowest rank of every nation, little more than the choice of working or starving; and the choice is, I suppose, equally allowed in every country. The *English* soldier seldom has his head very full of the constitution; nor has there been, for more than a century, any war that put the property or liberty of a single *Englishman* in danger.[81]

But lest we say that our parallel proves conclusively that Burns was an 'Augustan', not a 'Romantic', we should recollect that Johnson's essay is one of the most radical he ever wrote, and that there are points of correspondence even between Johnson and Blake. Nor have we altogether exhausted the soldier's mythopoeic features. His ludicrous willingness to 'meet a troop of Hell' stands for man's defiance of both Nature and Super-Nature as surely as does Tamburlaine's defiance of Death and the Gods at the end of

Part II of Marlowe's play. If *Love and Liberty* is Burns's drama of the mind, it is a private theatre of the absurd that he has created. The soldier is poor, he is a victim of man's inhumanity to man, but he is still Herculean; and his vision of himself clattering on his stumps to the sound of the drum unites the comic with the heroic in the same way as the grim twentieth-century humour of John Crowe Ransom:

> Captain Carpenter mounted up one day
> And rode straight way into a stranger rogue
> That looked unchristian but be that as it may
> The Captain did not wait upon prologue
>
> But drew upon him out of his great heart
> The other swung against him with a club
> And cracked his two legs at the shinny part
> And let him roll and stick like any tub.[82]

The trull, too, manages to be comic and heroic, realistic and mythopoeic at the same time. She holds by her ruling passion to the end — her delight is *still* in proper young men if she can get them; and if she can't, she will take the young in spirit. Her heart rejoices at her 'sodger laddie' because of his surviving military qualities, his 'knapsack a' in order' and the tidily braced 'mealy bags' on his arms: when one considers the primary meaning of the noun 'brace', one wonders if Burns is glancing ironically at Achilles, or remembering some illustration of Mars which he has seen. However shamelessly she may extort cash from the sentimental or the 'unco guid' in her professional life, she will abandon herself utterly to a man of her own sort, while it lasts: 'Here's to thee, MY HERO, MY SODGER LADDIE' — the toast is to him as person and social archetype, not as sex-object. Like the soldier himself ('First . . . ane sat . . . He ended'), she is given a mock-heroic touch ('martial chuck'), and she is his equal in force of personality. Though secondary and passive towards her 'old boy', in keeping with the approved relation between the sexes in respectable society, she has the ability to dominate the crowd, for she lays 'the loud uproar' simply by getting up on her feet. She positively glories in her whorish past, and we sense a flame of vitality behind the alcoholic haze. For all her predatory self-regard, the ravages of life have not daunted her any more than poverty and wounds have cowed her 'son of Mars'.

Each of the two songs we have been considering sketches in the past with a superb economy of detail, and ends with a turn towards

the singer's present, where suffering is temporarily annulled by
warmth and strong drink. 'A Highland Lad my love was born' is
also concerned with time. It puts before us a past that is genuinely
tragic, though it does so in an intentionally maudlin way. The
juxtaposition of past and present, of heroic illusion with the widow's
inconstancy, makes the outlaw's sacrifice even more poignant. Just
as one of the old soldier's guiding principles was loyalty to his
commanders, Wolfe and Curtis and Elliot, so the Highlander was
'faithfu' to his clan', destroyed inevitably by the 'lalland laws' he
held in scorn. And it is consistent with the expectations aroused
by the previous recitativos and songs that even *her* memories can
be obliterated in an instant by the joyous comfort of a hearty
can, and that we are meant to view the reversal sympathetically.
Professor Kinsley, however, places the emphasis somewhat differently.
Her 'sighs and sobs', he says, are 'carried with farcical briskness on
the runs of a reel tune. The music is a significant part of Burns's
statement about the undiscriminating, unfeeling animality of the
"merry core".'[83] Yet it should be noted that the direction 'Brisk'
which Professor Kinsley gives to the music in his edition is not
Burns's own. It doubtless applies to the traditional 'There's sax eggs
in the pan, gudeman' (SMM, 1796, 409), perhaps to the original
mal-marié(e) 'O an ye were dead, gudeman' from which the tune gets
its name, and certainly to the music as a reel tune (*Caledonian Pocket
Companion*, 1752, IV, 24); but it does not hold good of all the stanzas
of this fine lyric of character. Indeed, an intelligent singer can hardly
help introducing variations of tempo and feeling. The first line of st.
iv (105), describing her husband's exile, must be taken slowly and
affectingly, with a gradual increase in speed in lines 106-7, to the
ecstatic happiness of line 108 – 'Embracing my John Highlandman'.
Lines 109-10 must again be slow, lines 111-12 positively tragic,
and lines 113-14 drawn out and nostalgic; while the very last
couplet must be sung energetically, with the jollity of total absorp-
tion in the present, despite all that has happened formerly. In other
words, the last couplets of sts. iv, v and vi contrast in mood and
meaning with the first couplets of these same stanzas, and it is
necessary for the differences to be reflected in performance, otherwise there would be no 'tone poetry'.[84] While her cateran was alive
the widow's guiding principle, like his, was Fidelity, but now it has
lost all meaning for her, as the developing action shows. She is
apparently quite willing to go off with the fiddler to share his life as
a vagabond entertainer, until the caird's brute force prevails. But it
is not, or not necessarily, a case of just one night with the tinker. He
wants her to be with him for some time to come, wherever he goes,

and we are meant to take his generosity (once more, Burns singles
out that traditional *heroic* virtue) as genuine:

> If e'er ye want, or meet wi' scant,
> May I ne'er weet my Craigie!
>
> (lines 179-80)

We are of course not told what happens to them in the future; all
we can be certain of is the Caird's stated intention, at that fleeting
instant.

The Bard's words in the first of his two songs are meant for all
the beggars — for the Widow, the Caird (to whom he has, in a
gesture that outbids all the others in generosity, just given one of
his Deborahs as a consolation prize), and himself:

> But for how long the Flie may stang,
> Let Inclination law that.
>
> (lines 226-7)

The 'Bard of no regard' and acknowledged legislator of the group is
in fact an itinerant ballad-singer; he carries round with him a
pedlar's pack of broadsides of the kind examined in Chapter VIII;
it is one of these, presumably already printed, that ends the whole
work. Does it, or does it not, constitute a 'paean in praise of sheer
anarchy'; does it, or does it not, put forward a fundamental criticism
of eighteenth-century Scottish and British society? The Merry-
Andrew's song is highly relevant here. Professor Kinsley, following
John C. Weston, would like to exclude it from his text on general
scholarly grounds: it is found in one MS. in Burns's holograph but
was written at a different time from the surrounding text, and the
cantata's action is altogether more pointed without it. But the
work's ideas are much less clear if it is deleted. Its message is
identical with a passage I have already quoted from *The Beggar's
Opera*: that there is 'such a similitude of manners in high and low
Life, that it is difficult to determine whether (in the fashionable
Vices) the fine Gentlemen imitate the Gentlemen of the Road, or
the Gentlemen of the Road the fine Gentlemen'.[85] In other songs
Burns elaborates the parallels through his verbal irony ('unblushing
fair', 'heaven o' charms', 'the wee Apollo'. 'Adown my cheeks the
pearls ran', 'And go wi' me an' be my Dear' [Marlowe], 'So sung
the bard', 'brighter scenes of love', 'variorum', 'decorum'), and
through the irony of action: the widow reneges on her statement
that she will never forget her cateran, just as propertied widows in a
higher sphere may forget their protestations that they will never

remarry; and when the fiddler feigns to 'snirtle in his sleeve' at his loss and shows he is a 'man o' spunk' by wishing unison between her and his rival, the point perhaps is that affectation and disguise can be as necessary for beggars as they are for ladies and gentlemen. When discussing the poem's verbal paradoxes and fusion of 'violently opposed levels of usage', Professor Kinsley says 'Folk-poetry constantly mixes common speech and romance (and romantic) diction, and it usually does so incorrectly'.[86] *Love and Liberty*, however, is not folk-poetry but a consciously articulated work of art by an educated (though self-educated) man of letters, drawing its sustenance from (i) the vernacular narrative tradition going back to *Christis Kirk on the Green* in the sixteenth century,[87] and (ii) the popular lyric culture which has been the subject of this entire book, but more particularly its broadside strand. Broadsides themselves are what I have termed narrative lyrics of action. One may agree there is irony at the expense of the beggars; but there is even more at the expense of society as a whole.

Professor Kinsley finds that society 'stable' and 'relatively permanent'. Burns's imagery, and the past history of each beggar, prevent me from agreeing with him. The society outside the poem on which the society inside the poem is in part an ironical descant, was far from static. The old life in the Highlands had been destroyed, the clansmen increasingly uprooted, since the Forty-five. Only three years before Burns wrote *Love and Liberty* there had been serious economic distress in Ayrshire, and decent farmers, cottagers and labourers had been driven into mendicancy.[88] What chance was there for those who had been ruined before the seventeen-eighties began, the survivors of previous crises? As we have seen, the widow's song and her fate are a profound comment on the human consequences of the changes in Highland-Lowland relations. The Merry-Andrew's song extends the critique to Edinburgh, London, the Court itself: Poosie Nansie's is a miniature world with ramifications that lead outwards as far as the European continent and even Canada (the Heights of Abraham). The fool uses the Scots reductive idiom to poke fun at drunken philosophers and judges, showy mountebank preachers, the Premier in London. It is a society dominated by a hypocritical upper class and a hypocritical clergy, based on slaughter abroad and a kind of desperate gamesmanship at home: this explains why war, games of chance and religion are so important in the poem's imagery and verbal texture. By taking away his arm and leg, this 'relatively innocent' society has left the soldier no option but his present life. When his doxy says 'the Peace it reduc'd me to beg in despair', it is not against herself that the shaft is loosed, but against man's inhumanity which equates slaughter with prosperity and peace with abject poverty. It is the decay of the clans, happening alongside the growth in lowland wealth, that causes John Highlandman's criminal career and the raucle carlin's tragedy.

Burns's imagination sees a link between the generally approved rapine which nations and governments commit and the more un-lovely traits of the beggars. The fool is 'ty'd up like a stirk' (reduced to a brute beast) by authority and speaks of 'our mountebank squad' (military); the fiddler's heart is 'hol'd' and he rakes a name-less dame 'fore and aft' (naval warfare); the caird draws a 'roosty rapier' and is in fact an army deserter (line 170); the ballad-singer is enlisted in the *army* of Bacchus (line 200). Again and again, religion is held up to ridicule. The army chaplain is a conscienceless libertine, a 'sanctified sot' (line 69); the fool is 'abus'd in the kirk' for his sexual behaviour and observes that ministers are just show-men like himself; the fiddler asks the widow to 'bless' him with her 'heav'n o' charms' (a blasphemous correspondence) and 'prays' for 'grace' when threatened (both religious words and concepts, though of the simplest); the large bowl of liquor is the caird's 'faith' and 'hope'; and the final chorus, as well as being sung around the anacreontic bowl, also parodies a religious rite, with common cup, creed and grace.[89]

Finally, everything in the beggars' own world and in the rest of society too is subject to an eighteenth-century version of a medieval goddess, Fortune; everything is like a game of Chance. War itself depends on the throw of the 'bloody die', battle is a 'gallant game' (lines 34-5). When the widow says the chaplain left her first love 'in the lurch', she is using a metaphor that comes ultimately from the game of cribbage, and when the 'sanctify'd Sot' ventures his soul while she ventures her body, the terminology, of course, is again from gambling. The fool would even go so far as to 'venture' his neck; 'Whistle o'er the lave o't', the refrain of the fiddler's song, though it has several meanings, including a sexual innuendo, is clearly appropriate to a devil-may-care gambler's shrug at his losses; the ballad-singer will make a present of one of his Deborahs with the careless generosity of an aristocrat with his winnings, while the women in his life have deceived him with 'tricks an' craft', like those who cheat at cards. All the beggars, male and female, deceive settled folk with 'the ready trick and fable'; and the word 'variorum' in line 274, derived in the first instance from the official literary culture, but in drama meaning a 'changing scene', seems to carry its own connotations of shifting chance. Transformations from grave to gay, from wealth to poverty, are all in the luck of the game.

Like any other work of art, *Love and Liberty* must be judged on
what it alone says, and not by other works of the same poet, or by
what we know of his opinions from his letters. Of course Burns the
man, as lover, husband and father, was 'too serious and responsible
. . . to be content with the beggars' "life of pleasure . . . no matter
how or where" '90 — and so, no doubt, were the majority of common
folk who sang songs praising beggars and outlaws in the centuries
before Burns wrote. The life of pleasure was a great popular dream,
which Burns intensified and converted into a work that makes a
complex and original comment on the Scotland and Britain in
which he lived. I can only agree with Nibbelink that a transient
social unity *is* achieved by the end of the cantata; but its type of
communion is not so easily squared with the family spirit of *The
Cotter's Saturday Night* as this critic appears to think.91 They are far
from being totally animal and self-ridden during the main action
and *before* they are taken up into their dance of reconciliation. Of the
list of 'noblest Virtues' which, as we have seen, Burns found among
the dregs of humanity, only modesty is lacking in Poosie Nansie's.
The soldier is genuinely dauntless; the 'tozie drab' gives her whole
self — can honest madam do more?; loyalty has been the guiding
principle both of the thieving Highland Lad and of the widow, and if
she is now disloyal to his memory it is because 'history is to blame';
both fiddler and caird are prepared to *share* their lives and winnings
with the carlin if only she will go with them; the bard freely and
magnanimously presents one of his attached females to the fiddler.
The temporary synthesis of the Quodlibet is achieved not by an
ethical virtue but by a quality of personality, by pure Will. Like
any Tudor despot, like Tamburlaine in Marlowe's play, the
ballad-singer imposes order upon the rest by sheer inborn force of
character. What Professor Kinsley seems to feel is that such order is
a 'false consciousness' of the society within the poem, which is like
saying that the dance of reconciliation at the end of a Shakespearian
comedy is a false consciousness. It seems to me, on the contrary,
that the whole poem, reconciliation and all, expresses in very large
part a *true* consciousness not just of the 'society within the poem',
but of the real society in which Burns lived and had his being. And
it goes even further; it makes a satisfying work of art out of the
contradictions within any country or civilisation that has as its
social ideal, 'Fay ce que voudras', 'Let every man soap his own
beard'.92

The social character within the work is a profoundly critical
comment on Burns's Scotland, which he was to explore again, quite

seriously and indeed respectfully, in other poems such as *The Vision*. It is a comment which also happens to be the highest single achievement of the popular song culture of the eighteenth century.

REFERENCES

1.   This has long been recognised: but see in particular two articles by M. E. B. Lewis, ' "The Joy of my heart": Robert Burns as Folklorist' in *Scottish Studies*, XX (1976), 45-67 and 'What to do with "A Red, Red Rose" ' in *Scottish Literary Journal*, III (2), 1976, 62-75.
2.   For a detailed exploration of this point see J. Kinsley 'The Music of the Heart', in *Renaissance and Modern Studies*, VIII (1964), 1-52.
3.   Kinsley, 84.
4.   Kinsley, 196.
5.   *Museum* (1796), 417.
6.   Kinsley, 268.
7.   Kinsley, 194.
8.   Kinsley, 366.
9.   Kinsley, 603.
10.   Kinsley, 382.
11.   Kinsley, 217.
12.   Kinsley, 571.
13.   Kinsley, 320.
14.   Kinsley, 80.
15.   Kinsley, 292.
16.   Kinsley, 597.
17.   Kinsley, 485.
18.   Kinsley, 8.
19.   Kinsley, 204, 294.
20.   Kinsley, 503.
21.   Kinsley, 373.
22.   Kinsley, 398.
23.   *Merry Muses*, p. 52.
24.   Kinsley, 293.
25.   Kinsley, 353.
26.   Kinsley, 168.
27.   Kinsley, 211.
28.   Kinsley, 128.
29.   Kinsley, 491, 2, 3, 4.
30.   Kinsley, 425.
31.   Kinsley, 482.
32.   Kinsley, 484.
33.   Kinsley, 555.
34.   *P. & S.*, p. 1517
35.   *Oxford Dict. of English Nursery Rhymes* (Oxford, 1952 edn.), pp. 415-16.
36.   Kinsley, 592.
37.   Kinsley, 293.
38.   Kinsley, 430.
39.   Kinsley, 503.
40.   Kinsley, 236.

41. *Robert Burns's Commonplace Book 1783–1785*, edd. J. C. Ewing and D. Cook (Glasgow, 1938), pp. 7-8.
42. C. & W., IV, 433-4.
43. *Commonplace Book*, p. 8.
44. In *Political Works* (Glasgow, 1749), pp. 86, 100-1.
45. *Commentaries on the Law of Scotland* (Edinburgh, 1844), quoted in D. Macritchie, *Scottish Gypsies under the Stewarts* (Edinburgh, 1894), p. 1.
46. Quoted in Graham, II. 234. The best known literary portrait of a blue-gown is Edie Ochiltree in Scott's *Antiquary*. Meg Merrilies in *Guy Mannering* is a late representative of the gipsy-'traveller' type.
47. Graham, I, 234-7.
48. 'Epistle to Davie, a Brother Poet', lines 24 ff.
49. Alexander, p. 168.
50. There were periods of great hardship in the country areas in 1740, 1756, 1778, 1782-3, 1796 and 1799–1800, in spite of the generally increasing prosperity. See J. E. Handley, *Scottish Farming in the Eighteenth Century* (London, 1953), p. 35.
51. *Stat. Account*, Kinettles, IX, 201, (n.).
52. *Stat. Account*, Peterculter, XVI, 384-5.
53. W. Aiton, *General View of the Agriculture of the County of Ayr; with Observations on the Means of Its Improvement* (Glasgow, 1811), pp. 626-32, 638.
54. *TTM*, IV: (1740), p. 348.
55. *TTM*, IV: (1740), p. 374.
56. *P. & S.*, p. 1149.
57. Ben Jonson, *Works*, ed. C. H. Herford and P. & E. Simpson, 11 vols (1905–52), VII, 601-3, 567.
58. Beaumont and Fletcher, *Dramatic Works*, ed. Fredson Bowers *et al.* (Cambridge, 1966–   ) III, 263: Act II, sc. 1.
59. *Ibid.*, pp. 264-5.
60. *A Jovial Crew*, ed. A. Haaker (London, 1968), p. 61: II, ii, 254-62.
61. *Bagford Bds.*, ed. Ebsworth, I, 216-18.
62. *Ibid.*, I, 195-9.
63. Air v, sts. iii-iv.
64. Air iv, st. ii, lines 5-8.
65. *Ibid.*
66. *TTM*, IV: (1740), p. 374.
67. Northampton, U.S.A. (1963).
68. Marginal note by Thomas Stewart to the Alloway MS.; see *P. & S.*, p. 1148.
69. Above, p. 192.
70. Weston, *op. cit.*
71. Herd (1769), p. 47.
72. *TTM*, II: (1740), p. 78.
73. *Charmer* II (1751), 237.
74. Air xiv.
75. E. M. Gagey, *Ballad Opera* (New York, 1965), p. 42.
76. In his edition already referred to (Northampton, U.S.A., 1963) and in his article 'The Text of Burns' "The Jolly Beggars" ', *Studies in Bibliography* (Virginia), XIII (1960), 239-47.
77. 'Society at Poosie-Nansie's' in *Studies in Scottish Literature*, VII, Nos. 1 and 2 (July-October 1969), 124-7.
78. 'Burns and the Peasantry, 1785', in *Proceedings of the British Academy*, LX (1974), 1-21.

79.   *Ibid.*, p. 20.

80.   Cp. the events in the life of a typical mythical hero as listed by Lord Raglan in *The Hero* (London, 1936) and summarised by Robert Scholes in *Structuralism in Literature* (New Haven, 1974), pp. 63-4.

81.   *Works*, ed. Murphy (1824), p. 79, from *Idler*, 3rd edn. (London, 1767), ii, 325-30.

82.   'Captain Carpenter', sts. iii-iv, in J. C. Ransom, *Chills and Fevers* (New York, 1924).

83.   'Burns and the Peasantry', p. 17.

84.   The phrase is J. C. Dick's, in *The Songs of Robert Burns* (London, 1903), whose subtitle is 'A Study in Tone-Poetry'.

85.   Above, p. 200.

86.   'Burns and the Peasantry', p. 18.

87.   See James Kinsley's article 'The rustic inmates of the hamlet', in *A Review of English Literature*, I (1960), 13-25, and also A. H. Maclaine, 'The *Christis Kirk* Tradition: its evolution in Scots Poetry to Burns', *Studies in Scottish Literature*, II, Jul., Oct. 1964; Jan., Apr., 1965: 3-18, 111-24, 163-82, 235-50.

88.   See my *Burns*, pp. 17-18.

89.   Kinsley, p. 1162.

90.   'Burns and the Peasantry', p. 19.

91.   See above, n. 77.

92.   Unfortunately, this book was set before I was able to make use of A. H. Maclaine's 'Radicalism and Conservatism in Burns's *The Jolly Beggars*', *Studies in Scottish Literature*, XIII (1978, 125-43). Professor Maclaine concludes that both radicalism and conservatism are present in *Love and Liberty*; previous criticism, however, has over-emphasised the radicalism. The piece is 'at the same time both a celebration of and a satire on the beggar philosophy; the poet admires and laughs at his characters simultaneously'. The unique effect of the cantata comes from the tension between the narrator's voice and the beggars' songs, and indeed the narrator 'is consciously *making fun* of his beggars'. My own view is that narrator and beggars, when their voices are taken together, also make fun of the respectable and the polite. To be valid, an interpretation must be able to stand the test of performance. Now it is difficult to stage *Love and Liberty*, whether with Cedric Thorpe Davie's sung recitativos (as in the magnificent television production by Scottish Opera principals and chorus, January 1979) or in the Scotsound cassette version (SSC 037), with Robert Shankland speaking the recitativos and Jean Redpath singing both the doxy's and the pickpocket's songs, without making 'See the smoking bowl before us', and its values, the ideological as well as the formal climax of the work. Burns was more than the consummation of a dying Scottish tradition; he was, as Wordsworth and Keats knew, a harbinger of Romanticism. Some of the greatest achievements of European Romanticism were hymns of libertarian joy—the finales of Beethoven's fifth and ninth symphonies, the end of *Fidelio*, Blake's celebration of energy, the last act of *Prometheus Unbound*. In its own earthy and satiric fashion *Love and Liberty* moves towards a similar exercise of hope and joy. To appreciate the work fully one must welcome, not grudge, its emotional dialectic.

ABBREVIATIONS USED IN THE NOTES

Alexander	W. Alexander, *Notes and Sketches Illustrative of Northern Rural Life in the Eighteenth Century* (Edinburgh, 1877).
Bagford Bds.	*The Bagford Ballads*, ed. J. W. Ebsworth (Hertford, 1878).
BM	The British Museum, now the British Library.
Burns	T. Crawford, *Burns: a study of the Poems and Songs* (Edinburgh and Stanford, 1960: 1965; Edinburgh, 1978).
'Burns and the Peasantry'	J. Kinsley, 'Burns and the Peasantry, 1785', in *Proceedings of the British Academy*, LX (1974), 1-21.
Burns, *Notes*	*Notes on Scottish Song by Robert Burns*, ed. J. C. Dick (London, 1908).
Carlyle	*The Autobiography of Dr Alexander Carlyle of Inveresk 1722–1805*, ed. J. H. Burton (London and Edinburgh, 1910).
C. & W.	*The Life and Works of Robert Burns*, ed. R. Chambers, revised W. Wallace, 4 vols. (Edinburgh, 1896).
Commonplace Book	*Robert Burns's Commonplace Book 1783–1785*, eds. J. C. Ewing and D. Cook (Glasgow, 1938).
Congleton	J. W. Congleton, *Theories of Pastoral Poetry in England 1684–1798* (University of Florida Press, repr. 1968).
Creech	W. Creech, *Edinburgh Fugitive Pieces: with Letters, containing a comparative view of the modes of living . . . manners &c. of Edinburgh, at different periods* (Edinburgh, 1815).
Edgar	A. Edgar, *Old Church Life in Scotland: Second Series* (Paisley and London, 1886).
EUL	Edinburgh University Library.
FSNE	Gavin Greig, *Folk-Song of the North-East*, 1st and 2nd series (Peterhead, 1909 and 1914). Later reproduced in 1 vol. with *Folksong in Buchan* (Hatboro, Pa., 1963).
Fyfe	*Scottish Diaries and Memoirs 1746–1843*, ed. J. G. Fyfe (Stirling, 1942).
Graham	H. G. Graham, *Social Life in Scotland in the Eighteenth Century*, 2 vols. (London, 1899).
Greg	W. W. Greg, *Pastoral Poetry and Pastoral Drama* (London, 1906).

GUL   Glasgow University Library.

H. & H.   *The Poetry of Robert Burns*, ed. W. E. Henley and
                            T. F. Henderson (The Centenary Edition), 4 vols.
                            (Edinburgh and London, 1896–7).

Hecht-Hd.   Songs from David Herd's Manuscripts, ed. Hans
                            Hecht (Edinburgh, 1904).

Herd (1769)   *The ancient and modern Scots Songs, Heroic Ballads, &c.*
                            [ed. David Herd] (Edinburgh, 1769).

Herd (1776)   *Ancient and Modern Scottish Songs, Heroic Ballads, Etc.*
                            [ed. David Herd] 2 vols. (Edinburgh, 1776).

In Search of a Wife   *Boswell in Search of a Wife 1766–69*, ed. F. Brady and
                            F. A. Pottle (London, 1957).

Kinsley   *The Poems and Songs of Robert Burns*, ed. James
                            Kinsley (The Oxford English Texts Edition), 3
                            vols. (Oxford, 1968): also the Oxford Standard
                            Authors Edition, in 1 vol. (Oxford, 1969). Refer-
                            ences are to the numbers assigned the individual
                            poems, not to pages.

Letters   *The Letters of Robert Burns*, ed. J. de Lancey Ferguson,
                            2 vols. (Oxford, 1931).

LLL   *Love, Labour and Liberty: the eighteenth-century Scottish
                            Lyric*, ed. T. Crawford (Manchester, 1976).
                            References are to the numbers assigned the indiv-
                            idual songs in this anthology, not to pages.

Merry Muses   *The Merry Muses of Caledonia*, eds. James Barke and
                            S. Goodsir Smith (Edinburgh, 1959).

Museum   *The Scots Musical Museum*, ed. James Johnson, 6 vols.
                            (Edinburgh, 1787–1803). Reprinted 1839 and 1853,
                            and reproduced in 2 vols., Hatboro, Pa., 1962.

NLS   National Library of Scotland.

P. & S.   *The Poems and Songs of Robert Burns*, ed. James
                            Kinsley (Oxford, 1968), Vol. III (Commentary).
                            The references to *P. & S.* are to pages.

Pepys Bds.   *The Pepys Ballads*, ed. H. E. Rollins, 8 vols. (Harvard,
                            1929–32).

Ramsay-Fergusson   *Poems by Allan Ramsay and Robert Fergusson*, ed. A. M.
                            Kinghorn and A. Law (Edinburgh, 1974).

Ramsay of Ochtertyre   J. Ramsay (of Ochtertyre), *Scotland and Scotsmen in
                            the Eighteenth Century*, ed. A. Allardyce, 2 vols.
                            (Edinburgh, 1888).

Robertson, *Poems*   A. Robertson of Struan, *Poems on Various Subjects and
                            Occasions* (Edinburgh, n.d.–?1751).

Rogers   C. Rogers, *Social Life in Scotland from early to recent
                            times*, 3 vols. (Edinburgh, 1884).

Roxb. Bds.   *The Roxburghe Ballads*, ed. W. Chappell and J. W.
                            Ebsworth, 9 vols., The Ballad Society (Hertford,
                            1871–1902).

SRO	Scottish Record Office.
S.S.S.	[Peter Buchan] Sir Oliver Orpheus, *Secret Songs of Silence*, MS. (1832): Harvard College Library, MS. 25241.9.
Stat. Account	*The Statistical Account of Scotland*, ed. Sir John Sinclair, 21 vols. (1791–9).
St. Clair MS.	Song-collection made by Elizabeth St. Clair (the Mansfield MS.). Hornel Library, Broughton House, Kirkcudbright.
Stenhouse, *Illustrations*	W. Stenhouse, *Illustrations of Scottish Song* in James Johnson, *The Scots Musical Museum* (Edinburgh, 1839).
S.T.S.	Scottish Text Society.
Topham	[E. Topham] *Letters from Edinburgh* written in the years 1774 and 1775 (London, 1776).
TTM	*The Tea-table Miscellany* [ed. Allan Ramsay]. 4 vols. (Edinburgh, 1723–?1737; London, 4 vols. in 1, 1740). References are to the 1740 edition).
Watson's Collection	*A Choice Collection of Comic and Serious Scots Poems both ancient and modern . . . printed by James Watson*, 3 parts (Edinburgh, 1706, 1709, 1711; repr. in 1 vol. Glasgow, 1869, and by the S.T.S., ed. Harriet Harvey Wood, 1977).
Whitelaw	*The Book of Scottish Song: a comprehensive Collection of the most approved Songs of Scotland*, ed. Alexander Whitelaw (London, Glasgow and Edinburgh: n.d.).
Williams	Raymond Williams, *The Country and the City* (London, 1973: Paladin edn., 1975).

SELECT LIST OF SONG BOOKS AND MISCELLANIES PUBLISHED IN SCOTLAND (1662–1786)

All the books listed below were consulted in the preparation of this study, in addition to a large number of chapbooks and broadsides. All the asterisked items contain music; the unasterisked, words only.

*1. *Cantus, Songs and Fancies.* . . . *Printed by Iohn Forbes, and are to be sold at his shop* (Aberdeen, 1662).

*2. *Cantus, Songs and Fancies*, 2nd edn. (Aberdeen, 1666).

*3. *Cantus, Songs and Fancies*, 3rd edn. (Aberdeen, 1682).

4. *A Choice Collection of Comic and Serious Scots Poems.* . . . *Part I. Printed by James Watson* (Edinburgh, 1706).

5. *A Choice Collection of Comic and Serious Scots Poems.* . . . *Part II. Printed by James Watson* (Edinburgh, 1709).

6. *A Choice Collection of Comic and Serious Scots Poems.* . . . *Part III. Printed by James Watson* (Edinburgh, 1711).
[The whole collection repr. Glasgow (1869), and Edinburgh (1977) as Vol. 1 of the S.T.S. edition]

7. *The Edinburgh Miscellany: Consisting of Original Poems, Translations, &c. By Various Hands. Vol. I* (Edinburgh, 1720).

8. *The Tea-Table Miscellany.* . . . *Printed by Mr Thomas Ruddiman for Allan Ramsay* (Edinburgh, 1723).

9. *The Ever Green.* . . . *Published by Allan Ramsay.* . . . *Printed by Mr Thomas Ruddiman.* 2 vols. (Edinburgh, 1724).

10. *The Tea-Table Miscellany.* . . . Vol. II (Edinburgh, 1725). [No copy is known].

11. *Musick for Allan Ramsay's Collection of Scots Songs set by Alexr. Stuart.* . . . Vol. I (Edinburgh, 1726).

12. *The Tea-Table Miscellany.* . . . Vol. III (Edinburgh, 1727).

13. *The Tea-Table Miscellany.* . . . Vol. IV (Edinburgh, 1737). [No copy is known].

14. *The Phoenix.* . . . *Volume First* (Edinburgh, 1742).

15. *A Collection of Loyal Songs. For the Use of the Revolution Club* (Edinburgh, 1748).

16. *The Charmer; a Choice Collection of Songs, English and Scots.* . . . *Printed for J. Yair* (Edinburgh, 1749).

17. *A Collection of Loyal Songs. For the Use of the Revolution Club* (Edinburgh, 1749). [Title page identical with No. 15, but the contents are not]

18. *A Collection of Loyal Songs, Poems, &c.* (no place, 1750).

19. *The Charmer.* . . . *Printed for J. Yair.* Vol. II (Edinburgh, 1751).

20. *The Charmer.* . . . *The Second Edition. Printed for J. Yair* (Edinburgh, 1752). [Vol. I, and probably the only one published of this edition.]

*21. *Thirty Scots Songs for a Voice & Harpsichord. . . . the Words from Allan Ramsay. . . . Printed for, & sold by R. Bremner* (Edinburgh, ?1757).

*22. *A Second Set of Scots Songs for a Voice and Harpischord. . . . R. Bremner* (Edinburgh, ?1759).

*23. *The Free Masons Songs, with Chorus's in three & four Parts . . . to which is added Some other Songs proper for Lodges. . . . R. Bremner* (Edinburgh, ?1759).

*24. *The Songs in the Gentle Shepherd. Adapted for the Guitar. . . . R. Bremner* (Edinburgh, ?1759).

25. *The Tea-Table Miscellany: or a Collection of Choice Songs, Scots & English in Four Volumes. By Allan Ramsay. The Twelfth Edition* (Edinburgh, 1760).
[This seems to be the first complete edition published in Scotland to have survived. There was a complete London edition in 1740.]

*26. *Twelve Scots Songs for a Voice or Guitar. . . . R. Bremner* (Edinburgh, ?1760).

27. *Collection of Loyal Songs. For the Use of the Revolution Club* (Edinburgh, 1761).

28. *The Freemason's Pocket Companion . . .* [with] *a Complete Collection of Freemason Songs* (Edinburgh, 1766).

*29. *A New Collection of Scots and English Tunes . . . with some of the best songs out of the Beggar's Opera and other curious ballads . . . printed and sold by Neil Stewart* (Edinburgh, ?1762).

30. *A Collection of Songs. . . . Printed by A. Donaldson and J. Reid* (Edinburgh, 1762).
[Reissued 1763 for C. Wright as *A Collection of Bacchanalian Songs* and in 1775 as *The Buck's Bottle Companion.*]

31. *The Free Mason's Pocket Companion. . . . The Second Edition* (Edinburgh, 1763).

32. *The Black Bird. . . . By William Hunter, Philo-Architectonicae* (Edinburgh, 1764).

33. *A Choice Collection of Scotch and English Songs* (Glasgow, 1764).

34. *The Mevis: Being a Choice Collection of the Best English and Scots Songs* (Aberdeen, 1764).

35. *The Charmer. . . . The Third Edition. . . . Printed for M. Yair* (Edinburgh, 1765).

36. *The Free Masons Pocket Companion; Containing. . . . A large Collection of Songs, many of which were never before published* (Edinburgh, 1765).
[Contains 56 songs and 5 other poems.]

37. *The Free Masons Pocket Companion* (Glasgow, 1765).
[Contains 51 Masonic Songs and 43 other songs, Scots and English.]

38. *The Lark: being a Select Collection of the most celebrated and newest songs, Scots and English* (Edinburgh, 1765).

39. *The Linnet: A Collection of an Hundred and Thirty-Two Choice Songs* (Glasgow, 1765).

40. *The Chearful Companion. . . .* (Edinburgh, 1766).

41. *The Scots Blackbird, containing One Hundred and Seven Songs, Both Scots and English* (Aberdeen, 1766).

42. *The Lark: a Collection of Choice Scots Songs. . . .* (Edinburgh, 1768).

43. *The ancient and modern Scots Songs, Heroic Ballads, &c. . . .* (Edinburgh, 1769).
[The first edition of David Herd's Collection.]

44. *A Collection of Loyal Songs. For the Use of the Revolution Club. . . .* (Edinburgh, 1770).

45. *The Blackbird.* . . . (Edinburgh, 1771).

46. *The Freemasons Pocket Companion.* . . . (Glasgow, 1771). [Reprint of No. 37.]

*47. *A Collection of Scots Songs Adapted for a Voice and Harpsichord.* . . . *Printed and Sold by Neil Stewart* (Edinburgh, 1772).

48. *The History of Masonry; or The Freemasons Pocket Companion.* . . . *The Third Edition* (Edinburgh, 1772). [57 songs, 6 other poems.]

49. *The Chearful Companion.* . . . *A New Edition* (Edinburgh, 1774).

50. *Ancient and Modern Scottish Songs, Heroic Ballads, Etc.* . . . *In Two Volumes* (Edinburgh, 1776).
[The second, expanded, edition of David Herd's Collection.]

51. *The Nightingale: A Collection of Ancient and Modern Songs, Scots and English; None of Which are in Ramsay.* . . . (Edinburgh, 1776).

52. *The Gold-Finch, A Choice Collection of the Most Celebrated Songs, Scots and English, Many of which never before in Print.* . . . (Edinburgh, 1777).

53. *The Scots Nightingale; or Edinburgh Vocal Miscellany.* . . . (Edinburgh, 1778).

54. *St Cecilia; or, the Lady's and Gentleman's Harmonious Companion.* . . .(Edinburgh, 1779).
[Additional title page, *Wilson's Musical Miscellany.*]

55. *The Scots Nightingale: or, Edinburgh Vocal Miscellany.* . . . *The Second Edition, with the Addition of One Hundred Modern Songs* (Edinburgh, 1779).

56. *The True Loyalist; or, Chevalier's Favourite* (no place, 1779).

57. *The Chearfull Compainion.* . . . (Perth, 1780).

58. *The Scots Vocal Miscellany.* . . . (Edinburgh, 1780).

*59. *Thirty Scots Songs Adapted for a Voice and Harpsichord. The Words by Allan Ramsey.* . . . *Printed and Sold by N. Stewart* (?1780).

60. *The Universal Scots Songster* (Edinburgh, 1781).

61. *The Charmer.* . . . *Printed for J. Sibbald.* . . . 2 vols. (Edinburgh, 1782).
[Vol. II described as 'An Entire New Collection'.]

62. *The Gold Finch, or New Modern Songster. The Second Edition.* . . . (Edinburgh, 1782).

63. *St. Cecilia; or, the British Songster* (Edinburgh, 1782).

64. *The Chearfull Companion.* . . . (Perth, 1783).
[Basically a second edition of No. 57.]

65. *The Goldfinch, or New Modern Songster.* . . . (Glasgow, ?1783).

*66. *A New and Complete Collection of the Most Favourite Scots Songs . . . printed for & Sold By Corri and Sutherland.* . . . (Edinburgh, 1783).
[34 Songs.]

*67. *A New and Complete Collection of the Most Favourite Scots Songs.* . . . (Edinburgh, ?1783).
[Same title-page as *66, but a different collection, with 31 songs.]

68. *The Poetical Museum.* . . . *Printed and Sold by G. Caw* (Hawick, 1784).

69. *The Young Free-Mason's Assistant.* . . . (Dumfries, 1784).
[102 items.]

70. *The Gold-Finch.* . . . (Glasgow, 1785).
[83 items only: much shorter than the other *Goldfinch* volumes.]

*71. *The Songster's Favourite.* . . . *By Laurence Ding* (Edinburgh, ?1785).

72. *The British Songster.* . . . (Glasgow, 1786).

73. *The Chearful Companion.* . . . (Glasgow, 1786).
[A reprint of No. 40.]

*74. *The Musical Miscellany; a Select Collection of the most approved Scots, English and Irish Songs* (Perth, 1786).
[The first pocket-sized song-book with music to be printed in Scotland.]

Some of the most influential song-books containing Scottish material were, however, published in England. Apart altogether from the English editions of Ramsay's *Tea Table Miscellany,* the following should be noted:

*1. [T. Durfey] *Wit and Mirth* . . . *or, Pills to purge melancholy* (London, 1699: 4th edn., 6 vols., 1719–20). Contains some genuine Scottish airs, as well as many parodies and pseudo-Scottish words and tunes.

*2. *Orpheus Caledonius; or, a collection of the best Scotch songs set to musick by W. Thomson* (London, 1725). 50 songs.

*3. [W. Thomson] *Orpheus Caledonius* . . . 2 vols. (London, 1733). 100 songs.

4. *Orpheus: a collection of One thousand nine hundred and seventy-four of the most celebrated English and Scotch songs* . . . 3 vols. (London, 1749).

5. *The Union Song-Book: or, Vocal Miscellany. Being a Choice Collection of the most celebrated Scots and English Songs.* . . . *Printed by and for William Phorson* (Berwick, 1781). [266 items.]

6. *The Blackbird.* . . . *Printed for William Phorson* (Berwick, 1783). [173 items.]

Many chapbooks containing Scottish songs were printed in Newcastle-upon-Tyne.

GLOSSARY

SND denotes *The Scottish National Dictionary*, N.E.D. the *New (Oxford) English Dictionary*, O.G.S. *The Ordnance Gazetteer of Scotland*, ed. F. H. Groome, 6 vols. (Edinburgh, 1882–5). Other references are to Jamieson's Scottish *Dictionary*, (1808), Johnson's English *Dictionary* (1755), Kinsley's glossary to *Burns: Poems and Songs* (1968) and Eric Partridge, *Dictionary of the Underworld* (1968 edn.).

a', *adj., adv., n.* all
abee, *adv.* alone
ae, *adj.* one; only
aff, *adv., prep.* off, away
aft(en), *adv.* oft(en)
ain, *adj.* own
alackanie! *int.* alas!
amang, *prep.* among
an('), *conj.* (1) and; (2) if, whether
ance, *adv.* once
anither, *adj., pron.* another
asteer, *adj.* astir, stirring
Auchleck, *prop. n.* Gilbert Auchleck, cutler of Netherbow in Edinburgh, whose title in the Cape drinking club was Sir Launce
aucht, *n.* property
auld, *adj.* old
Auld Harry, *prop. n.* the devil (euph.)
awa('), *adv.* away
ay(e), ayes, *adv.* always
ayont, *prep., adv.* beyond, past

back, *v. slang* to support by a bet; cover the back, support
bairn, *n.* child
baith, *pron., adj., conj.* both
balou, balow, *n.* lullaby
band, *n.* bond, promissory note
bangstrie, *n.* violence to another's person or property (SND)
Bass, *prop. n.* Bass Rock, (in Firth of Forth)
beet, *v.* kindle, add fuel to fire (SND)
begunk, *n.* trick
beild, bield, *n.* shelter

belly-cheat, *n., cant* food, apron (Partridge); also *v.* (obscure)
ben, bien, *adj. cant* good
ben, *adv.* inside (see **but**)
bent, *n.* open country; to the bent *adv. phr.* flee(ing) one's creditors
benty, *adj.* covered with coarse grass
birken, *adj.* birch
birn, *n.* dry, heathy pasture
black, *adj.* dark-haired
blackmans, *n. cant* night (? literary variation of 'darkmans')
blaw, *n., v.* blow
blin, *v.* cease
bodie, *n.* person
bodle, *n.* 'a copper coin, of the value of two pennies Scots, or the third part of an English half-penny' (Jamieson)
bogie, *n.* marsh
Bogie, *prop. n.* ? aphetic form of Strathbogie
borrows-toun, *n.* royal burgh
bot, but, *prep.* without
bots, *n.* ? phonetic variant of 'pots'; a kind of ale
bou'd, *ppl. adj.* crooked
bountith, *n.* gratuity
bowie, *n.* pail
bowse, *n.* liquor; *v.* drink
brae, *n.* hill, high ground
braw, *adj.* fine, handsome, finely dressed
brecken, *n.* brake, bracken, fern
breed, *n.* bread
brink, *v.* move violently

brose, *n.* oatmeal mixed with boiling water or milk; *nonce v.,* make this dish

bucklin-kame, *n.* comb for holding up the hair

bughtin(g), *n.* folding (of sheep)

burn, *n.* well, stream; **burnie,** *dim.*

busk, *v.* dress, prepare

buss, *n.* bush

bussy, *adj.* busy

but, *prep.* without

but(t) and ben, *adv. phrase* in the kitchen and in the parlour; backwards and forwards, in and out

ca', *v.* drive (of nail)

ca' thro', *v. phrase* get work done

cadgie, *adj.* sportive

caird, card, *n.* pedlar, tinker, gipsy

camsterry, *adj.* cantankerous

canty, *adj.* joyous, lively

capuchin, *n.* 'a female garment, consisting of a cloak and hood, made in imitation of the dress of capuchin friars' (Johnson)

carks, *n. pl.* carcases (stage Highland-Eng.)

carl(e), *n.* fellow

carlin(e), *n.* old woman

cauk, *n.* chalk; 'wi caulk and keel', by fortune-telling, i.e. 'pretending to be dumb and making magic signs with chalk' (SND)

cauld, *adj.* cold

causey, *n.* street

chap, *n.* buyer, customer

cheates, *n. pl., cant* things, objects

chine, *n.* backbone

claithing, *n.* clothing

clap, *v.* pat, embrace

claw, *v.* lacerate, beat

cleading, *n.* clothing

clink, *n.* money

clout, *n.* cloth; *v.* patch; *ppl. adj.* mended

cly the jarke, *cant phr.* to be whipped (Partridge)

cockernonie (-y), *n.* hair gathered in a band or fillet (a symbol of virginity)

cock laird, *n.* landholder who cultivates his own estate

cod, *n.* pillow

coff, *v.* buy; **coft,** *pret.*

cog(g), -ie, *n.* wooden drinking-cup girded with metal bands

coggin(g), *v.n.* motion of teeth on a wheel

coup, *n.* blow, upset

crack, *n.* moment, short space of time

crackmans, *n. cant* hedge (Partridge)

craig, *n.* crag, rock; **craigie, -y,** *adj.* craggy

craigie, *n.* throat

Crief(f), *prop. n.* town in central Perthshire and the seat of the criminal courts of the Stewards or Seneschals down to the abolition of heritable jurisdiction in 1748. O.G.S., following Scott, speaks of '"the kind gallows of Crieff"', whence sometimes of a morning a score of plaids had dangled in a row' at the western end of the town. In revenge for these executions, the clans burned Crieff in 1716 and destroyed several houses in 1745

cronon, *n.* crooning (stage Highland-Eng.)

crudle, *v.* cause to curdle

cry up, *v. phr.* praise

cust, *v. pret.* cast

cuts, *n. pl.* lots (in gambling)

cuttie, -y, *adj.* short

cuttie gun, *euph.* short pipe

cuttie mun, *comp. n.* spoon with a short handle (euph.)

cuttie stoup, *n. plur. (euph.)* a pewter vessel holding the eighth part of a chopin or quart (Jamieson)

daff, *v.* dally

deal, *n.* plank sawn from a log of timber

deel, de(')il, *n.* devil

dell, *n. cant* young girl

dike, *n.* wall

dink, *adj.* neat, trim

ding, *v.* drive, force

dinnae, *v. and neg. part.* don't

dirgie, *n.* dirge, 'funeral feast, mainly of drink, taken gen. after the burial '(SND)

distain, *v.* discolour, dye

dit, *v.* close, shut

docups, *n. pl.* ? articles of dress

doited, *ppl. adj.* muddled, senile

dominie, *n.* schoolmaster

dool, dule, *n.* pity, sorrow; *interj.* alas

dortie, (-y), *adj.* pettish, saucy

dorts, *n. pl.* sullen humour(s)

douk, *v.* duck

doup, *n,* buttocks

dowie, -y, *adj.* doleful

doxy, *n. cant* beggar's harlot (Partridge)

drumlie, -y, *adj.* troubled, gloomy

duddie, -y, *adj.* ragged

duddies, *n. pl.* rags

dunt, *v.* thump, throb

dyvour, *n.* bankrupt

eastlin, *adj., adv.* easterly

ee (*pl.* een), *n.* eye

e'en, *n.* evening

eild, *n.* age

eithest, *sup. adv.* most easily

Emelius, *prop. n.* ? coinage from *lat.* 'melius', better

eneugh, *adv.* enough

ettle, *v.* aim, attempt

eye-brie, *n.* eyebrow

fa', *v.* (1) fall; (2) befall; (3) take, have a right to, deserve

fain, *adj.* glad, content

fainness, *n.* pleasure

fand, *v. pret.* found

faugh, *n.* 'in the old *infield* and *outfield* system of farming, a part of the *outfield* ground which was tilled and left fallow alternately for four or five years at a time' (SND)

fee and bountith, *n. plur.* wages and gratuity

fendy, *adj.* active (in finding food)

ferly, *v.* marvel

fient ane, *strong neg.* the devil of a one

firstan, *adj.* first

firy-fery, *n.* bustle, state of excitement

flae, *n.* flea

flie, *n.* insect; ? Spanish fly, cantharides

flyed, *pa. pple.* frightened

forsta', *v.* understand

fou, fu', *adj.* full, drunk; *adv.* fully, very, quite

fou nappy, *adj. plur.* drunk with ale

fouth, *n.* abundance

frae, *prep.* from

frolick a vapour, *v. phr.* cheer away a fit of depression

fu' lies me o' you, *v. phr.* you are very pleasing to me

fur, *n.* furrow

gab, *n.* mouth, volubility

gaberlunzie, *n.* beggar's wallet, beggar, begging trade

gae, *v.* go, walk; **gaen, gane,** *pa. pple;* **gaun,** *pres. pple*

gage, *n. cant* quart pot of drink (Partridge)

gan, *n. cant* mouth (Partridge)

gang, *v.* go, walk

gar, *v.* make, cause; **gart,** *pret., pa. pple*

gaud, *n.* rod or goad

gate, *n.* way, road

gawkie, *n.* booby

geck, *v.* toss the head, flout

gee, *n.* huff; **take the gee** 'become pettish and unmanageable' (Jamieson)

gie, *v.* give; **giein,** *pres. pple,* **gae, gied,** *pret.;* **gien,** *pa. pple*

gif, *conj.* if

gingle, *v.* jingle

girdin', *n.* striking; euphemism for sex-act

gowan, *n.* daisy

gowk, *n.* fool

graip, *n.* dung-fork

gree, *v.* agree

greet, *v.* weep; *pret.* **grat**

greetie, *n.* little cry

groat, *n.* silver coin of little value, 3d. Scots

ground, *n.* bottom

gruip, *n.* hollow behind stalls of horses or cattle for receiving dung and urine

gryce, *n.* pig

gudeman, guid man, *n.* head of household, husband

gully, *n.* and *attrib.* large knife

ha', hae, *v.* have

hacket-kail, *n.* chopped colewort

ha(u)d, *v.* hold, keep

haffet, *n.* side of the head

hag, *n.* 'moss-ground formerly broken up' (*Statist. Account*)

hain, *v.* spare

hald, *n.* holding. refuge

halesome, *n.* wholesome

halflens, *adv.* half, partly, nearly

hame, *n. adv.* home; **hamely,** *adj.* homely, plain, friendly

hangie, *n.* the hangman

hantle, *n.* a considerable number or quantity

hap, *n., v.* wrap

Harman-beckage, *coll. n.* constables ('not cant, but a term coined by Jonson', Partridge)

haslock, *n.* wool on a sheep's neck

hause-rig, *n.* the second furrow made in ploughing (SND)

hech, *int.* 'an exclamation, akin to a sigh, gen. expressive of sorrow, fatigue, pain, surprise or contempt' (SND)

heckle, *n.* comb for splitting flax-fibres

herd, *n.* shepherd

hernane sell, *pron. plur.* her [my] own self (stage Highland-Eng.)

heugh, *n.* steep hill or bank

heuk, *n.* hook, sickle

hinder, *adj.* last

hing, *v.* hang

hinny, *n., adj.* honey

hodin, *n.* undyed, rough woollen cloth

hodling, *ppl. adj., v., n.* denoting 'a quicker motion than toddling' (Jamieson)

hooly, *adv.* slowly, moderately

howm, *n.* level, low ground on the banks of a river

huskiebae, *n.* usquebaugh, whisky

hynd, *n.* farm-labourer

iceshogle, *n.* icicle

ilk(a), *adj.* each, every

ingle, *n.* fire (on hearth)

in-knee'd, *adj.* with the legs bent inwards at the knees

I'se, *pron.,* and *v.* I shall

jee, *v.* move, vacillate

jimp, *adj.* neat, slender

jo, *n.* sweetheart

kail, kale, *n.* borecole, or soup made from that vegetable

kail-yard, *n.* vegetable garden

kebbeck, kebbuck, *n.* cheese

keckle, *v.* laugh uproariously

kee, *n. pl.* cows (English dialect)

keek, *v.* look, peep

keeking-glass, *n.* looking-glass

keel, *n.* ruddle, a red ochre used for marking sheep

keep a mail, *v. phr.* keep her food (meal) down

kent, *n.* pole for leaping ditches

kill, *n.* kiln for drying grain

knight of the post, *n. phr.* professional perjurer

knotting, *n.* the fancy work now called 'tatting'

laden, *v.* load

laft, *n.* loft

lage, *n. cant* water, weak drink (Partridge)

laigh, *adj.* low

lairds in the abbey, *n. phr.* bankrupts who could seek sanctuary in Holyrood Abbey, Edinburgh

lane, *adj.* lonely; *after poss. prons.* -self

lang, *adj.* long

lap, *v. pret.* leapt

lave, *n.* remainder, rest

lav'rock, *n.* lark

lay her bale, *v. phrase* put down her bundle (euph.)

leacher, *n.* lye, wood-ashes through which water has passed

leal, leel, *adj.* loyal, true

lee, *n.* meadow

lee-rigg, *n.* meadow ridge

leesome, *adj.* compassionate; *adv.* easily, pleasantly

leez me on, *v. plur.* dear is to me, I love

lem[m]an[e], *n.* sweetheart

leugh, *v. pret.* laughed

libkens, *n., cant* lodgings

lick, *v.* beat

limmer, *n.* 'a woman of loose manners' (Jamieson), jade, hussy

link, *v.* walk briskly, trip

loaning, *n.* 'strip of grass running through arable ground, serving as pasture, milking-place and driving road' (Kinsley)
lo'e, loo, *n.* love
loon, *n.* young boy
loot, *v. pret.* let
low, *v.* flare up
lown, *n.* worthless fellow
lug, *n.* ear
lyart, *adj.* grey

main, *n.* moan
mair, *adj., adv.* more
maist(-ly), *adv.* mostly
makin o's, *v. phr.* fondling
mallison, *n.* curse
mantie, *n.* gown (from manteau, infl. by place name Mantua); **make mantie,** dress-make
marrow, *n.* companion, mate
maun, *v.* must; **mauna,** must not
maut, *n.* malt
mautman, *n.* maltman
mavis, *n.* thrush
mawking, *n.* hare; or ? 'a half-grown female, esp., when engaged as a servant' (Jamieson)
meal-po[c]k[e], *n.* meal bag
meikle, mickle, muckle, *adj.* much
menȝie, *n.* crowd
mercat, *n.* market
merk, *n.* old Scottish silver coin, 'which by the 18th century was equivalent to 13⅓d. sterling' (SND)
Merse, *prop. n.* 'in loose popular phraseology, it is all the low country between the Lammermuirs and the river Tweed . . . the eastern part of what were formerly termed "the marches" ' (O.G.S.)
minny, *n.* mother
mirk, *n.* darkness; *adj.* dark
misca', *v.* miscall
Miss John (Mess John), *n.* clergyman
mity, *adj.* infested with mites
mort, *n. cant* wench
motie, *adj.* spotty
mou, *n.* mouth
mucking, *n.* cleaning out

multure, *n.* fee for grinding grain
muzzle-pin, *n.* pin for muzzle, the clevis or bridle of a plough
my lane, *adv.* alone

nae, *adj., adv.* no, none; *adv.* not
nane, *pron., adj., adv.* none
neist, niest, *adj. adv.* nearest, next
neive, nieve, *n.* hand, fist
Netherbow, *prop. n.* in Edinburgh, continuation of High Street towards the Canongate
nice, *adj.* fastidious
nig[g]le, *v. cant* have sexual intercourse
nip a Jan, *cant phr.* cut a purse (Partridge)
norland, *adj.* northern
nowt, *n. pl.* black cattle
nurice, *n.* nurse, nurse's

o', *prep.* of
o'er, our, ower, owre, *prep., adv.* over; *adj., adv.* too
o'erlay, *n.* necktie, cravat
ohon, *interj.* alas (stage Highland)
onie(-y), *adj., pron.* any
or, *conj., adv.* before
out-shinn'd, *adj.* with the legs bent outwards at the shins
owsen, *n. pl.* oxen
oxter, *n.* crook of arm; *v.* give [her] an arm

pare, *adj.* bare (stage Highland-Eng.)
paroquet, *n.* parakeet
parritch, *n.* (and nonce *v.*) porridge
pauky, pawky, *adj.* cunning, crafty
pe, *v.* be (stage Highland-Eng.)
peckage, *n. cant* food (Partridge)
pettitoes, *n. pl.* trotters, feet
pirn, *n.* bobbin of a spinning wheel
plaiden, *n.* cloth with check or tartan pattern
planting, *n.* plantation
play, *n.* sexual intercourse (euph.)
pleuch, *n.* plough
pockmahon, *interj.* ('**mahon**'=devil, from '**Mahoun**', Mahomet)
poind, *v.* distrain
possing, *v. noun* washing clothes by lifting them from the tub and kneading them

prie, *v.* taste, try
prop, *n. cant* ? leg
pund, *n.* pound

quean, quine, *n.* girl

randy, *n.* obstreperous beggar
range, *n.* stir (of water in cauldron)
raploch, *adj.* coarse
raucle, *adj.* crudely vigorous
reel, *v.* travel, roam
reesk, *n.* waste land yielding only
  rushes and coarse grass; **reesky,**
  adj, formed from n.
refe, *n.* robbery
rig(g)s, *n. pl.* ridges
rigwoodie, *n.* the rope or chain that
  crosses the back of a horse when
  yoked in a cart; *adj.* withered,
  hag-like
rin, *v.* run
ring, rung, *n.* stick, cudgel
ringle-ey'd, *adj.* wall-eyed
rock, *n.* distaff
rom-bowse, *n. cant* wine (Partridge)
row, *v.* roll
ruck, *n.* a heap of corn or hay
Rumple, *prop. n.* Rump [parliament]
runkled, *ppl. adj.* wrinkled

sae, *adv.* so
saft, *adj.* soft
sair, *adj., adv.* sore(ly)
sald, *v. pret., pple* sold
sang, *n.* song
saugh, *n.* willow
saul, *n.* soul
scaul, *v.* scold
scaulding, *ppl. adj.* well-scrubbed,
  spotless
scour, *v.* hurry
scrimp, *v.* deprive
scug, *v.* screen
scurry, *v.* roam, wander
seam, *v.* fit (one plank to another)
sell out, *v. phrase* dispose of one's
  army commission by sale
sest, *pa. pple* taxed
sey, *v.* assay, try
shave, *n.* slice
shilling-hill, *n.* where the chaff is
  winnowed from the corn

shooling, *n.* shovelling
shoon, *n. pl.* shoes
shoy, *n.* joy (stage Highland-Eng.)
sic, *adj.* such
siller, *n.* silver, money
sin, *conj.* since
skeeg about, *v. expr. as n.* rhythmic
  strokes
skelp, *v.* strike, thrash
skew, *n. cant* cup, bowl
skipper, *n. cant* barn, shelter with or
  without roof
skyre, *v.* to frighten
sla(-ee), *adj.* sly, clever
sma', *adj.* narrow, slender
smirky, *adj.* with a good-natured,
  smiling face
sna(w), *n.* snow
snirtle, *v.* snigger
snood, *n.* band or fillet for binding
  young woman's hair; *v.* to bind
  the hair
so(d)ger, *n.* soldier
sonsie, -y, *adj.* buxom, comely
sorn, *v.* 'to obtrude one's self on
  another for bed and board'
  (Jamieson); *n.* **sorner**
souter, *n.* shoemaker
spaw, *n.* spa
speir, spier, *v.* ask
spring, *n.* lively tune
stane, *n.* stone
stang, *v.* sting
starn(ie), *n.* star
stauling ken, *n. cant* drinking den
  where stolen property exchanged
sta(w), *v. pret.* stole
steek, *v.* close, shut
steer, *v.* stir, move to
stent, *v.* restrain, confine, stretch,
  overtax
stirk, *n.* young bullock
stob, *v.* stab
stot, *n.* young bullock
stoup, *n.* tankard, measure, pitcher
Stra(th)bogie, *prop. n.* district in
  N.-W. Aberdeenshire
strae, *n.* straw
strake (hands), *v.* strike
stud(d)y, *n.* anvil
stumpie, *n.* short, thick member;
  reel o' stumpie, sexual
  intercourse (euph.)

sud, *v. pret.* should
suthron, *adj.* southern, English
swons, *v. pres.* swoons
syne, *adv., conj.* then, since

tae, *n.* toe
tail-tree, *n.* piece of wood that goes behind horse's tail for keeping back a stuffed cloth used as saddle; penis (euph.)
tak, *v.* take
tap-knot, *n.* bow of ribbon worn on top of head
tat, *conj., rel.* that (stage Highland-Eng.)
te, *art.* the (stage Highland-Eng.)
temper-pin, *n.* 'wooden screw used in regulating the tightness of the band of a spinning-wheel' (N.E.D.)
tent, *v.* watch over
thae, *dem. pron., adj.* those
thieveless, *adj.* useless
thouse, *pron. and v.* thou shalt
thornie-dike, *n.* hawthorn hedge
thrawart, *adj.* perverse
three-girred cap, *n. phrase* cup with three bands
thripling kame, *n.* comb-like implement for splitting flax or hemp
thumpin', *adj.* strapping, fine
tick, *n.* credit
tiff, *n.* order, trim
tight, *adj.* well-formed, strapping
til(l), til't, *prep.* to; to it
tine, *v.* (*pret.* -t) lose
tinkler, *n.* tinker
titter, *adv.* rather
toolie, *v.* quarrel, fight
toom, tuim, *adj.* empty
toun, *adv.* down (stage Highland-Eng.)
tozie, *adj.* tipsy
trouse, *n.* 'close-fitting trousers, worn with stockings' (Kinsley)
trump, *n.* jew's harp, trumpet
trunkies, *n. pl.* clothes-chests
turner, *n.* 'a copper coin formerly current in Scotland in value two

pennies Scots money and equivalent to a bodle' (Jamieson)
twa, *numer. adj., n.* two

unco, *adv.* very

wa'(w), *n.* wall
wad, *v. pret.* would (have)
waff, *adj.* stray
wa(u)krife, *adj.* wakeful
wale, *v.* choose; *n.* choice or choicest thing or quality
wan, *v. pret.* won
wardly, *adj.,* worldly
warst, *sup. adj.* worst
wauk, *v.* wake
waur, *v.* worst, get the better of
wean, *n.* child
wede, *v. pa. pple* weeded
westlin, *adj.* western, westerly
wha, *pron.* who; **wham,** whom; **whase,** whose
Whig-mig-morum, *nonce n.* political altercation
whilk, *pron. adj.* which
whirlie-wha, *n.* whirligig; penis (euph.)
whittle, *n.* knife
whorle, *n.* the fly of a spinning 'rock'
will, *n.* in phrase **'a will'** spontaneously
win, *v.* dwell
winna, *v.* will not, won't
wist, *v. pret.* knew
withershins, *adv.* in contrary direction, contrary to the course of the sun
woo, *n.* wool
wood, *adj.* mad
woody, *n.* gallows
worthies, *n. pl.* pamphlets on biography of protestant martyrs
wynd, *n.* lane, alley

yellow-mou'd, *adj.* yellow-mouthed, jaundiced, naggingly jealous
ye'se, *v. and pron.* you shall
yirth, *n.* earth
yoaking, *v., n.* coupling (with sexual innuendo)
yowe, *n.* ewe

INDEX

NAMES AND TOPICS

FIRST LINES AND TITLES

(Including the titles of Songs, Poems, Tunes, Novels and Plays, but
not of song-books cited purely as references)